HAD IT COMING

ALSO BY ROBYN DOOLITTLE

Crazy Town

HAD IT COMING

COMING

What's Fair in the Age of #MeToo

ROBYN DOOLITTLE

ALLEN
LANE

ALLEN LANE
an imprint of Penguin Canada,
a division of Penguin Random House Canada Limited

Canada • USA • UK • Ireland • Australia • New Zealand •
India • South Africa • China

First published 2019

www.penguinrandomhouse.ca

LIBRARY AND ARCHIVES CANADA CATALOGUING IN PUBLICATION

Title: Had it coming / Robyn Doolittle.
Names: Doolittle, Robyn, author.
Identifiers: Canadiana (print) 20190101059 | Canadiana (ebook)
20190101296 | ISBN 9780735236592 (hardcover) |
ISBN 9780735236608 (HTML)
Subjects: LCSH: Sexual consent—Canada. | LCSH: Sexual
ethics—Canada. | LCSH: Sex and law—Canada. | LCSH: Sex—Political
aspects—Canada. | LCSH: Sex—Social aspects—Canada.
Classification: LCC HQ32 .D66 2019 | DDC 306.70971—dc23

Book and cover design by Kate Sinclair
Cover image: CSA-Printstock / Getty Images

Printed and bound in Canada

10 9 8 7 6 5 4 3 2 1

For Joel,
my love, my best friend, and a true partner

CONTENTS

INTRODUCTION

IN WRITING A book about #MeToo, I could have gone two ways.

The first, the easy route, would have been to lean into my own frustrations, anger, and indignation at the world, developed during thirty-four years of living as a human female. I could have collected those grievances—all those times that a man took credit for my work or a date pushed too far, or that time in a taxi when I barely escaped from the driver. I could have harnessed all the memories of men telling me to "Smile!," of my ideas not being taken seriously on account of my gender, of having my butt patted on the street or on public transit or at a bar. And I could have rolled it all in with the gnawing reality that in 2019 women continue to earn less for the same work as men, represent only a quarter of House of Commons seats, and—as of 2018—total exactly one CEO among the top hundred most influential companies in Canada. That situation doesn't even begin to approach the level of inequality for women of colour or for women in countries where by law they're second-class citizens, where they're under the thumb of male guardians, where their access to education is limited, where they're routinely subjected to sexual violence as part of domestic life, or civil strife, or war. And then I could have taken that Molotov cocktail of resentment, lit it on fire, and lobbed it into the world, screaming, "Burn it all down!" That's a book that would have earned me a lot of love on Twitter. It would have been simple to talk about and promote. The fury that many women are experiencing and voicing right now is real and warranted, and writing 70,000 words about why would have been cathartic.

But that is not the book I've written.

At the time I started researching this book, I'd already spent more than two years immersed in many of these issues. I'm a journalist with *The Globe and Mail*, and in the summer of 2015 I began investigating how police handle sexual assault allegations. As part of that research, I interviewed well over a hundred people connected to the criminal justice system—sexual assault complainants, police officers, lawyers, judges, sexual assault nurses, academics, activists, and front-line support workers. I'd read through thousands of pages of court transcripts and police files. Building on what I'd learned through that reporting, I turned my mind to #MeToo. I thought I'd have firm opinions on everything related to the movement, but the more I read, the more I pushed myself beyond the confines of like-minded social media silos, the more open conversations I had with those in my social and business circles, the more I realized that that approach wasn't going to cut it. It's been done. I came to see that a more useful and honest book about #MeToo wouldn't shy away from the tough questions that the movement has raised.

Unfortunately, as a culture we aren't very good at having nuanced, complicated discussions. The public space is not a safe venue to talk about controversial subjects. Social media has seen to that. Instead, people are talking it out in private, with friends they trust not to rip them apart on Twitter. My goal with this book is to bring those discussions into the open.

At this extraordinary moment of change in how men and women interact, the path forward isn't simple. It's important, I believe, to uncover and evaluate the facts, to expose outdated myths that pervade institutions, and to bring rigour, openness, and compassion in equal measure to this very important conversation. I've come to embrace the complexities and messiness that comes with those tough conversations. So rather than lighting a match to that oily rag, with this book I've tried to make the case for progress as well as healthy debate.

CHAPTER 1

KOBE BRYANT AND ME

I WAS EIGHTEEN when police in Eagle, Colorado, arrested Kobe Bryant on accusations that he'd raped a woman in a hotel room. I don't remember how I heard about it, but I do remember my first thought upon learning the news: "Well, what did she expect going to a hotel room with an NBA player?"

The woman was nineteen, barely a year older than I was at the time. She'd been working the front desk at a mountain lodge when Bryant checked in on June 30, 2003. The twenty-four-year-old basketball all-star was in the area for knee surgery. He arrived late with a small entourage and asked the woman to show him around the facilities. After the tour, she escorted Bryant back to his room. He invited her in. They chatted for a bit. Flirted. And when he kissed her, she kissed him back. It was flattering, she later told police, that the famous Los Angeles Laker seemed interested in her. She was okay with the kissing.

But then Bryant started to grope and fondle her. The teen-ager moved towards the door, but Bryant blocked her path. "I try and walk to the side, and he would walk with me," she told police. That's when, she alleged, the six-foot-six shooting guard put his hands around her throat and squeezed—not hard enough to close her windpipe, but hard enough to make it clear that he was in control. Bryant removed his pants. He bent her over a chair. When he removed the teenager's underwear, she again protested, but he ignored her. "Every time I said 'no' he tightened his hold around me," she told police.

The woman told police that Bryant proceeded to rape her. He did so with one hand gripping her throat while she wept. When she was eventually able to leave, Bryant's T-shirt was stained with her blood. Almost immediately, the woman bumped into a friend, the hotel bellman. She tearfully recounted that Bryant had choked and raped her. A sexual assault examination performed fifteen hours later revealed two one-centimetre lacerations and several smaller tears in her vaginal region. The injuries were "consistent with penetrating genital trauma." Officials also documented a bruise on her jaw.

Bryant initially lied to investigators and said he'd never had sex with the teenager, but he changed his story after police indicated that they had physical evidence from the rape kit. In his new version of events, Bryant admitted that they'd had sex, but he claimed it was consensual—and in fact, *she* had been the one to initiate it. The ensuing media coverage trumpeted Bryant's athletic accolades, questioned the complainant's character, and minimized the severity of the allegations by sprinkling basketball references throughout stories that were otherwise about rape. "On the hardwood, he often controls the court. But facing allegations of felony sexual assault by an unnamed nineteen-year-old woman, basketball superstar Kobe Bryant may find himself on another court where three-point plays don't count," NBC News reported after the arrest. The headline in the *Los Angeles Times* reassured fans that they had reason to doubt their star's accuser: "Alleged victim in Bryant case is a 19-year-old graduate of local high school who is said to be fun-loving, outgoing and emotional." The Associated Press story painted a portrait of a man deserving of compassion: "Sitting not far from the court, where everything comes so naturally to him, Kobe Bryant found it tough just to speak. After waiting several seconds to gather himself, the Los Angeles Lakers' guard choked back tears and his voice quivered. 'I'm innocent.'"

The next year and a half brought merciless exposure for the young woman. An American supermarket tabloid, the *Globe*, published a front-page photograph of the girl, taken at her high school prom, with curled blond tendrils falling beside her cheeks and a corsage on her wrist. In the picture, she's hiked up her satin skirt, exposing a mid-thigh garter. Her full name appears in all caps alongside the headline "Kobe's Accuser: Did She Really Say No?" On numerous occasions, court staff mistakenly released confidential details about her. For example, they emailed reporters' transcripts of a closed-door discussion about the complainant's sexual history. When it came out that traces of another man's semen had been found inside her, Bryant's defence used it to attack the woman's credibility. The woman had already disclosed that she'd had sex two days before the incident, but the defence asserted that she'd also had intercourse after the encounter with Bryant, which accounted for her vaginal injuries. (Her lawyer called the assertion "patently false.")

In September 2004, prosecutors in Eagle County announced that they were dropping the charges against Bryant. "The victim has informed us, after much of her own labored deliberation, that she does not want to proceed with this trial," District Attorney Mark Hurlbert explained. Bryant issued an apology that contained no admission of guilt: "Although I truly believe this encounter between us was consensual, I recognize now that she did not and does not view this incident the same way I did." The following year, attorneys for the woman and Bryant reached a civil settlement.

When I was eighteen, I didn't know most of these details and obviously didn't care enough to find out. I felt no connection to this woman, despite the fact that she was practically my age, that I'd spent the last three years working at a hotel in my own small town, that my high school girlfriends and I had taken that exact same photo in our prom dresses, that there is no question I would have been giddy if a famous athlete had flirted with me. Instead I felt safe in my sense of superiority, confident that I'd never be so foolish. Or weak. I wasn't one of those girls: slutty girls, dying-for-attention-from-men girls, girls who made the rest of us look bad. I remember talking about Kobe Bryant's arrest with guys. I always made it clear that I was one of the good ones. I got it. Don't worry—I'm cool. This girl had gone to a hotel room with an NBA basketball player at night. What did she think was going to happen?

This, all of it, is what rape culture looks like: my baseless suspicion, the sympathetic press coverage, the slut-shaming, the cavalier attitude of court staff towards a sexual assault complainant, the fact that Bryant's career carried on without consequence. Let's not forget that on March 4, 2018, the first Academy Awards in the era of #MeToo, Kobe Bryant won an Oscar.

I'VE BEEN A reporter with *The Globe and Mail*'s investigative team since 2014, and I've spent much of that time looking into the criminal justice system and the way that Canadian police treat allegations of sexual assault. Before I began this work, rape culture wasn't something I really thought about. I wasn't a denier. Like every woman I know, I've experienced gender-based harassment and discrimination. And I've always identified as a feminist. In fact, I'd probably have considered myself a vocal one. I'd just never spent much time considering the root causes: the ways that men—and women—normalize sexual violence by perpetuating outdated attitudes. It was only when I discovered that police were systemically neglecting sexual assault cases—despite the fact that this crime is among the most serious in the Criminal Code, second only to homicide—that my job forced me to think about it.

In the summer of 2015, I was looking for my next story, and at the time the country was transfixed by the ongoing sexual assault saga of former CBC Radio host Jian Ghomeshi. Ghomeshi had been arrested the previous November on accusations that he'd abused multiple women. Coverage of the story had been relentless and went beyond the nuts-and-bolts news developments. Writers used the case as a means to explore subjects that still weren't typically allotted prominent space in mainstream media—subjects such as consent, victim stereotypes, rape myths. The story evolved into a mass debate about whether the courts were rigged against sexual assault complainants. Women in my life were convinced this was the case. It certainly felt that way. But was it actually true?

The standard line from police officers, defence lawyers, and even some Crown attorneys is that sexual assault cases are inherently difficult to investigate and prosecute: usually only two people are involved, and there's often no visible evidence of harm. As such, few complaints result in charges and even fewer end with convictions. Defenders of the status quo say that, short of upending the entire justice system, these challenges are inescapable. This is the point where the conversation always stalls. The problem seems too big and abstract.

In that dilemma I found inspiration for my next investigation. I'd need to find a path into the story that was not only focused but also far-reaching enough to have an impact. Could I prove conclusively that sexual assault cases, en masse, were being mishandled? Could I quantify rape culture?

It turned out that the answer was yes. And it was the beginning of my personal awakening.

Over the course of more than a year and a half, I filed hundreds of freedom of information requests to collect crime statistics from 873 police jurisdictions across the country. The data showed that, collectively, Canadian law enforcement was disproportionately dismissing sexual assault complaints as "unfounded"—a police term that means the detective thinks the accusation is either false or baseless. In other words, it's not that police can't find a suspect or that there isn't enough evidence to lay a charge. The term means that they think the incident didn't happen. And 19.39 percent of sexual assault allegations were being discarded in this way.

"Unfounded" would become the name of the series I went on

to write. And what I learned was that, compared with the number of common physical assault files closed as unfounded, Canadian law enforcement dismissed nearly twice as many cases of sexual assault. That's a staggering rate, with serious public policy implications. If legitimate sexual assault complaints were indeed being thrown out, it would create the impression that police receive fewer such reports than they actually do. In turn, this would artificially inflate the charge rate, distorting the true picture of how many allegations end with an arrest. Canadian police claimed that 42 percent of sexual assault accusations ended with a criminal charge. Once the "unfounded" files were factored in, that number dropped to 34 percent.

Now I had to figure out why the dismissal rate was so high.

I interviewed more than a hundred experts—front-line advocates, legal scholars, criminologists, trauma specialists, Crown attorneys, defence lawyers, nurses, and police officers— and then investigated fifty-four specific sexual assault cases that had been reported to police. I spoke with the complainants, the witnesses, the officers involved, and in some cases the accused. I collected police files, medical records, surveillance footage, and court documentation when available, as well as emails, texts, and social media messages pertaining to the allegations.

Among those cases, it was startling to see how the same patterns recurred. I found files closed with almost no investigation. Basic steps that would have been taken with any other police file—such as collecting video surveillance, interviewing witnesses, gathering forensic evidence, questioning the suspect— were routinely skipped. Sometimes complainants waited months to be contacted for their first interview. I noticed a shocking number of detectives who either didn't understand or were content to ignore Canadian consent law. I spoke with several complainants who said the officer had outright accused them of lying. Others were lectured about drinking too much, questioned about unrelated sexual history, and challenged about why they hadn't fought back more or called for help.

I saw the same disturbing practices repeated across the country. It explained why police were discarding one out of every five sexual assault accusations as bogus. (Numerous academic studies have shown that the false-reporting rate for sexual assault is, at most, 8 percent, which is less than the false-reporting rate for auto insurance claims.) I spent twenty months reporting on this story and then another year and a half documenting the measures being taken in response to it. My research proved that rape myths and stereotypes—the oxygen that keeps rape culture alive—were polluting the Canadian justice system.

I REMEMBER THE day when it finally clicked for me.

I'd been covering a trial where the complainant had been so drunk at the time of her rape that she'd struggled to stay awake just minutes beforehand. The accused had picked her up—literally, since she couldn't walk unassisted—at a bar about fifteen minutes earlier and then guided her to his nearby hotel room. They hadn't met before. A judge found the man guilty, thanks in no small part to the hotel elevator's security camera, which showed the woman basically passed out, leaning against the wall. (Without that footage, I doubt the man would have been convicted. The courts have struggled to establish the line where intoxication crosses into incapacity.) Around the same time as this trial, I happened to rewatch one of my favourite movies from university, *The 40-Year-Old Virgin*. In case you haven't seen it, after Steve Carell confesses to his friends that he's never had sex before, there's a scene where his buddies take him to a nightclub to teach him how to get laid. "In every man there's a code written that says, 'Tackle drunk bitches,'" one of the guys tells the wide-eyed and innocent Carell. Heeding this advice, our hero hones in on a woman who's so hammered that she later pukes in his face. I'd watched this scene a hundred times and had never given it a second thought, but now I saw how problematic it was. What a horrible message.

It was as though I could finally see the Matrix. I started noticing rape culture everywhere.

"Rape culture" is a term that feminists coined in the 1970s to describe the societal framework that enables sexual violence by blaming victims and excusing perpetrators. Rape culture is judging women for wearing revealing clothing and measuring masculinity in terms of sexual conquest. It's the endless number of love scenes in movies that start with a no and end with the woman relenting. It's how Monica Lewinsky, a twenty-two-year-old intern, got branded as a home-wrecking whore while the forty-nine-year-old philandering president of the United States enjoyed soaring popularity.

I thought back to Kobe Bryant and my suspicion of the young woman. I Googled the case and read it again through my educated, adult eyes. I was embarrassed and guilt-ridden. The nauseatingly sympathetic press coverage, the slut-shaming the complainant endured, the court staff's seemingly offhand approach to her privacy, the failure to hold Bryant accountable—how had I not seen it?

This is what makes rape culture so dangerous. It feels normal. The mindset is so entangled in day-to-day assumptions that it becomes camouflaged by its ordinariness. To me, this will be the lasting legacy of #MeToo. The movement exposed the deeply ingrained rot. Now, we're all being forced to confront uncomfortable questions about why we've given tacit approval to the devaluing of women's safety and sexual autonomy. Why is it that we've decided that unwanted flirting, touching, kisses, catcalls, and sexual advances at work are acceptable inconveniences in a woman's life? And why is it that public institutions like universities, police services, the courts, and legislative bodies have been given a pass on their dismal track records around sexual violence? Trying to take on these issues presents a whole new set of challenges.

How do you go about stopping sexual misconduct? Do we need to change our laws? Is this more about education? And what do we do with the perpetrators, especially when the allegations aren't criminal in nature? This last point, which has raised questions about due process, the presumption of innocence, and the right to a second chance, has perhaps generated the most controversy. Essentially what we're all trying to figure out is what's fair in this new era?

THE #METOO MOVEMENT has been years in the making. When it finally broke through in October 2017 with the Harvey Weinstein scandal, it exposed rape culture. The first step to solving a problem is acknowledging you have one. Then the hard work can begin. #MeToo marked the beginning of that journey.

Opinions are divided on where to go next.

Among the #MeToo-Too-Far cohort, people argue that the issues are overstated and that the attempts to address this supposed misogyny are tearing down pillars of Western democracy, among them free speech and the right to due process. Oscar winner Michael Haneke, an Austrian filmmaker, told a Vienna-based newspaper that the movement had become a "witch hunt." "Any form of rape or coercion is punishable," he said, but "this hysterical pre-judgment which is spreading now, I find absolutely disgusting." Polarizing Canadian psychology professor Jordan Peterson remarked to the *Toronto Sun* that "#MeToo has been an assault on the English common law," alleging that the presumption of innocence was being lost.

And these types of views aren't held solely by men. Older feminists were among the first to push back. In January 2018, actress Catherine Deneuve and writer Catherine Millet were among one hundred French women to sign an open letter published in *Le Monde* denouncing the movement. "Rape is a crime, but trying to seduce someone, even persistently or cack-handedly, is not." The writers lamented the men who'd faced career repercussions "when all they did was touch someone's knee or try to steal a kiss." Men have been vilified for "talking about intimate subjects during professional dinners or for sending sexually charged messages to women who did not return their attentions." Polls suggest that this is not an uncommon sentiment. A survey for *The Economist* by public opinion company YouGov found that 18 percent of Americans believe false accusations to be a bigger issue than unreported or unpunished attacks, and that about a third of the population believes that women who complain about sexual harassment are doing more harm than good.

Then there are people like me, who believe that rape culture exists, that it's damaging, and that it needs to end, but who also have reservations about certain elements that have emerged during the debate.

I am dismayed, for example, by the chill on open discussion around the issues raised by #MeToo. "Call-out" culture—in which those who violate codes of acceptable thought and behaviour are banished to the digital pillory for a mass public shaming—is real and toxic. This trend began years ago, thanks to social media, and the result is that people refrain from thoughtful discussions out of fear of saying the wrong thing and being branded as "unwoke."

The #MeToo movement has forced a long overdue conversation about sexual violence and misconduct. Unfortunately, we've never been in a worse position to conduct such a delicate debate. Political partisanship is the highest it's been in decades; public trust in institutions—notably in government and media—continues to plummet; and social media has left us measuring our worth via followers, likes, and retweets. It's an environment that incentivizes the extreme. There's no room for nuance when the animosity is so thick and so little about these issues is easily settled.

Just look at the case that came to define all sexual assault cases in Canada—the trial of Jian Ghomeshi.

CHAPTER 2

THE #METOO PIONEER

ON SUNDAY, OCTOBER 19, 2014, Canadian media critic Jesse Brown dropped a teaser for listeners of his Canadaland podcast. Sometime soon, Brown said, his website was going to publish a "monster" scoop that would be "worse than embarrassing for certain parties." Brown was referring to a piece about a secret Canadian surveillance program, but that's not what CBC Radio host Jian Ghomeshi thought when he learned of the promo.

For months the Canadaland team had been looking into allegations that Ghomeshi had abused, harassed, and sexually assaulted women. Ghomeshi knew he was being investigated and so did his bosses at the CBC, but the host had assured them that the story was bogus and that he could prove it. With Canadaland's bombshell now apparently imminent, network management asked to see Ghomeshi's exonerating evidence.

So, on the Thursday, CBC executives met with the host's lawyers at the firm's downtown Toronto office. Ghomeshi's team shared graphic texts, emails, photos, and a video, which Ghomeshi believed would confirm that his sexual partners had been willing participants in rough, bondage-dominance encounters. Instead, the CBC executives were horrified. One clip reportedly showed a large bruise along the side of a woman's body. A text message referenced a "cracked rib." The executives left feeling that it was "much bigger than we ever thought," the *Toronto Star* later reported.

The next day, Friday, Ghomeshi was put on leave while the CBC figured out what to do. He was one of their biggest stars, a personality the network had spent years building up and promoting. They knew he couldn't stay, but his sudden termination was going to attract a lot of attention. A spokesperson told reporters that Ghomeshi had "to deal with some personal issues." Initially, media connected the break to the fact that the host's father had recently passed away. Ghomeshi himself seemed to play along with this theory, tweeting, "Thanks for all the well wishes, you guys. I'm ok. Just taking some much needed personal time." But the charade was short-lived. On Sunday the CBC announced it was cutting ties with its star.

The news stunned.

By Canadian celebrity standards, Jian Ghomeshi was as big as it gets. Posters of his grinning face decorated downtown Toronto. The indie-folk-rock-singer-turned-broadcaster was involved in a seemingly impossible number of ventures. By day, Ghomeshi's arts and entertainment affairs show, *Q,* aired in Canada and on 120 public radio stations in the United States, including in such mega markets as New York and Chicago.

Owing to Ghomeshi's brand, *Q* regularly attracted A-list celebrity guests—Jay-Z, Leonard Cohen, Paul McCartney, and Adele among them. An impressive feat for a Canadian public-radio culture show. By night, Ghomeshi fronted marquee cultural events—the Polaris Music Prize, the Giller Prize, CBC's Canada Reads—and in his spare time, the host managed the indie-pop singer Lights and wrote a bestselling memoir, *1982*. Although he was forty-seven, Ghomeshi was the CBC's best connection to young audiences.

The country wondered, "What could have possibly caused the CBC to fire him?"

Shortly after news of Ghomeshi's departure broke, the host offered an explanation in a lengthy statement on Facebook:

> I've been fired from the CBC because of the risk of my private sex life being made public as a result of a campaign of false allegations pursued by a jilted ex-girlfriend and a freelance writer . . . I have always been interested in a variety of activities in the bedroom but I only participate in sexual practices that are mutually agreed upon, consensual, and exciting for both partners. . . . We all have our secret life. But that is my private life. That is my personal life. And no one, and certainly no employer, should have dominion over what people do consensually in their private life.

Ghomeshi's legions of fans were apoplectic. His post quickly attracted more than a hundred thousand likes. For a nanosecond, Ghomeshi appeared as the victim, but public opinion changed quickly. Late Sunday night, the *Toronto Star*—which had partnered with Jesse Brown months earlier—published allegations from three women that Ghomeshi had been violent towards them during sexual encounters. A fourth—who had worked with Ghomeshi at CBC—alleged the host had sexually harassed and groped her in the office. Then another woman told the CBC's *As It Happens* that Ghomeshi had once thrown her to the floor "and started closed-fist pounding me in the head repeatedly until my ears were ringing." Four more women came forward to the *Star*, including actress Lucy DeCoutere, who alleged that Ghomeshi had choked and slapped her on a date. (Ghomeshi denied the allegations of violence.)

On October 30, four days after Ghomeshi's firing, Canadian journalists Antonia Zerbisias and Sue Montgomery created the hashtag #BeenRapedNeverReported in support of Ghomeshi's accusers. Among the first tweets, from @AntoniaZ, was "1970: My friend's friend from out of town 'forgot his wallet' in his hotel room, it will only take a minute. #BeenRapedNeverReported." The hashtag garnered nearly eight million impressions around the world in less than twenty-four hours. Toronto police chief Bill Blair made a public appeal for any victims to come forward. Several did. And on November 26, 2014, Jian Ghomeshi turned himself in. He was charged with four counts of sexual assault and one choking-related offence.

The attention the case attracted was astounding. Ghomeshi's celebrity ensured that the arrest would be big news, but a number of other factors doused the spectacle in gasoline. Ghomeshi had spent years studiously cultivating his image as a sensitive, thoughtful progressive. That he'd cloaked himself in feminism for so many years enraged people. It didn't help—at least from my vantage point—that he wasn't particularly well-liked by women in Toronto media. Personally, I'd never heard any rumours of violence, but the word was out that at work, Ghomeshi was obnoxiously demanding and at parties overly flirtatious, verging on creepy. But likely more than anything else, the Ghomeshi scandal was compounded by events unfolding in tandem south of the border.

On October 16, 2014—three days before Jesse Brown's "monster" scoop promo on Canadaland—comedian Hannibal Buress told a joke at the Trocadero Theatre in Philadelphia that went like this: "Bill Cosby has the fucking smuggest old black man public persona that I hate. He gets on TV: 'Pull your pants up, black people. I was on TV in the eighties. I can talk down to you because I had a successful sitcom.' Yeah, but you raped women, Bill Cosby, so—brings you down a couple notches. 'I don't curse on stage.' Well, yeah, you're a rapist, so—" Buress continued, "I've done this bit on stage, and people don't believe. People think I'm making it up . . . trust me. You leave here and Google 'Bill Cosby rape.'"

It was true. In January 2005 a woman named Andrea Constand, a former employee of Cosby's alma mater, Temple University, told police that the comedian had lured her to his Philadelphia mansion by promising to discuss her career. Instead he drugged and sexually assaulted her while she was immobilized. When Cosby's lawyer called the allegations "preposterous," California attorney Tamara Green—who'd met Cosby in the 1970s when she was working as a model—decided to speak out. "He did exactly the same thing to me," she told the *Philadelphia Daily News* in February 2005. The Montgomery County district attorney declined to press charges, citing a lack of "credible" evidence. He also noted that Constand's delay in reporting weighed against her. So Constand launched a civil suit instead, which included depositions from thirteen women making similar allegations. The story was widely covered, but the public, the courts, and the entertainment industry didn't seem to care. Networks kept running *The Cosby Show* and the comedian continued to tour to packed crowds. Cosby retained his status as "America's Dad." And this was the way it was for nine years—until Buress's stand-up routine.

It wasn't the first time the comedian had told his Cosby joke, but on that occasion, someone posted the set online. The firestorm was instant. Venues refused to host Cosby. More women came forward. *New York* magazine put thirty-five of Cosby's accusers on its cover, lined up one by one, four rows deep. *The Cosby Show* was pulled from syndication. By the end of 2015, Cosby was charged in the sexual assault of Andrea Constand. A jury convicted him in April 2018.

Was it a coincidence that both the Cosby and Ghomeshi stories broke at the same time? Did the former fuel the latter? Or were these events merely the first signs of the #MeToo shift.

In Canada, the Jian Ghomeshi sexual assault trial became a proxy for all sexual assault trials, a litmus test of the criminal justice system. It was as if the country's attitude towards sexual violence was itself on the docket. If the judge found Ghomeshi not guilty, it would be proof that victims didn't matter. Everything was riding on the trial—except that it wasn't the right case to shoulder that pressure.

THINGS GOT UNDERWAY on February 1, 2016, at Old City Hall court in downtown Toronto. Many major news outlets live blogged the proceedings in minute-by-minute detail. The country could follow along in real time as, one by one, the complainants took the stand and their testimony fell apart.

There were inconsistencies—like one woman's statement that Ghomeshi had driven a yellow Volkswagen Beetle while in fact he hadn't leased it until months after the alleged incident—and misleading answers. Ghomeshi's legal team was led by the tiny but terrifying Marie Henein, famous for her legal brilliance, clever tactics, and penchant for wearing sky-high stilettos to court. She presented the complainants with evidence that contradicted earlier sworn statements: namely, their claims that they hadn't had contact with Ghomeshi after the assaults. Embarrassing emails—which neither the police nor the Crown prosecutor had been made aware of—were presented in court. One witness acknowledged that she'd deliberately misled police about a later sexual encounter with Ghomeshi. And then it emerged that two of the complainants had secretly discussed the specifics of the case with each other, which one denied under oath until presented with evidence to the contrary. "It's time to sink the prick," wrote one complainant. "I'll do whatever I can to put this predator where he belongs."

The revelations were devastating to the Crown's case. As the *National Post*'s Christie Blatchford observed, "It's now apparent the case was built upon the self-serving and carefully edited allegations of dishonest complainants, two of whom appear to have been colluding and gleefully anticipating Ghomeshi's ruination, and raised up on the gossamer wings of unproven allegations in the press and on social media."

When Justice William B. Horkins issued his verdict on March 24, 2016, it was equally inflammatory. Each complainant, he charged, had been confronted with evidence that contradicted previous sworn testimony. There were "inconsistencies and questionable behaviour" as well as instances of "outright deception," Justice Horkins said. Memory gaps are to be expected, given that the alleged incidents occurred more than a decade earlier. What is not acceptable is the "shifting of facts" from one telling to the next, he said. Jian Ghomeshi was found not guilty on four counts of sexual assault and one count of overcoming resistance by choking. Afterwards, hundreds of protesters congregated outside the downtown courthouse, chanting, "We believe survivors." They then marched to Toronto police headquarters. The blowback continued online. "If the threshold for conviction was not met here, nobody has a hope in hell of getting their abuser convicted. #IBelieveSurvivors," tweeted Canadian sexual violence activist Julie Lalonde. Writer Carla Ciccone shared, "If u see this shit show of a verdict as anything less than a failure of our justice system, u are a part of the problem. #IBelieveSurvivors." The headline in Salon read "Jian Ghomeshi's Not-Guilty Verdict: Victim-Blaming Is Alive and Well in Sexual Assault Cases." In the Huffington Post, Angelina Chapin wrote, "[This] verdict reinforced the myths that women who misremember details, omit evidence and contact their abusers are not credible victims."

But here's the unpopular—to some, painful—truth: according to virtually every legal mind I've interviewed since the ruling, the Ghomeshi verdict was the correct one. I know this statement is a declaration of war in many circles, but it shouldn't be. Elaine Craig, a law professor at Dalhousie University who specializes in feminist legal theory, wrote a book called *Putting Trials on Trial* that dissected the ways rape myths and stereotypes taint our court system, and she barely touched on the Ghomeshi trial. When I asked her about this, she said, "The evidence introduced during the trial did not establish proof beyond a reasonable doubt, and there were a number of frailties and inconsistencies in the complainants' evidence." Craig did question whether the complainants had been properly informed about things like the impact of speaking with each other before the trial or giving multiple statements to the media about their experiences. But that doesn't change the fact that, given the circumstances, an acquittal was appropriate.

Although we didn't yet have a name for what was happening, Canadians' reaction to Jian Ghomeshi's arrest was the first sign that something in the culture had changed. The case might not have been the right one to expose weaknesses in the Canadian court system, but it did inspire conversations about power and consent that we'd never had before—at least not publicly. And although Ghomeshi had been cleared in a court of law, in the court of public opinion—a barometer of ethical and moral crimes—he was guilty as charged. He lost his job and his status and remains a pariah to this day. He is the original #MeToo casualty, something Ghomeshi himself acknowledged in an ill-advised piece he wrote for *The New York Review of Books* in 2018: "One of my female friends quips that I should get some kind of public recognition as a #MeToo pioneer. There are lots of guys more hated than me now. But I was the guy everyone hated first."

IN ONE VERSION of the #MeToo origin story, actress Alyssa Milano fired the first shot of the revolution on October 15, 2017, via Twitter: "If you've been sexually harassed or assaulted write 'me too' as a reply to this tweet"—reigniting a call to action that civil rights activist Tarana Burke coined in 2006.

Ten days earlier, *The New York Times* had exposed Hollywood mega-producer Harvey Weinstein as a serial sexual abuser of women. Up till then, Weinstein, a man of immense power and influence, had been able to leverage his connections to keep rumours about his behaviour out of the headlines. As co-founder of Miramax and the Weinstein Company, he'd amassed a personal fortune of at least $240 million; his films had racked up a staggering 341 Oscar nominations and 81 wins. Meryl Streep referred to him as "God" when she accepted the Best Actress Award at the 2012 Golden Globes. Weinstein had also championed progressive politics, hosting lavish fundraisers for Democrats and building close connections to both the Clintons and the Obamas. All that changed with the *Times* blockbuster by reporters Jodi Kantor and Megan Twohey, who revealed that Weinstein had spent decades sexually harassing women who worked in the film industry. Actress Ashley Judd went on record to say that when she was a young actress, Weinstein had invited her to his hotel room for a business breakfast meeting. He answered the door in a bathrobe, pressured her to let him give her a massage, and asked if she would watch him shower. "How do I get out of the room as fast as possible without alienating Harvey Weinstein?" Judd told the newspaper, recounting her thoughts at the time. Less than a week after the *Times* story, an even more damning exposé by Ronan Farrow in *The New Yorker* featured allegations from thirteen more women, including three accusations of rape. Soon after, actresses Rose McGowan, Gwyneth Paltrow, and Angelina Jolie spoke out about their own bad experiences. (Weinstein has denied any criminal acts.)

Then came Milano's tweet. As the hashtag whipped around the globe millions of times over, giants in every industry—men who had once seemed untouchable—began to fall. Actor Kevin Spacey, comedian Louis C.K., media men Charlie Rose and Matt Lauer, head of Amazon Studios Roy Price, Senator Al Franken, and the list goes on and on. (Vox keeps an ongoing tally of notable figures in arts, business, politics, and media who have been accused of sexual misconduct. It's currently at 263.) From #MeToo came Time's Up, an organization founded by celebrities to address inequality in the workplace and to raise legal funds for victims of sexual harassment. At the Golden Globes that January, actresses arrived in black gowns to protest Hollywood's sexist culture.

But this social awakening didn't start in October 2017—or with Alyssa Milano. The forces that enabled the Weinstein story to gain traction had been building for years.

IT WAS THESE same forces that propelled so much of the response to my Unfounded series in the *Globe*. Within days of its launch, Prime Minister Justice Trudeau vowed action. The federal government went on to pledge $100 million in funding to end gender-based violence. Citing the series, more than a hundred police services collectively audited 37,000 previously closed cases. Thousands were identified as having been miscoded and more than four hundred were reopened. As well, new policy, training, and oversight measures were rolled out across the country. If the series had run even five years earlier, it's hard to imagine such change. It's why people often tell me how lucky I am that the series ran in the same year as #MeToo.

The timing wasn't a coincidence, though. In the years preceding the famous hashtag, a series of events on both sides of the border had already directed the public's attention to these issues. I started working on Unfounded because of Jian Ghomeshi's arrest in 2014. The focus on that story was intensified by the simultaneously unfolding revelations about Bill Cosby. Then in 2015, a second high-profile scandal erupted in Canada regarding a sexual assault case—this time about a judge. Federal Court Justice Robin Camp faced calls for his removal from the bench after it came to light that he had asked a complainant why she didn't just "keep [her] knees together" to avoid being raped. And then at the Academy Awards in February 2016, Lady Gaga stood on stage in locked arms alongside dozens of sexual-abuse survivors as she belted out the power ballad "Til It Happens to You"—the title song from *The Hunting Ground* documentary, a harrowing indictment of universities' failure to address campus sexual assault. Hollywood gave her a standing ovation—its own moment would be less than two years away. By that summer, things were in motion. That was when Fox News forced the resignation of its all-powerful chairman, Roger Ailes, after former anchor Gretchen Carlson filed a lawsuit alleging that she was pushed out after rebuffing Ailes's repeated sexual advances. And June 2016 was when the world learned about Brock Turner, the Stanford University student who sexually molested an incapacitated woman behind a dumpster at a frat party. That woman wrote a seething victim-impact statement read by millions around the world. It famously began, "You don't know me, but you've been inside me."

Fast forward to February 2017 and the launch of my Unfounded series. That same month in the United States, a site-reliability engineer named Susan Fowler wrote a blog post detailing the toxic culture of sexism and harassment at the car-sharing service Uber, her former employer. Her story went viral, inspired scores of consumers to delete the app, eventually took down the CEO, and kickstarted a debate about misogyny in Silicon Valley. In April 2017 the country's highest-rated cable news host, Bill O'Reilly, was fired after *The New York Times* broke the story that Fox had paid out millions to silence sexual harassment allegations made against its star. The move would have been unthinkable even a few years earlier.

Someday a historian will plot out the march towards #MeToo and pinpoint the moment when the rules changed. It certainly wasn't in 1959, when twenty-four-year-old Elvis Presley began dating fourteen-year-old Priscilla Beaulieu and no one blinked. Or in 1992, when Woody Allen emerged unscathed from having been publicly accused of molesting his seven-year-old adopted daughter, even after admitting to a consensual affair with the adopted daughter of his longtime partner, Mia Farrow—twenty-one-year-old Soon-Yi Previn, whom he later married. Or in 1994, when no one cared that twenty-seven-year-old R&B star R. Kelly began a relationship with (and secretly married) fifteen-year-old Aaliyah. Or in 2000 and 2002, when more allegations surfaced that the singer had engaged in sexual activity with minors. The singer wouldn't face his comeuppance until the 2019 release of the documentary series "Surviving R. Kelly," which laid out in damning detail the ways that he had preyed upon teenage girls. (He denied the allegations.) But sometime between Kobe Bryant's forgotten rape case in 2003 and Roger Ailes's ousting in 2016, people's willingness to turn a blind eye to sexual harm came to an end. In the aftermath of Weinstein's downfall, societies around the world have been forced to reassess attitudes towards women. It's happening at a scope and speed not seen in decades. In the early days of the reckoning, the focus was on sexual violence, harassment, and exploitation. The direction of blame centred on the individual perpetrators, but then evolved to the institutions that have ignored and enabled the harm. The discussion has since branched out to include broader issues of gender discrimination, power dynamics, and the fight for equal pay and representation in business and elected office. Each of these ills stems from the same pool of misogyny. It shouldn't be surprising that women are sexually harassed in the workplace, given how they're treated in the areas of compensation and promotion. In its most evil iteration, sexism manifests itself as rape culture.

These conversations aren't new. They've just spilled into the open. Now the question is, What will—and should—the world look like when the ground stops shifting?

CHAPTER 3

THE LAWS AREN'T THE PROBLEM

ONE OF THE most surprising things I learned while investigating the handling of sexual assault complaints in the criminal justice system is that Canada already has some of the most progressive laws in the world—and it's been that way for two decades. Even the country's most activist lawyers and scholars agree on this point. Among the dozens of legal experts I've interviewed on the subject—Crowns, defence attorneys, judges, law professors, criminologists—none had serious complaints about the law. In fact, most are proud of it.

Beginning in 1982 and continuing through the decade, Parliament passed a series of amendments to the Criminal Code that dramatically improved the country's laws governing sexual violence. First came the repeal of rape and indecent assault offences and the creation of three gender-neutral sexual assault charges. The government also abolished the requirement for corroborating evidence, meaning that a judge no longer needed additional and independent outside evidence to convict an accused. Then the doctrine of "recent complaint" was removed, meaning that if a victim hadn't immediately run or cried for help after an attack, judges and juries could no longer view that as undermining the complainant's credibility. Finally, rules were put in place to limit the ways in which a complainant's sexual history could be used in court. In the ensuing years, Canadian courts responded with a number of enlightened—and binding—judgments that nudged the law in an even more progressive direction, including strong language from the Supreme Court denouncing rape myths and stereotypes.

Today, Canada operates with what's called an "affirmative" consent standard. This means that individuals engaged in sexual activity need to be sure their partners are agreeing to it. Rather than waiting for a no, both parties need to indicate yes—and individuals who are incapacitated by alcohol or other factors aren't considered capable of consent. In Canada, a victim isn't required to resist an attack or scream for help for the event to be considered sexual assault. Nor do complainants need to appear visibly upset while recounting the incident later in order to be believed. The law officially recognizes that there is no set "rule on how people who are the victims of trauma like a sexual assault will behave." Other jurisprudence has discounted the notion that a person who has consented to sex in the past is more likely to consent to sex later, an update intended to address the "unchaste" woman stereotype. Taken together, these laws should provide all the tools necessary for the justice system to

arrest, prosecute, and convict sexual assault assailants. And yet
at every stage of the process, from the police investigation to the
trial to the final judgment, issues persist.

In Canada, the laws aren't the problem. It's the willingness
to enforce them.

MADDIE CURLED UP on her side and stared blankly at her
bedroom wall, shifting between sadness, anger, and worry.
Her temples throbbed and her joints ached. She needed a drink
of water but she didn't want to move. So instead she lay there,
cycling through the previous night again and again, as if thinking about it hard enough would change the outcome.

She reached for her phone on the nightstand. There was
a text from him.

"Sorry for all this. i didnt know if you wanted this or not
but i made sure, i asked like 5 times and stuff and yeah, my
apologies I feel like a huge dick I dont know if it because of,
you know youre too drunk or what not," he wrote. "You didnt
deserve that drama, not one bit."

She could hear her parents downstairs, banging around
in the kitchen getting breakfast ready. Maddie badly wanted to
talk to her mom, but when she imagined what her mother's
face would look like hearing the news, the prospect was too
painful. So instead she typed out a text message to her: "If you
can't remember saying 'no,' is it rape?"

An instant later she heard footsteps flying up the stairs.
Her mother pushed open the door, her eyes wide with worry.
She lay down next to her daughter and held her. Maddie dis-
solved in tears. "Okay, what happened?" her mother asked,
trying to sound calm.

That night Maddie and her parents sat in a room at police headquarters, waiting for a detective. The space was decorated like a grandmother's living room—muted green walls, framed floral art, a potted plant, faux wood furniture, a cream couch with burgundy swirls—except that it was outfitted with a video camera that recorded everything said and done within its walls.

Maddie sat hunched forward on the couch, her arms wrapped around her stomach. Her unwashed blond hair was pulled back from her face in a half ponytail. She'd had only about three hours of restless sleep. Maddie was tired, hungover, afraid, and confused.

"Just be honest," her mother said.

"I feel fucked up because I know [him] and everyone knows [him]," the eighteen-year-old replied. "I honestly don't think [he] knew . . . that it was wrong."

"I think he did, because he texted you first thing this morning, right?" her dad said.

Maddie stole a glance at her phone. Friends were texting, asking what was going on.

"I haven't thought about how I feel about the situation because that's all I keep thinking about—what's going to happen to [him]?" Maddie said. "I don't want to ruin his life . . . it's not fair."

At that moment, a police constable, a tall woman in a hot pink blazer with spiky brown hair, walked into the room. "You ready?" she asked the teenager. Maddie smiled. Her mother got up and kissed her on the cheek. "We won't be far away," she said as she and her husband headed into the hall.

The officer took a seat on the opposite side of the room and pulled out a notebook. She introduced herself in a gentle, sing-song voice, the way a grade two teacher might address a new class of children.

"So, I've asked you here this evening to sit down and just have a chat with you about the incident that you found yourself in last night. . . . My job is to find a solution to the problem. And jail isn't always a solution to the problem, and being charged and having a criminal record isn't always a solution," she began. "It might be a stern talking-to. And when I talk to him, he might go, 'Holy crap, I didn't even real-ize she wasn't an interested party. . . .' All I want to do is just gather as much information about what you can recall and we'll go from there."

Maddie nodded as the officer spoke. She later told me she had no idea what was supposed to happen, but she trusted the investigator. She told her the same story she'd told her parents that morning.

The night before, Saturday, October 10, 2015, she and some friends were driving around town, dropping in to vari-ous parties. Sometime after two a.m. they went somewhere new. By that point, Maddie said, she was very drunk. She told the police officer that her memory was shaky. She knows she decided to leave the party to get something from the car, and a guy—I'll call him Eric, but that's not his name—went with her. "I'm not even sure how we ended up in the car. I started just getting whatever it was. And then he just grabbed me. Like grabbed my face, and then I don't really—I have no idea if consent was given. At all. And then, I just, I don't really remember much at all, just that he was on top of me and then, I didn't have pants on."

The next thing Maddie remembered was that one of her friends was banging on the window. "He was like 'This isn't right, get off, get out of the car. We're going home' and I was just crying." Later in the interview, the investigating officer circled back to when the two first got into the car. Maddie said she couldn't recall exactly what they'd talked about—probably music. Then she remembered him saying something like "You're too hot for me" and "I don't want you to regret this." The officer asked what she'd been thinking in that moment. Maddie said that she hadn't really said anything, that she was "confused" and "shocked" by what was happening. The officer wanted to know what she specifically did when Eric kissed her. "I kissed him back, but I wasn't really, like, thinking or moving." Maddie said she had no memory of the time between the kiss and the moment she realized she had no pants on and he was on top of her. The officer never asked the seventeen-year-old how much she'd had to drink, but she did ask Maddie about what Eric had consumed.

Two days later the case was passed on to another constable, who interviewed several people from the party. One of Maddie and Eric's mutual friends told that officer that on a scale of one to ten, between sober and completely obliterated, both had been about a "nine and a half." Multiple witnesses told him that Maddie had told them she didn't remember consenting, although one felt that she obviously must have known what was going to happen because she agreed to go to a car with him while drunk. They said that it seemed like a ruse—an "excuse"—to leave the group to go have sex.

Four days after the party, the investigator contacted Eric, who by then was back at college, out of the city. The interview, which lasted about twenty minutes, was conducted by phone. In Eric's version of events, Maddie was the instigator, the one who'd "jumped" him. At other times in the interview, he insisted that he'd asked her permission before things escalated to sex. The officer never challenged any of Eric's claims. Nor did he specifically address the text message that Eric sent to Maddie the morning after, even though Eric alluded to the message himself, saying that he'd apologized because he didn't want what happened to become a "big deal"—because (to him) it wasn't.

"Did she say anything to suggest that she didn't want to do this?" the officer asked.

"No."

The officer asked Eric if he'd told Maddie "I don't want you to regret this." Eric agreed that he had. And so, the officer continued, did he think he'd done anything wrong?

"I don't believe so," Eric replied, although in hindsight, he conceded that maybe it hadn't been the best idea. The officer concluded the interview by telling Eric that "this sort of thing can happen" and that in future, he should make sure that he and any of his sexual partners are clear about what they're agreeing to.

Eric told the officer people were saying he raped Maddie.

"If you had consent, it's not rape," the officer reassured him.

The case was closed without any charges.

IT WAS ONLY when I heard stories like Maddie's through my Unfounded reporting that I appreciated how lucky I'd been during my own teenage and university years. How many times had my friends and I drunk too much at a party or at a bar? It had never occurred to me that I had been in danger of anything other than a hangover. How many near-misses had I had in my youth? I included Maddie's case in an Unfounded story that examined the ways sloppy police work can derail sexual assault investigations. There were a litany of problems with the way her complaint was handled, none of which I found to be uncommon. But of all the case files I've seen, this one best crystallizes the disconnect between the written law and what's happening on the ground.

The first police officer ended Maddie's initial interview by telling the teenager that she didn't think charging Eric was the best option, because he likely "misunderstood" that she hadn't consented. "You have to take a little bit of responsibility as well, right?" she said. "And you unfortunately drank too much. You unfortunately found yourself in that position."

The officer's comments are a textbook case of victim-blaming and are totally inappropriate. What's more, she seemed to be closing the investigation before interviewing a single witness—including the suspect. But the most striking aspect of the interview is that the police officer fundamentally failed to grasp Canadian law. (And because of that, she seemed unmotivated to investigate Maddie's claim.)

In May 2017 the Office of the Independent Police Review Director—which oversees allegations of police misconduct in Ontario—concluded that both constables made "a critical error" relating to their "understanding and application of 'consent.'" With Canada's affirmative consent standard, the officers should have been focused on collecting evidence to determine whether Maddie had indicated she wanted to engage in sexual activity, either through words or actions—not whether she said no. Furthermore, in Canada, a person who is so intoxicated that they don't understand what's going on can't consent to sex. A witness told police that Maddie and Eric had both been extremely inebriated—a nine and a half out of ten— and yet neither officer bothered to investigate whether Maddie had the capacity to consent. This despite the fact that Eric's texts the morning after the incident suggested he was aware that Maddie's "ability to consent was compromised," the OIPRD report states. Instead, at least one of the officers seemed more concerned with how much *Eric* had had to drink. Maddie's intoxication was used against her. Eric's was seen as a mitigating factor.

Through decades of case decisions, the laws around consent have been refined, clarified, and strengthened. But what I learned while reporting on Unfounded is that many of the police officers tasked with investigating sexual assault didn't seem aware of these developments.

I interviewed a thirty-eight-year-old nurse named Kelly, for example, who told me she'd been violently raped at an acquaintance's house. Police records showed that the detective was skeptical of Kelly's story, in part because of the way she acted. Why hadn't she screamed for help when others were in the home? Why didn't she run out afterwards? Kelly told the officer that she was afraid the man, who was much bigger than she was, would hurt her more than he already had. The officer didn't buy it, and the case was thrown out.

I spoke with a university student named Melodie whose allegation was dismissed because the suspect told police *he* thought the encounter was consensual. "'He doesn't feel like he raped you,'" Melodie recalled the detective saying. Legally, an accused can try to make the argument that he honestly believed the complainant was a willing participant, but it's not enough for him to just *decide* it was consensual. He has to be able to provide concrete examples of ways she indicated yes. It seems the officer didn't know this. After CBC reported on the story, the file was reassigned to a new officer and the suspect was charged with sexual assault and a choking-related offence.

I also interviewed a twenty-eight-year-old named Stacey, who told police that a man she'd been dating forced her to have sex. She says she told him outright that she didn't want to, but when it was clear that he wasn't going to stop, Stacey asked him to put on a condom out of concern for her health. In a video of her police interview, the detective—a woman—concluded that Stacey asking for a condom could be seen as a sign of consent, erasing all her earlier refusals. "You know, sometimes women—or even just people in general—even though you're thinking he may get the hint that 'I don't really want to do this,' guys don't," the officer told her.

In other cases I looked into, the officers simply skipped basic investigative steps—including interviewing witnesses, collecting surveillance footage, and running forensic tests on physical evidence. Eventually, I came to see this as an extension of the problems around understanding consent. When a sexual assault allegation fit the folktale rape story—a bad man in the bushes and a virtuous victim—I saw officers move mountains to catch the perpetrator. It was the messy cases where they seemed unmotivated; they seemed to think that the allegations weren't that serious. It was drunk teenagers having sex. Or a misunderstanding. I think those officers viewed the incidents as ethical, rather than criminal violations, even though the law would disagree.

As part of my series, I interviewed Crowns from across the country, and several I spoke with shared a similar opinion. "I think with a lot of these cases, especially the ones that aren't so black and white, among these guys [police officers] there is a feeling, 'Why should one stupid night ruin your life?'"

That attitude seemed to permeate Maddie's file. From the outset, the investigating officers appeared preoccupied with how an accusation like that might affect the accused, Eric. It was apparent from the police reports that the officers viewed the incident as a case of teenagers making bad decisions. In fact, the report cites the supervising sergeant referring to the allegation as "drunken teenage sex." I think that mindset prevented them from conducting a proper investigation. To be clear: the specifics of the case—Maddie's memory gaps and the uncertainty around the line of incapacity—would always have made a conviction difficult, but her complaint should have been treated seriously. That was the point of my Unfounded project. It wasn't about sending more people to jail; it was about making sure that sexual assault allegations—even the difficult ones—are thoroughly investigated.

In that respect, there has been progress since Unfounded was published.

IN THE MONTHS after my series ran, Canadian police services pledged to audit more than 37,000 previously closed sexual assault files. In the fall, the country's largest force, the Royal Canadian Mounted Police, invited me to its headquarters in Ottawa to meet with some of the officers assigned to go through those cases. "For the files we've reviewed, there's some that are really, really well done," said Sergeant Wendy Smith, who was leading the audit. But, she said, they were finding problems. It was clear some investigators had been influenced by myths and stereotypes. Others appeared to misunderstand consent law. Some were unaware of how trauma can impact a victim's behaviour and ability to recount an offence—for example, a file where the investigator noted "authenticity" concerns with a victim's statement because she couldn't tell the story chronologically. These issues weren't necessarily common, Smith told me, but they came up often enough to be notable.

As part of its case audit and new training plans, the RCMP developed a twenty-page "Best Practices" guide for sexual assault investigators. It includes a breakdown of consent laws and how they apply to specific situations, information about how trauma can affect a victim's account, and a checklist to ensure a thorough investigation. I had similar meetings with other big police services, and every time, I was surprised by how sincere they seemed. After all, I hadn't had high expectations of how police would react to the series.

Here's why: three months before the *Globe* published Unfounded, I emailed more than a hundred Canadian police services to let them know exactly what my series was going to allege. I highlighted how that particular force's unfounded rate compared with the national average and gave each agency an opportunity to respond to any specific acts of wrongdoing involving its police officers that I'd uncovered. I also included fifteen basic questions, which I explained were designed to help me form a clearer picture of what was happening on the ground in each jurisdiction. Among the questions I asked were these: Does your service have a dedicated sex assault unit? Is it mandatory for officers to receive specialized training before investigating sexual assault? Do senior officers ever review sex assault cases to determine whether the investigation was thorough? The response was not encouraging.

Only eighteen police services provided answers. More than a dozen others promised to reply but never did, and seventeen formally declined to answer, including the country's largest agencies, the RCMP and the Ontario Provincial Police. Of those, ten police services emailed me the exact same two-hundred-word statement, which included the following line: "We do not believe it is in the public interest to pull staff from their core duties to respond to your request."

I was shocked. It was obvious that some police services had banded together to try to stonewall my investigation. (Remember, I'd already spent more than a year battling many of these services to release the unfounded numbers.) In fact, I found emails from the head of the Ontario communications branch suggesting that police services form a united front and decline to address the issues my series raised. I was later able to prove that a national network of media relations officers from dozens of Canada's largest police services had spent weeks coordinating this non-response. Included in the hundreds of pages of email conversations released to me through a freedom of information request: "I am rather tired of spending hours and hours of time gathering all this detailed information and statistics for reporters who will only use it to write negative stories about police. Why should we participate?" one wrote. "I totally agree," replied another. "It's partly our responsibility to educate [the reporter] and perhaps she may second guess some of the conclusions she seems to be making," said a third. (The first comment was written by the manager of corporate communications at one of the country's largest police services. In 2017, taxpayers paid her $147,194.22.) These communications officers appeared as ambivalent about public accountability as some of the detectives did about enforcing Canadian sexual assault laws.

So when my Unfounded series appeared, I was fully expecting police services to go on the attack, or, at best, to ignore it altogether. But that didn't happen. Within days—as police boards, politicians, community groups, and regular citizens demanded action—police services were clamouring to make pledges of reform. Police chiefs were calling me on my cell phone and apologizing for ignoring my requests. The *Globe* had put together an online look-up tool so that Canadians could search their local police service's unfounded record. Whenever a police service had refused to participate, the *Globe* had noted it. Now some of those departments were begging me to retroactively include their statistics. Apparently, they'd been facing backlash in their own communities (as well as from within their own ranks—certain individual officers had tried for years to convince their superiors that the service needed a new approach to handling sexual violence). Week after week, police services held press conferences announcing new oversight measures, policies, and training initiatives. It was remarkable.

The *Globe* had presented the country with indisputable evidence that police were mishandling sexual assault complaints. But I don't think the subsequent policy changes were inevitable, given that this wasn't the first time police had been called to account for high unfounded rates. In the 1980s, criminologist Julian Roberts was hired by the federal Department of Justice to look at that very issue. Numerous other academics have conducted similar studies and written similarly damning reports. Statistics Canada spent years cautioning police services about the improper use of the unfounded code. But little changed in law enforcement practices.

To me, the sudden about-face that followed the publication of the Unfounded series was a sign that police leadership hadn't recognized how far public attitudes had shifted on sexual violence. If the internal emails from the communications officers were any indication, Canadian law enforcement officials had been expecting to sit back and do nothing—even after being presented with volumes of evidence that sexual assault investigators either didn't understand the law or had been wilfully misusing it. That people found this unacceptable seemed to catch police chiefs off guard. Advocacy groups have spent decades asking police to make the kinds of changes they're making now, but it wasn't until the wider public got on board that things began to change.

CHAPTER 4

FLASHPOINTS

THROUGH THE CENTURIES, laws have evolved as attitudes change. These shifts don't always happen in perfect
lockstep, but they're reliably connected. It's why historical
court cases serve as a fascinating window into the values of the
past. This is especially evident in sexual assault trials.

One such case in April 1858 involved a farmer in rural
Ontario suing his teenage daughter's Sunday school teacher for
the tort of "seduction." Most rape cases from this era were handled in the civil system, if they were dealt with at all. And since
in 1858, women were considered chattel, sexual assault was
considered a property crime against the woman's father. This is
how a *Globe* newspaper article explained the allegations: "In
July, 1856, [the teacher] watched her going into the woods to
look after the cattle, followed her and accomplished his purpose, although she struggled." Similar incidents occurred over

the following year, the story continued and, ultimately, she became pregnant with his baby. In addressing the jury, the judge warned that most women in the teenager's situation will cry rape in order to "screen themselves" from scandal. "[The judge] spoke in severe terms of the conduct of the girl and the neglect of her parents towards her," the reporter noted.

Canada enacted its first Criminal Code in 1892. (Before that the country borrowed from the British system. Through the decades the laws shifted. Legislatures enacted statutory requirements for corroboration. The constant was the deep skepticism of a woman's word.) At that time, the statute addressing sexual violence was limited to "rape," defined as a man's "carnal knowledge of a woman who is not his wife without her consent" and where consent hadn't been obtained through threats or "fraudulent representations." Courts also relied on a series of statutes passed by the various colonial entities—for example Upper Canada, Nova Scotia, Quebec, etc.

Even as women won the right to vote, the right to hold office, the right to practice law, progress was slow. Nearly a century after that Ontario farmer sued his daughter's Sunday school teacher for violating his "property", Canadian courts were still treating women as lesser human beings.

Take a random sentencing hearing in Toronto from November 1951. Four teenage boys had been convicted in a brutal gang rape of a fifteen-year-old girl. The attack lasted three hours and the suspects had apparently held down the victim's younger sister throughout. When it came time to decide on a punishment, Justice Gale reminded the youths that the maximum penalty for rape was death or life imprisonment, "but I do not intend to send you to the penitentiary," he said. Instead, they were being sentenced to a number of months in reform school. "I think that fundamentally you are all decent," the judge concluded. (The *Globe* ran an editorial criticizing the light sentence and was then found in contempt of court because a hearing involving a fifth accused was still in progress.)

This not-so-subtle sexism pervaded our country's criminal justice system for most of the twentieth century. The saga of Gerald Regan, who served as premier of Nova Scotia from 1970 to 1978 and who later became a federal cabinet minister, illustrates how recently that kind of thinking prevailed. Beginning in the mid-1950s—just a handful of years after Justice Gale reassured four gang rapists that they were good lads deep down—and continuing over the next two decades, Regan was alleged to have sexually abused scores of women. The accusations didn't become public until the early 1990s, when the RCMP announced it was investigating past sexual misconduct claims against the former premier. In 1994 the CBC's investigative program *The Fifth Estate* tracked down more than a dozen of the alleged victims. The following year, the then sixty-six-year-old Regan was charged with sixteen criminal offences, including rape, attempted rape, unlawful detention, and indecent assault. More charges were later added. A total of twenty-two women came forward to police. Most didn't know one another. Many told a similar story of being cornered, molested, and attacked. The women were babysitters, a journalist, a housekeeper, a dishwasher, a government secretary, a page in the Nova Scotia legislature.

The RCMP focused its case on the allegations of thirteen complainants. Regan's lawyer, the late, legendary Edward

Greenspan—a mentor to Jian Ghomeshi's lawyer Marie Henein—was ruthless. At one point he mused about placing ads in newspapers across the country asking for tips regarding the women's histories. In 1998 Regan was found not guilty of eight offences. (A judge had stayed the others.) The verdict was appealed, and through legal manoeuvring by the Crown, the case climbed all the way to the Supreme Court. By April 2002, however, it was all over: prosecutors announced they were abandoning the case after some complainants declined to press forward. To illustrate the tenor of discussion at the time, in February 2002 the *National Post*'s George Jonas had this to say: "The chances of a male accused of a sexual offence receiving a fair trial in Canada's matriarchal justice system [are] better than the chances of a Jew receiving a fair trial in Nazi Germany, but only just." If that sounds over the top, writing in *The Globe and Mail*, Ian Hunter, a professor emeritus at the University of Western Ontario's Faculty of Law, remarked:

> The trial of Mr. Regan reminds me of the 1930s trials of old Bolsheviks in Russia. . . . Mr. Regan's real offence is to have betrayed the feminist orthodoxy to which, as a Liberal politician, he invariably paid lip service. Yes, I know, the age difference, the power imbalance etc., but Mr. Regan is from a different era, when unwarranted indiscretions led to a slap on the face, not to relentless state prosecution. Is it fair to apply, retroactively, the standards of this era to the conduct of a previous one?

When the case collapsed, the tone of the coverage was more of the "Ordeal Ends" and "Prosecutors Give Up" variety (headlines in *The Globe and Mail* and *Vancouver Sun*, respectively) than the burning outrage you'd expect in today's post-Weinstein world, less than twenty years later. Sexual assault laws are mostly the same; what's changed is public sentiment.

Law professor Elaine Craig thinks a crucial difference between then and now is the emergence of social media platforms like Twitter and Facebook. "Some of the perceptions that you saw with Regan—like arguments from the defence that the pendulum has swung too far in favour of complainants—continue today. But I think it's undeniable that the form and volume of public engagement on this issue takes a different shape now because of social media," Craig told me, pointing to the reaction to the #MeToo hashtag.

Craig isn't confident that Regan's trial would play out differently if it were held today, but she said the commentary about it would take a very different form.

Social media provides a venue for everyone to express opinions—not just those with access to the editorial pages of a mainstream newspaper. In the past, the wider implications of a legal case centring on sexual violence would be debated among the elites in the op-ed pages. This was the case with the trial of Steve Brian Ewanchuk, the outcome of which would make it one of Canada's most pivotal sexual assault cases in history.

Although Ewanchuk lacks the name recognition of a Jian Ghomeshi, his 1995 trial had a lasting impact. The proceedings wound their way up to the Supreme Court of Canada and established some of the most significant principles in our modern laws. Not only that, but the case ignited a very public dispute between two prominent judges about whether feminism had hijacked the criminal justice system. For the first time since the legal reforms of the 1980s, a sexual assault trial asked Canadians to take stock of their values around sexual violence and power.

IT BEGAN IN June 1994 when Ewanchuk arranged to meet a seventeen-year-old girl in the parking lot of an Edmonton mall under the pretense that she'd be interviewing for a job. Ewanchuk ran his own woodworking business and had said he was looking for some help. He conducted the interview in his van, and then invited the girl to see some photographs of his work that he kept in a trailer hitched to the back. After she climbed inside, he followed and shut the door. The teenager testified that she believed it was locked and became frightened, although she tried to hide it so as not to "egg on" Ewanchuk. (The court heard that the teenager weighed about 105 pounds and stood barely five one, while Ewanchuk was over six feet tall, twice her age, and "two to three times" her size.)

Inside the trailer, she mentioned she had a young baby and a boyfriend. Ewanchuk asked if she was a friendly and affectionate person like him. He began making more aggressive sexual advances. He told her he wanted a massage, and she complied. Then he massaged her shoulders, stomach, and the area near her breasts. She pushed him away with her elbows and said "no." Ewanchuk assured the girl that he wouldn't hurt her and began massaging her again. He exposed his penis and rubbed it against her pelvic area. With each advance, she told him "no" or "please, stop." Her ordeal lasted two and a half hours.

In November 1995 Justice John Moore found Ewanchuk not guilty of sexual assault, arguing that even though the teenager had said no—three times—her rebuffs left room for Ewanchuk to believe she was a willing participant. It seemed reasonable to the judge that Ewanchuk believed he had "implied consent." Explained Moore: "[She] is a credible witness, and I know that she was afraid. . . . However, she successfully kept all her thoughts, emotions, and speculations deep within herself. She did not communicate most of [them]." It was noteworthy, he added, that she never asked to leave the trailer and that when she finally did, Ewanchuk let her walk out.

Alberta's Court of Appeal upheld the decision in February 1998 in a two-to-one split. Justice John McClung delivered the reasons for judgment. "The Crown tried to prove that what occurred did so against her apparent consent, but [the prosecution] did not succeed," he began. "She was afraid, but she wanted Ewanchuk to think otherwise. She succeeded." It is worth mentioning, the judge continued, that the girl didn't enter Ewanchuk's trailer "in a bonnet and crinolines." She'd had a baby and was living with her boyfriend. In an earlier time, he said, a young woman might deal with an unwanted suitor by dropping "a well-chosen expletive, a slap in the face or, if necessary, a well-directed knee"—not a criminal complaint.

But the Crown argued the case up to the Supreme Court. And on February 25, 1999, the country's highest court ruled that there was no such thing as "implied consent"—meaning that a person can't assume that a sexual partner has consented simply because the partner is silent or has stopped resisting. A person must agree to engage in sexual activity and that can be expressed through words or actions. The justices also took the unusual step of finding Ewanchuk guilty of sexual assault. This landmark decision became known as the "no means no" case, and put on record that outdated notions were no longer welcome in the criminal justice system.

"This case is not about consent, since none was given. It is about myths and stereotypes," declared Justice Claire L'Heureux-Dubé. Myths such as that women fantasize about being rape victims; that a no actually means "yes" or "try again" or "persuade me"; that a woman who does not want to be raped could fight off her attacker; that rape isn't as bad for women who've already had sex; and that women often deserve to be raped because they've acted a certain way or dressed provocatively.

Why, Justice L'Heureux-Dubé asked, had Justice McClung highlighted the fact that the complainant had a baby and was living with a man out of wedlock? His comments could be taken as a suggestion that she was a person of questionable character and, by extension, less worthy of belief. For Canadian feminists, Justice McClung's statements were all the more painful because of his pedigree. John W McClung was the grandson of one of Canada's most tenacious suffragettes, Nellie McClung.

The Ewanchuk case drew national attention, particularly after Justice McClung broke all protocol and publicly slammed Supreme Court Justice L'Heureux-Dubé in a letter to the *National Post*. He suggested that views like hers could explain the high rate of suicide among men in Quebec, her home province. As the backlash began to swell, he said in an interview that he "was just trying to give my friend Claire a prod because of her consistent anti-male response on these matters." McClung later apologized.

It's worth noting that when Justice Moore acquitted Ewanchuk in 1995, it wasn't the first time the man had stood accused of sexual assault. In November 1969, at the age of nineteen, Ewanchuk raped a sixteen-year-old girl he'd offered to drive home after she missed her bus. Two months later, he did it again to another girl. And then another woman two years later. And he sexually assaulted another in 1986. In each case Ewanchuk was charged, convicted, and sent to jail. In 2003, four years after the Supreme Court decision, Ewanchuk began molesting a seven-year-old girl. It continued into 2004. He was once again found guilty of sexual assault in November 2005.

THE EWANCHUK CASE is an example of a flashpoint trial that triggered national debate and helped to clarify an ambiguity in the law. It's credited with establishing Canada's affirmative consent standard. It made clear that what matters in consent is what's happening in the mind of the complainant, not in the mind of the accused. Today that's a foundational principle of the sexual assault provisions, said Lisa Dufraimont, a professor at York University's Osgoode Hall Law School and an expert on evidence in criminal proceedings. "It's an important case for championing the interests of the complainant," she told me. "The [original] trial judge came in and said, 'Even though she didn't agree in her mind, with the way she acted, I'm going to take that as consent, I'm going to [infer] consent.'" The Supreme Court's overturning of that decision, then, represented a fundamental paradigm shift. "I think this—the subjective understanding of consent as something that exists in the complainant's mind—was the intention of Parliament when they rewrote the Criminal Code," Dufraimont noted, "but we need cases to spell things out for us in our legal system."

In other instances, high-profile cases can reveal subtle shifts in how the justice system operates outside of official changes to the law. Consider the trial of Halifax taxi driver Bassam Al-Rawi, who in 2017 was found not guilty of sexually assaulting an extremely drunk female passenger.

On May 23, 2015, Constable Monia Thibault was on patrol in a sleepy residential neighbourhood of Halifax when she spotted a taxi idling on a street corner. It was one twenty a.m. and the street was empty and dark. Constable Thibault walked closer and noticed the rear window was fogged up. She looked inside and saw a woman passed out in the back seat, naked from the breasts down, her legs spread open and propped up on the two headrests. The driver, meanwhile, was leaning back in the fully reclined front seat, fumbling with something in his lap. It looked to Thibault as if he was trying to conceal a pair of pants and blue underwear. "I noticed his zipper was undone and his pants were halfway down his backside. I placed him under arrest for sexual assault," the officer later testified during the two-day trial.

The female passenger was unconscious. The officer had to shake her awake. "She was very confused as to where she was," Constable Thibault told the court. The woman told the officer that she'd been out with some friends at a downtown bar. She recalled getting into a cab, but she couldn't "remember anything after that." Thibault collected the woman's pants at the scene and noticed they were damp—she had urinated on them. Toxicology tests recorded her blood alcohol level at about three times the legal driving limit. DNA swabs identified her DNA around Al-Rawi's lips.

Court testimony revealed that, because she'd been so intoxicated, security staff at the bar had refused to let her back in after she'd briefly gone outside. Evidence showed she'd travelled in the taxi for only ten or eleven minutes before Thibault approached the cab. The young woman testified that she had no idea why she'd be in the south end of Halifax; she lived on the other side of town.

In his closing submissions, Crown attorney Ronald Lacey told Judge Gregory E. Lenehan that even if the court found that there was consent, the complainant clearly did not have the capacity to agree to sexual activity, as she was too intoxicated.

Al-Rawi's defence attorney, Luke Craggs, argued that consent was not the issue. Rather this was a case where the Crown had not proven beyond a reasonable doubt that the complainant had been sexually assaulted. (Al-Rawi himself never took the stand.) In his closing arguments, Craggs had an answer for every troubling bit of evidence. On how her DNA ended up on the driver's face: "I would submit the more logical inference . . . is that [she], intoxicated, uninhibited, exercising questionable judgment, did something to Mr. Al-Rawi to get it on his face, maybe a kiss, maybe licking his face. . . ." On why the cab had driven off in a direction so far from her home: She hadn't wanted to go home, the attorney argued, referencing conversations she'd had with her friends at the bar. On why Al-Rawi had parked on a dark side street: "Her friend recalled her saying she needed to use the bathroom. I mean, a side street seems like a logical place to pull over . . . squat against a tree, and relieve yourself." On why Al-Rawi's pants were down: "I mean, it looks kind of like how we feel after Christmas when we eat too much and suddenly we can't get into our pants anymore." On why Al-Rawi seemed to have possession of most of her clothing: "It is reasonable to infer from all of the . . . evidence that [she] drunkenly removed her own clothing and threw it at Al-Rawi and threw it in the front of the car." And on how her legs came to be resting, spread open, on the two headrests: "[The complainant] just put them up there for some reason."

Three weeks later, Judge Lenehan announced he had reached a verdict.

There was no question, he said, that the woman was unconscious and incapable of consenting at the time the officer came upon the cab. "What is unknown, however, is the moment [the complainant] lost consciousness." To this question, the Crown had no answer. The Crown also couldn't determine if she had consented, because she didn't remember. And as for the idea that the woman was too drunk to agree to sexual activity regardless—even if she was awake—Judge Lenehan concluded that it was his understanding that a severely intoxicated person could be "capable of appearing lucid."

"Taxi drivers are therefore under a moral obligation to not take advantage of intoxicated people," he said. "Once he saw she had peed her pants, he knew she was quite drunk. He knew going along with any flirtation on her part involved him taking advantage of a vulnerable person. . . . [But] a lack of memory does not equate to a lack of consent. . . . I am left with no alternative but to find Mr. Al-Rawi not guilty."

Even five years ago, a case like Bassam Al-Rawi's would likely have died as a news blip: Cab Driver Found Not Guilty of Sexually Assaulting Intoxicated Woman. But Judge Lenehan reached his controversial decision in March 2017 in a post-Ghomeshi world and a month after the *Globe*'s Unfounded series, when public attention on the topic was high.

People were outraged.

The Al-Rawi acquittal drew condemnations from across the country—in newspaper columns and editorials, from politicians, academics, and advocates, and on social media. Hundreds gathered to protest in downtown Halifax. A few days after the verdict, Al-Rawi was accosted on a bus by Halifax transit riders who called him a "disgusting rapist." An Instagram post about the incident went viral, prompting a statement from the Halifax Regional Police urging calm. Meanwhile, the Nova Scotia Judicial Council was inundated with complaints demanding a review of Judge Lenehan's conduct. A dozen Nova Scotia women's agencies joined calls for the judge's removal from the bench.

Lenehan did become the subject of a judicial investigation, but the committee ruled that his behaviour did not meet the test for misconduct. However, in a unanimous decision, the Nova Scotia Court of Appeal overturned the acquittal, concluding that Lenehan had erred in law when he found that there was no evidence of lack of consent. The court ordered a new trial, which is pending.

For Lisa Dufraimont, the Al-Rawi case reveals how the courts' approach to sexual assault cases has changed in recent years. The Osgoode Hall evidence expert told me that she believes the Court of Appeal got it right in finding that Judge Lenehan had ignored significant circumstantial evidence of the complainant's non-consent. But in a different political climate, she said, a Crown may well have elected not to appeal. Sexual assault cases involving alcohol are always considered difficult, and judges are given considerable latitude in determining "beyond a reasonable doubt." So even though Judge Lenehan's legal errors would have also been errors a decade ago, the Crown might have accepted the not guilty verdict. "I think it's fair to say that there are those in the legal community even now who would have thought it would be hard to appeal on Al-Rawi," she told me.

Still, what cases like Al-Rawi's show, Dufraimont continued, is that the legal community is making a concerted effort to prosecute these challenging files.

IT'S THANKS TO the reforms of the 1980s and judgments such as the Ewanchuk ruling that Canada's legal system is among the most forward-thinking on the subject of sexual violence. Elsewhere in the world, the recent surge of public outrage has meant that officials are just beginning to turn their attention to updating archaic laws. But it often takes one of these flashpoint cases to draw public attention to the wrong.

That was the situation in California following the 2016 conviction of Brock Turner, the former Stanford University swimmer who was convicted of sexually assaulting "Emily Doe" behind a dumpster at a frat party while the girl was unconscious from alcohol consumption.

The trial became a global scandal after the Santa Clara County District Attorney's office decided to release Doe's statement in its entirety after the sentencing hearing. "You don't know me, but you've been inside me, and that's why we're here today," Doe's letter began. In 7200 scorching words, she eviscerated Turner's version of events, the defence's reliance on rape myths, and the entire culture's culpability in perpetuating stereotypes about women and sex. Her letter voiced the griev-ances of a generation of women. After BuzzFeed posted a copy on its website, Doe's words were viewed 11 million times in four days. It sparked impassioned debate about consent, drink-ing culture on university campuses, and privilege, and exposed the many hidden loopholes within California's sexual assault statutes.

Emily Doe, who was twenty-two at the time, had planned on staying home that Saturday night but made a snap decision to go to a frat party with her younger sister who was in town visiting. She drank at the party, forgetting that her alcohol tolerance had diminished since she was in college. Hours after the attack she woke up on a hospital gurney with blood caked on her hands and elbow, pine needles in her hair, and no mem-ory of how she got there. Her blood alcohol was estimated to be three times the legal driving limit.

She'd been rescued by two Swedish graduate students, Peter Jonsson and Carl-Fredrik Arndt, who were biking past the Kappa Alpha fraternity party on January 18, 2015. They noticed a male "thrusting" his hips into the body of a half-naked, motionless woman. Doe and Turner were in a clearing between a dumpster and a basketball court. Jonsson told the court that the woman "looked asleep," and that when Turner saw them approaching, he ran away "as fast as he could." The Swedish students ran him down and phoned the police. The twenty-year-old Turner, mean-while, testified that Emily had verbally consented to the sexual activity and denied that she'd been unconscious.

Within days, a jury of eight men and four women returned with a verdict: Brock Turner was guilty. Sentencing would be held a few months later. Prosecutor Alaleh Kianerci had asked for six years, but the district attorney's office began bracing itself for a major letdown after learning that the probation officer was recommending a "moderate" sentence as Turner had also been drunk. Turner had no criminal record, and it was the official position of the State of California that the sexual assault of a drunk person was not as bad as the sexual assault of a sober person. In other words, state-sanctioned victim-blaming. It was one of the dated laws that would be changed as a result of the Turner trial.

When the sentencing day came Judge Aaron Persky imposed a lenient six-month jail sentence. Turner ended up serving three.

It was an unsurprising decision, Jeff Rosen, the district attorney in Santa Clara County, told me: "Most judges would have done the same thing . . . because that's how these cases were viewed by the probation department, by the bureaucracy, by the court insiders, if you will, whereas I think the public viewed this differently." In fact, two years after Emily Doe's letter ricocheted around the globe, California voters took the astonishing step of recalling Persky over his Turner decision, making him the first judge in the state to be recalled since 1932. It was salient evidence of Rosen's point—the public was fed up with the status quo on sexual violence.

More changes followed in the wake of the trial. California lawmakers proposed new legislation to amend California's sexual assault-sentencing guidelines closing the loophole that allowed judges to hand down lighter sentences to offenders convicted of assaulting an unconscious or intoxicated victim. It also set mandatory minimums for sexual assault convictions. A second bill inspired by the case expanded the definition of rape to include penetration with any foreign object rather than just a sex organ. Both California bills passed with broad bipartisan support, a noteworthy feat considering the state of partisan politics and the politically charged nature of this kind of reform.

"That was the law for a long time and nobody questioned it," Rosen said. Had it not been for Emily Doe's galvanizing letter, there wouldn't have been the political will to make these changes, he said. "I'm not sure what set off the #MeToo movement, but I certainly think this case was a part of that."

CANADIAN POLITICIANS HAVE also taken note of the public unrest around high-profile sexual assault cases—most notably *R. v. Ghomeshi*—and have responded by proposing legislative changes.

In June 2017, then justice minister Jody Wilson-Raybould introduced Bill C-51. It aimed to amend the Criminal Code in a number of ways, the most controversial of which was to limit the ability of an accused person to enter into evidence any private records belonging to the complainant that the accused happens to possess. Although the wording of the legislation is vague—it's not entirely clear what "records" means—defence lawyers across Canada decried the proposal, declaring that it was clearly intended to prevent the situation that arose during Jian Ghomeshi's trial. In court the former CBC host's accusers had been presented with their own emails on the witness stand—emails that proved parts of their sworn testimony weren't true. In a criminal trial, the Crown is required to hand over all the evidence they have to the accused. But the defence has never been required to do the same. Bill C-51, lawyers have warned, would create a "reverse disclosure" situation that would drastically curtail an accused's ability to defend themselves.

"Under the new law, an accused person will be required to disclose to the Crown and the complainant any records that will be used to challenge the complainant's credibility or reliability. Let's cut to the chase—these are the new Ghomeshi rules," Michael Spratt, a partner at the Ottawa criminal law firm Abergel Goldstein & Partners, wrote in *Canadian Lawyer*. "In other words, the legislation will tip off a liar that records exist exposing their lie and then gives them a chance to come up with an explanation."

Some academics (including Lisa Dufraimont), along with a number of notable defence attorneys, have cautioned government against making these changes. Before the reforms of the early 1980s—and rulings such as *R. v. Ewanchuk*—the Canadian justice system was indeed heavily biased against complainants, they concede, but the fixes have already been implemented. Canadian laws are up to the task.

The problem with the proposed legislation, Dufraimont said, is that in the rare instance when complainants lie in court, Bill C-51 may give them the tools to avoid detection. Marie Henein would not have been able to elicit a spontaneous reaction from the witness about an email that proved she had misled police.

There is never going to be a perfect system where every guilty person is convicted and every innocent person is acquitted, Dufraimont told me. There is no perfect law that's going to rid the world of sexual assault. People don't stop committing crimes because the government passes stricter sentencing rules.

"I think what's really needed is a deeper cultural change. Respect for others. Respect for women and children," she said. "Ultimately, I think things like campus initiatives around consent training will do a lot more to prevent sexual assaults than any changes to the law."

CHAPTER 5

CONSENT: IT'S NOT AS SIMPLE AS TEA

ROUGHLY THREE MONTHS after the Harvey Weinstein grenade launched the first feminist cultural reckoning of my lifetime, I was at home thumbing through Twitter on my iPhone when suddenly my entire feed seemed be talking about the same thing. A website I'd never heard of, Babe.net, had published a piece entitled "I went on a date with Aziz Ansari. It turned into the worst night of my life."

As I read those words, I felt that stab of grief that was becoming so familiar: another famous man, whose work I really enjoyed, was turning out to be an utter creep. Thus far, the list of #MeToo casualties included Oscar winner Kevin Spacey, comedian Louis C.K., actor James Franco, and broadcaster Matt Lauer—accused, respectively, of sexual assault, masturbating in front of unwilling women, sexually exploiting female acting students, and sexually harassing subordinates, including exposing himself to a female employee and then, when she failed to acquiesce, reprimanding her for it.

The thought of Ansari being included among this rogues' gallery was especially painful. This was the guy who co-wrote *Modern Romance*, the bestselling book about relationships in the world of texting, sexting, and Tinder. Ansari publicly identified as a feminist. A week before the Babe.net story dropped, he showed up at the Golden Globes proudly displaying a Time's Up pin on his lapel. He won best actor in a comedy that night for his role in the quirky Netflix show *Master of None*, a series he created, which tackles male-female power dynamics with nuance and thought. *Master of None* devoted an entire episode to exploring casual misogyny. In one brilliant scene that every woman can relate to, Ansari's character, Dev, is at a bar with his girlfriend, Rachel, and two other friends, Arnold and Denise, when he's approached by a work colleague. The man shakes hands with Dev and Arnold but ignores the women entirely. When Rachel and Denise balk at this afterwards, Dev's reaction is to downplay the slight as unintentional, which infuriates Rachel: "There are a lot of subtle little things that happen to me and all women, even in our little progressive world. And when somebody, especially my boyfriend, tells me that I'm wrong without having any way of knowing my personal experience, it's insulting."

What I'm getting at is that Ansari had always presented as the ultimate "male ally," a man who not only draped himself in the flag of feminism but who championed female voices and challenged men to think about the world from a woman's perspective. The Babe.net headline was crushing. I clicked on the link and prepared to mourn an idol.

The article began in a familiar way. "Grace," a twenty-three-year-old photographer, had met Ansari at an Emmy Awards after-party the previous September. A week or so later she went to the comedian's Manhattan apartment and they shared some wine. "It was white," Grace told the writer of the piece. "I didn't get to choose and I prefer red, but it was white wine." (You could practically see the writer underlining the sentence and writing a little star in the margin: *foreshadowing—Ansari does not care about what Grace wants.*)

The story followed Grace and Ansari to a dinner and then back to Ansari's apartment. Once inside he kissed her, they began making out. Ansari took off their clothes, although Grace told the writer she felt uncomfortable about how fast things were moving. When he announced he was going to get a condom, Grace spoke up: "Whoa, let's relax for a sec, let's chill." Ansari went back to kissing her and then performed oral sex briefly. Afterwards he asked her to do the same, and she did, Grace said. This first encounter lasted about ten minutes but Ansari's advances continued throughout the night, despite Grace giving "non-verbal cues" that she was "uncomfortable and distressed." Said Grace: "Most of my discomfort was expressed in me pulling away and mumbling. I know that my hand stopped moving at some points . . . I know I was physically giving off cues that I wasn't interested." Finally, Grace told Ansari that she didn't "want to feel forced," to which he replied, "Of course, it's only fun if we're both having fun" and suggested they "chill" on the couch. But once there, he motioned to his penis and Grace performed oral sex again. "I think I just felt really pressured," she said. Grace eventually announced she wanted to leave and Ansari called her an Uber.

The next day, the piece continued, Ansari texted Grace to say it was fun meeting her and Grace replied with a lengthy message, part of which read, "Last night might've been fun for you, but it wasn't for me . . . You ignored clear non-verbal cues; you kept going with advances. You had to have noticed I was uncomfortable . . . it may have seemed okay. But I didn't feel good at all." Ansari wrote back, "I'm so sad to hear this. . . . Clearly, I misread things in the moment and I'm truly sorry." The story concluded with Grace telling the Babe.net writer that she believed what happened in Ansari's apartment that night constitutes a sexual assault.

As a piece of journalism, in my opinion, the story was disastrous. It was poorly reported and rife with irrelevant asides (like the unwanted white wine) that were apparently included as evidence of Ansari's bad character. To me, they read as red flags that the reporter was comfortable contorting banal facts to better buttress a desired narrative. It made evaluating an already thorny case even more challenging.

Even assuming that everything happened exactly as the writer had described, I didn't consider Ansari's actions significant misconduct—let alone sexual assault. He wasn't her boss. There was no suggestion she was drunk. He wasn't threatening. It didn't sound like a date I would want to be on, but I was struggling to classify this as a #MeToo story. I text-messaged three of my smartest girlfriends, asking: what am I missing?

"There was such a lack of enthusiastic consent here," one replied. All types of misbehaviour need to be on the table for discussion if things are ever going to change, another added. There was a clear power imbalance, because of Ansari's celebrity, and he would have been aware of that, said the third. My friends were united in the idea that if a man wants to pressure a date for sex after she's made it clear she's not into it, he should be prepared for the consequences. Essentially, what they were saying is that Ansari had it coming.

Until then, the voices complaining that #MeToo had gone too far were mostly coming from the fringes. Babe.net brought backlash to the mainstream. Two columns defending Ansari were shared widely online. In a piece for *The Atlantic* headlined "The Humiliation of Aziz Ansari," Caitlin Flanagan wrote, "Apparently there is a whole country full of young women who don't know how to call a cab . . . and last night they destroyed a man who didn't deserve it." In a *New York Times* op-ed Bari Weiss said, "I'm apparently the victim of sexual assault. And if you're a sexually active woman in the 21st century, chances are that you are, too."

Equally eloquent voices took up the other side. "Perhaps what is especially threatening about Grace's story is that it involves a situation in which many men can imagine themselves. But this is a reason to discuss it more, not to sweep it under the rug," wrote Anna North in Vox. "Listening to Grace doesn't mean deciding all men should go to prison, or should lose their jobs. It does mean admitting that many men behave in exactly the ways their culture tells them to behave."

The Babe story exposed a generational fracture among feminists, with younger women tending to be more sympathetic to Grace's feelings and older women seeming more likely to fall in line with Caitlin Flanagan's thinking. At its core, this was a debate about consent and what that word means in the modern world.

In Grace's mind, what occurred in Ansari's apartment had been a "sexual assault." Her choice of words pulled the conversation into a legal realm, but to say Ansari's actions were illegal is a real stretch. It's not against the law to cajole someone into having sex. It may not be very nice, but if the person voluntarily agrees, it's not sexual assault. To me, at issue is whether the comedian violated a moral code. Nailing down the line between an ethical violation and a legal one isn't always easy when it comes to consent. For example, is having sex with a willing but really drunk partner illegal? No, provided the person isn't so drunk that the Criminal Code would consider the person incapable of understanding their actions. The point between severely intoxicated and incapacitated is fuzzy. You can be slurring, stumbling, even falling down or experiencing a memory blackout and still be capable of legal consent. On one side of that line, having sex with that drunk person can be described as not very nice. On the other side, it's rape.

This is why many academics and sexual health educators are trying to push the conversation in a new direction, where the focus is on sexual pleasure and being a good partner, not avoiding arrest. Farrah Khan, an advocate and educator, is one of those people. "If we keep setting the bar at 'Don't break the law' we're going to continue to have problems," Khan told me one afternoon.

I'd gotten to know Farrah Khan well in my years reporting on Unfounded. She's a femme, queer Muslim woman in Toronto with a master's in social work and a long résumé: among many other things, she runs Ryerson University's sexual violence support and education office, co-chaired Ontario's Roundtable on Violence Against Women, and sat on the Trudeau government's Gender Equality Advisory Council ahead of the G7 summit. Khan is one of the few advocates I've met who's adamant that a solution must involve men, and that a person who "causes harm"—she doesn't like the term "perpetrator"—shouldn't automatically be sent off to "rapist island," provided the person is willing to do the work to reform. (Of course, this excludes serious, serial abusers.) To some this might seem obvious, but it's a pretty controversial stance in other corners. For all these reasons and more, when Khan told me she was going to be running a consent training session at Queen's University during frosh week, I cancelled my Labour Day plans and decided to make the trip.

AT TEN A.M. on the first Sunday in September 2018, the lineup of first-year students ran five deep and stretched all the way around the Queen's Athletic and Recreation Centre. The residence dons, identifiable by their lime green T-shirts, marshalled the bleary-eyed teens to their seats in the bleachers. Most had moved into residence the day before and many looked as though they hadn't yet been to bed. A DJ blasted pop music, and at the front of the gym, two twenty-foot screens projected the first slide of the presentation: "Pleasure Principles" with Farrah Khan. Wiggling across the top of the screen were four GIFs: a banana, an eggplant, a peach, and a floppy piece of pizza that seemed to be licking up and down. (A GIF is an image file that can be a short little animation. As for the food, if you grew up in the era of sexting, you would recognize each as an R-rated invitation.)

"What's the pizza?!" one of the boys asked Khan, who was waiting by the front.

"What do you think it is?" she replied mischievously. (It's a tongue. And the peach is a bum. And the banana and eggplant are self-explanatory.)

At Queen's University, 95 percent of new students live in residence, giving school administrators a unique opportunity to communicate a message to all its first years. Khan's talk was considered mandatory, and had been built in to the week's orientation schedule. At this morning's presentation, nearly fifteen hundred students—half of all the young adults in residence—packed into every row of the gym. The other half would see an identical presentation at two p.m.

Once the last group of students had settled in, Khan strolled to the microphone in a knee-length red summer dress and chunky Adidas basketball sneakers. She is thirty-nine but speaks teenager fluently.

She began by asking how many of them had sat through a sex education class in high school. Then she clicked to a screenshot from the movie *Mean Girls*, where Coach Carr is talking to the students about the urges they might be feeling: "But if you do touch each other, you will get chlamydia and die." Everyone laughed.

"In high school," Khan continued, "when you were learning in sex ed., you learned about three things, right? You learned don't get pregnant, how to use condoms, or, the last one, is don't have sex. . . . But did anybody learn about anything else? Like pleasure?"

Two guys put their hands up and chuckled to each other.

"I want us to talk about pleasure if we're going to talk about sex," Khan said. "The thing that we know about sexual violence is one of the ways to address it is to actually know what we like and what we don't like."

The students were hooked. The guys wanted to learn about pleasing the girls. The girls wanted to learn about staying safe. By framing a discussion of consent around pleasure, Khan got the students thinking about the concept from an ethical standpoint rather than a legal one: consent as a positive—fun sex!—rather than as something associated with rape and police and court. The issues were the same. Consent is about making sure your partner is a willing and active participant in sexual activity. Ensuring that both of you are enjoying the experience accomplishes this task. Do you want to try this? Do you like this? Does this feel good?

Khan talked to the students about supporting and protecting each other. If a friend gets really drunk at a party, make sure you don't leave them alone. If you're out at a club and a guy is trying to grind on a friend, you could say something to him—or just pull your friend away and head to the bathroom. Be each other's squad, she told them. (At this point Khan cued up a GIF of fluffy alpacas moving together as a group.)

"What I like about alpacas is if you go for one, they all come for you," she said.

Maybe that creepy dude grinding up on a girl at the bar is your friend, she continued. "Don't be afraid to take a minute to 'call him in.' We live in a 'call-out' culture right now," where everyone is quick to publicly and mercilessly denounce each other online for real or perceived bad behaviour, Khan said. This is a different strategy. This is about finding an appropriate moment (maybe not when everyone is around) and taking that friend aside because you care about them and you want to let them know that what they did isn't okay. Maybe they don't know it's not okay, she said. (I stole a glance at the teens sitting around me. Not a single one was staring at his or her phone. They were taking in every word.)

And what about that even trickier scenario, Khan asked, where it's clear that a friend *has* had too much to drink and she's going home with a guy? Yes, her squad should check in and look out for her, but what about the guy's friends? "In this kind of situation, it's not just about supporting the person who's been drinking; it's also the person leaving the bar with them. Because what I want us to remember is that the person leaving the bar with them is someone we also care about," Khan said. "You actually do a favour for your [guy] friend by saying 'You know what, maybe it's not the night tonight. You know, maybe you should just go home.'"

This was another area where Khan has flipped the script.

She was taking up a current debate—about the extent to which it's up to women to avoid risky situations (like getting drunk at a bar) versus whether the onus should fall squarely on men not to commit harm—and adding another layer. Khan was asking men to avoid putting themselves in a situation where they could end up being accused of sexually assaulting someone. (Obviously, not all perpetrators are men and not all victims are women—I'm using these pronouns for clarity's sake and because statistics show that they're by far the most common.)

The message was clear: if one or more parties is extremely intoxicated, there are risks for everyone involved, so why not just go home? The responsibility doesn't lie solely with the woman or the man; it lies with both. Additionally, their respective groups of friends also need to shoulder some responsibility. Safety is a community issue, she argued.

As Khan wrapped up at around eleven a.m., I turned to a group of first-year students behind me. Callum, Laura, Tiffany, and Tina all lived on the same floor of the dorm and came from different parts of Ontario. All had been born in the year 2000. I wanted to know what they made of the presentation. Did they think they had a good understanding of what consent is now? Had they ever heard anything like this before? Each readily recited the basics, in the same way that I might have rhymed off the provincial capitals when I was their age: Consent is freely given. It can't be forced from someone through a threat or by a person in a position of power. People can't consent if they're totally drunk or unconscious. Consent can be withdrawn at any time. And just because you agree to one act doesn't mean you're agreeing to go all the way.

I was impressed.

Callum told me that he'd spent the summer working as a camp counsellor, and that during their training, the entire staff was shown a video about consent.

"They did that for us too, before prom—that tea video," Laura said.

"Yeah, that was it. The tea video," Callum said.

Actually, in the preceding six months all four had been shown the tea video, by either an employer or a teacher or both. You might have seen it too. It comes up often at the conferences and training sessions I've attended since getting into this area of reporting. The roughly three-minute "Tea Consent" video has been viewed more than seven million times on YouTube.

It opens with some simple black lettering on a white background: *Consent: It's Simple as Tea.* A man's voice begins to narrate: "If you're still struggling with consent, just imagine: instead of initiating sex, you're making them a cup of tea. You say, 'Hey, would you like a cup of tea?'"—there's a black-and-white drawing of a stick figure holding up a little mug—"and they go, 'Oh my god, I would LOVE a cup of tea!'"—another stick figure is smiling enthusiastically with their arms in the air—"then you know they want a cup of tea." But what if they say they aren't sure? (Now the little stick figure is looking at a steaming cup indifferently.) The voice explains: "Then you can make them a cup of tea or not, but be aware they might not drink it, and if they don't drink it, then—and this is the important part—don't make them drink it. Just because you made it doesn't mean you are entitled to watch them drink it."

The video cuts to one stick figure pouring tea into the other confused-looking stick figure's mouth. A big red line is drawn through the scene. The video continues: You can't get annoyed at them for not wanting tea. So what if they say they want tea and change their mind? "Sure, that's kind of annoying, as you've gone to all the effort of making the tea, but they remain under no obligation to drink the tea." And what if they're unconscious? The video shows the one figure asleep as the other forces tea down their throat. "Don't make them drink the tea . . . unconscious people don't want tea. Trust me on this." And what if that person had some tea with you on Saturday—does that mean you can always expect that they're going to want to drink your tea? Obviously not. "If you can understand how completely ludicrous it is to force people to have tea when they don't want tea, and you're able to understand when people don't want tea, then how hard is it to understand it when it comes to sex? Whether it's tea or sex, Consent Is Everything."

The video—produced in 2015 as part of an awareness campaign by the Thames Valley Police in the United Kingdom—has been universally praised as the perfect way to simplify a complicated topic. The analogy is especially convincing in the case of the incapacitated tea-slash-sex partner. But for Trent University professor Terry Humphreys, who's spent years researching the complexities of the issue, the tea video doesn't do much to help us understand the vast majority of real-life sexual scenarios.

Most people aren't talking through consent; they're relying on body language, he told me. And yet most of the messaging we hear on the subject focuses solely on verbal communication. Think about public awareness campaigns like "no means no" and "yes means yes" (or, "Would you like a cup of tea?"). The result, Dr. Humphreys said, is that students have a really good understanding of the technical definition of consent, but when it comes to their personal lives, it plays out much differently.

"The whole way we understand sex and the scripts we use to engage in sex says very little about talking. It's mostly nonverbal. I'll approach you this way. I'll touch you on your shoulder and then if you don't pull away, I know I can continue to the next level. It's a dance of intimate behaviour between two people, but with a lot of room for interpretation," he said. It's flirting over dinner, jokes back and forth, the establishment of a rapport. This part of the tango gets going long before the big finale. If and when a date escalates to sexual activity, that rhythm continues. Someone may move closer. Then there's a kiss. Does the person pull away? Do they kiss back? Maybe they move a hand to the other person's chest or caress their face. "I don't believe there's any one single cue that people are looking at. I think they're assessing a whole cluster of cues throughout the night. There's a whole context."

That's why when someone says he knew a partner wanted to have sex because "she smiled at me" and people respond with horror, Dr. Humphreys always feels sorry for the guy. "People are reacting: 'Oh my God, he thought he had consent because she smiled?' But he doesn't have the language to talk about the hundred little cues before that."

I asked the four university students from Khan's Pleasure Principles seminar about this. "So you've obviously had to sit through a lot of these sessions. How would you go about establishing consent? How do you make sure the other person is into it?"

Callum spoke up first: "I feel like a lot of it is sort of not really communicated consciously. It's not like people are going up to each other and saying 'Is this okay? Is this okay? Is this is off the table?' That'd be awkward. I think a lot of things are communicated without words."

The girls agreed.

"I feel like you really just end up going with it," Tina said.

THE RESEARCH SHOWS that this is exactly how most adults have sex.

In one influential study, 378 psychology students at the University of Kansas were asked to read two sexual scenarios and to imagine themselves as both the one initiating activity and the one consenting. Researchers handed the students a questionnaire that included thirty-four specific behaviours to consider as an indication of consent. Those actions ranged from explicit verbal signals—"I want to have sex with you"—to indirect verbal signals—someone asking if they should get a condom—and to non-verbal types of communication, including undressing, returning a kiss, smiling, and fondling. The questionnaire also offered something the researchers called "no response signals": allowing the person to take off your clothes, not stopping the sexual touching, and not saying no, among other things. The researchers found that the students relied on a range of verbal and non-verbal actions to show their (hypothetical) partners that they were willing participants. But—and read this next quote twice—the study found that "both women and men reported using no response, e.g., not resisting, more frequently than other signals."

The report was published in 1999, so it's dated, but studies conducted since then have reported similar findings. One 2017 study by a team of researchers primarily from Binghamton University in New York asked 145 heterosexual male university students to read a series of vignettes depicting sexual situations. The stories included a mix of verbal and non-verbal cues of consent—such as "pulls you closer to her" or "says 'I want you'"—as well as verbal and non-verbal cues of refusal—"pushes away from you" and "says 'Let's not do this right now.'" The researchers also offered examples of passive responses, such as "tenses up and doesn't say anything" and "stops responding but doesn't resist you in any way." And then they included contextual factors, such as whether alcohol was involved, the woman's attire, whether there had been a previous sexual relationship, and the level of intimacy before an interaction. What the team found was that men picked up on both verbal *and* non-verbal signs of refusal, but when there was a passive response, they filled in the gaps by assessing the context of the situation. If the woman came back to his apartment after a date, or if they had had sex before—the men read these as signs that she was interested in having sex. Basically, if the man believed that the woman desired him, then she was consenting. As the study's author, Richard E. Mattson, told me, "[For the men] she was consenting to sex by virtue of the situation. . . . She's not saying no or yes in those circumstances, so people were drawing on other things to make those decisions."

The study also measured its volunteers' key personality traits and found that men who held ideas suggestive of hypermasculinity—now fashionably referred to as "toxic masculinity"—were more likely to ignore cues of refusal or passivity. "There are certain types of gendered sex roles that are pretty ubiquitous within North American culture. Essentially, the woman is the gatekeeper of sex and her job is to throw up obstacles, and the man is the pursuer, so the courtship routine is almost a predator and prey situation. Men, to varying degrees, buy into this," Mattson said. (I think some women buy into it, too. We're conditioned from a very young age to believe that the ideal sexual scenario is one in which the strong man takes charge.)

Further muddling the already confusing relationship between consent and desire are the numerous studies that have found men to be more likely than women to view a situation as sexually charged. In the original 1982 study, whose findings have been replicated since, a man and a woman who'd never met were asked to have a five-minute get-to-know-you conversation while another couple—also an unacquainted man and a woman—watched. Both couples were later asked to assess the conversation using a set of behaviours (such as the level of flirting) connected to sexual intention. The result was that the men perceived more sexual intent in the conversation than the women did, and reported being more sexually attracted to the women than the other way around. Pair these findings with Mattson's work, and you can see the dilemma: men think desire is equal to consent, but men aren't always able to accurately assess desire.

It's important to remember that, for the most part, what we're talking about here is consent from an ethical perspective. At the best of times, sexual assault cases are challenging. A scenario where a person communicates non-consent through inaction isn't likely to end up before a judge—even though, technically, Canada's affirmative consent standard requires an indication of yes that doesn't need to be spoken. In the Aziz Ansari case, "Grace" clearly gave verbal and physical cues that she wasn't interested in having sex. She said she pulled away, stopped moving her hands, and told him to "chill" and that she didn't "want to feel forced." At the same time she reciprocated kissing, was passive while being undressed, and received—as well as twice performed—oral sex. She completely lacked desire, but Ansari could reasonably argue he believed she had consented.

Lisa Feldman Barrett, a psychologist and neuroscientist at Boston's Northeastern University, has studied the way mood impacts perception. The brain, she told me, is wired to predict and anticipate what the body is going to need next. It's responsible for the fact that right before you go to stand up, your brain will raise your blood pressure so that you don't faint. In a May 2018 *Time* magazine piece, Dr. Barrett wrote about this phenomenon—the brain projecting itself forward in time, predicting what it will see—in the context of how it could play a role in cases of mistaken consent. "The brain actually changes the firing of its own neurons to anticipate what it will encounter next," she told me. Sometimes, this can be so powerful that it can cause people to see things that aren't present.

In the article, she recounted the famous study by cognitive psychologists Daniel Simons and Christopher Chabris in which the researchers asked volunteers to watch a video of people passing a basketball and to count the tosses. The participants were so focused on the task that many didn't notice a man in a gorilla costume ambling across the frame. The volunteers' brains didn't see what was in plain sight. Barrett linked this finding with her own research, in which she found that people who are in a good mood are more likely to view others in a positive light, as more trustworthy and attractive. The reverse is true if they're in a bad mood. In a sexual situation, she said, this might cause one party to view a situation through "desire-coloured glasses." Taken together it's a recipe for miscommunication, with potentially very serious consequences. "In many cases, without verbal consent, two people's brains can perceive exactly the same events very differently. They can, in effect, be experiencing different situations," Dr. Barrett wrote in *Time*. "As a woman, I'm immediately skeptical that men can't tell the difference between consensual and nonconsensual activity. It seems like an easy out. . . . As a neuroscientist, however, I'm forced to consider another alternative, however distasteful." In our conversation, she added that although words aren't always clear, they're less likely to be misunderstood than body movement.

Not everyone is convinced.

Dr. Melanie Beres, a Canadian sociology professor at the University of Otago in New Zealand, researches the complexities of consent. She told me that studies pointing to miscommunication as a cause of acquaintance rape are overly narrow. The scenarios put to volunteers are always tightly controlled—short vignettes, for example, or five-minute conversations between strangers—and this is the wrong approach, she said. There's a growing body of research that assesses consent through a different—she would say more reliable—lens, and it's the area that Dr. Beres herself works in. To academics like her, the evidence overwhelmingly shows that people are communicating just fine when it comes to consent. The problems arise when one party chooses to ignore the message.

"My research is focused on whether people understand each other's willingness to participate in sex and the answer to that, I think, generally is yes. . . . We refuse sex in the same way that we refuse other social invitations," Dr. Beres said. "Let's say someone offers you some food and you aren't interested. You might say 'Maybe later' or 'I just ate,' and they'll understand you don't want food." This translates to sex, too. People communicate that they aren't interested in something in all sorts of ways. They hesitate, hedge, or mumble. They make excuses or change the subject. They give noncommittal responses. Sexual situations are typically drawn out. People aren't making a decision based on one thing. So even if a partner misreads one lack-of-interest cue, that won't be the only signal, she told me. This is why it's better to evaluate consent by looking at a prolonged scenario, where there are lots of opportunities to register someone's refusal.

Dr. Beres pointed to a 2006 study by a trio of Australian researchers who analyzed two focus-group conversations between heterosexual men in which a male moderator asked them to talk through refusals of both sexual and non-sexual scenarios. For the latter, when asked how they'd go about declining a friend's request to go to a pub on a Saturday night, the men often chose an approach designed to, as one put it, "let 'em down softly," such as a white lie like "I'm having dinner with my grandparents" or "No, thank you. I'm feeling seedy from last night." In the sexual scenarios, the men were asked how they'd go about telling a partner they didn't want to have sex that night. Again they fell back on soft language that would spare a partner's feelings, such as "I don't think this is a good idea" and "This isn't quite what I expected tonight." Another suggested calling her a cab to send the message. When they were asked about the reverse scenario—how they'd recognize that a date wasn't interested—the volunteers said they'd be able to pick up on unwillingness if she started checking her watch and talking about how late it was, became cold, pushed him away, or isn't flirting back. One said that you "generally undress each other to some degree and if she's not ripping your shirt off, you know, and you try and rip hers off [and] she doesn't respond in the same way, then you know it's a pretty good sign and you're not on the same level." Some men gave more explicit examples, such as being slapped in the face. The study was a small one, but its findings are in line with other research that suggests men actually do have a sophisticated understanding of the subtleties of refusals.

In 2009, Dr. Beres published a paper that reached similar conclusions. She'd conducted two dozen unstructured interviews with twenty-one young adults about a range of topics, including their dating history, their casual sexual experiences, and how they evaluated interest in engaging in sexual activity. The responses showed that both the men and the women evaluated consent on an ongoing basis throughout an interaction and recalibrated their expectations based on a partner's behaviour. "In some of those conversations, they'd say something like 'If I go home with someone from the bar, then that means they're interested in sex.' So then I'd say, 'Okay. Have there ever been times when you went home with someone and sex didn't happen?' And every single one of them would say, 'Well, yeah,'" Dr. Beres told me. The volunteers described subtle, non-verbal gestures, such as becoming tense or stiff or pulling away, as evidence of refusal. In reverse, the participants said they interpreted a partner pulling them closer, sighing, or moaning as evidence of consent. "I was really surprised when I started doing this research how articulate men were in being able to talk about this," Dr. Beres said. For most, an uncomfortable partner was an immediate sign to stop. "A couple of them talked about it differently. If they noticed she was getting uncomfortable, [one] said, 'You don't ask about it, because that kills it. You go back and you try again.' But it wasn't that he wasn't aware of those signs. He was acutely aware."

IT SEEMS TO me that both lines of research—that people are horrible at reading body language; that people are perfectly capable of reading non-verbal cues—could be true. It's possible for two people to have very different reads on the same

situation and it's also likely that some individuals are deliberately ignoring unspoken signs that a partner is uncomfortable.

In either case, the status quo isn't working and there's no
obvious quick fix. Most consent education campaigns only add
to the confusion by conflating consent as a legal concept with
consent as an ethical practice. Among the buzziest campaigns
circulating now is "Consent is as easy as FRIES." Consent is:
Freely given; Reversible; Informed; Enthusiastic; and Specific.
Some of these are consistent with the legal definition, but
there's no law that says you have to be excited about having
intercourse. (Think of a couple in a long-term relationship.
There are all sorts of reasons why one partner may agree to
have sex, even though they aren't feeling very "enthusiastic"
about it.) I've encountered well-intentioned student activists
at two large Canadian universities whose frosh presentations
include warnings that consent must be sober. In addition to
not being true in either the legal or the ethical sense, that's not
realistic advice for many first-year university students. They
may as well be pitching abstinence.

This wishful thinking is Dr. Humphreys's concern. Current
consent education campaigns don't reflect the way most people engage in sex. It's all "no means no" and "yes means yes,"
but as we've seen, people rarely communicate consent with
words, he told me. Ideally, adults would be having more verbal
communication in the bedroom, but that will require a big
shift that isn't going to happen on its own. "What it requires
is probably a multi-pronged approach," he said. "Yes, we need
to bring awareness to this. But if you really want to see change,
you need to go back to the public school sex-ed curriculum and
start there. That's where you can have more of an influence."

But where the education system is concerned, there isn't much hope either. Many school boards in Canada don't explicitly teach the concept of consent prior to high school, and attempts to do so have been met with controversy.

In Ontario, Canada's most populous province, the Liberal government of former premier Kathleen Wynne spent massive amounts of political capital pushing through an updated sex-ed curriculum that specifically addressed the issue. Under the revised teaching guidelines, students would begin learning about the general concept of consent as early as grade two, while kids as young as six would be taught that they can say no if someone does something that makes them uncomfortable. In grade six, students would learn about communication skills within a relationship. They would be taught that only a clear "yes" is a sign of consent, while silence, uncertainty, or a "no" means that the person hasn't given consent. In grade seven, discussions about communication would move on to the context of a romantic partner. And by grade eight the curriculum would explicitly address consent during sex. Students would learn that if a partner agrees to one type of sexual activity, it doesn't automatically mean agreement to others. In other words, this curriculum would have prompted students to think about all the issues that Dr. Humphreys says are essential in order to prevent sexual assault.

On February 23, 2015, following years of consultation with thousands of parents and parent groups, then Liberal education minister Liz Sandals unveiled the revamped curriculum at a news conference. Social conservatives and religious groups were furious. Charles McVety, the president of Canada Christian College, called the document "radical." The pro-life

Campaign Life Coalition organized protests at the legislature. Various fringe groups were feeding parents misinformation—for example, that the new curriculum would require Grade 1 students to view flash cards of genitals. In May, more than twenty thousand students were kept home from classes to protest the curriculum. At Toronto's Thorncliffe Park elementary school—where there's a large religious community—only ten percent of students showed up to class.

Nevertheless, the Wynne Liberals stood by the new curriculum and it remained in place for three years—until they were voted out of power in June 2018. Three months before that, when former Toronto city councillor Doug Ford won the leadership of the Progressive Conservative Party, he vowed to scrap the revised sex-ed lessons—a move that solidified his support among social conservatives in the province. He made good on that promise after becoming premier. In September, when Ontario students returned to school, teachers were instructed to revert to the 1998 curriculum—a document that included not a single mention of the word "consent." And given what Dr. Terry Humphreys told me, this doesn't bode well for how well these kids will understand the concept when they come of age.

Moreover, the difference between legal and moral consent remains a puzzle to many. In my four years of reporting in this area, I've learned that it's not just regular people and university students who don't understand the distinction. The people whose job it is to know that line don't get it either.

CHAPTER 6

THIS IS WHY
SHE DIDN'T SCREAM

THAT THERE IS such widespread confusion around consent—
including among some police officers and judges—poses an
obvious challenge to the criminal justice system. Sexual assault
cases usually centre on whether both parties agreed to the activity. Credibility is on trial: two narratives pitted against each
other. Judges and juries almost always have to make a determi-
nation based on scant physical evidence, which puts significant
pressure on detectives to conduct rigorous investigations that
will help point to the more plausible version of events.

That was the element missing from so many of the sexual
assault investigations I reviewed. Routinely, police seemed to
decide how seriously to investigate a case based on their initial
conversations with a complainant. I watched videos of several

interviews and read the transcripts of others. It was often obvious right away that the detective didn't think the allegations were worth pursuing. So it wasn't surprising to later read in the investigation's final report that police hadn't interviewed any witnesses, or tried to contact the suspect, or canvassed for any surveillance footage.

Reviewing those interviews showed me how important first impressions are to a police officer. If a complainant recounted what happened in a detailed and coherent way, I'd see detectives react positively, going above and beyond to prove a case. But if the individual's account was confusing or unsure, the file was much more likely to be written off without a proper investigation.

The tragedy is that seriously traumatized people sometimes struggle to remember details of their ordeal. They may not be able to tell a coherent story. And they may describe conduct that seems counter to how you'd think a person might act while being attacked. They may report, for example, that they felt frozen or unable to speak. Those behaviours are consistent with the actions of a person who was truly terrified. But many police officers, Crown attorneys, and judges are not well versed in an area of science known as the "neurobiology of trauma." In fact, historically the way police have been taught to investigate sexual assault makes them inherently suspicious of witnesses who can't repeat a story in chronological order or whose version of events is full of holes. That lack of understanding about how trauma manifests itself is a possible explanation for why so many sexual assault cases are being dismissed as false or baseless.

In the last decade, we've witnessed an explosion of awareness about how traumatic events can alter the way our brains and bodies function. Memory, speech, actions, emotions—they can all be affected. Today, across North America, law enforcement officials, military personnel, campus police, school administrators, counsellors, Crown prosecutors, and judges are being urged to educate themselves about the effects of trauma— and it might just change everything.

THE FIRST TIME I heard the term "neurobiology of trauma" was in 2016 in an interview with a Crown prosecutor. I wanted to know what she thought about the state of sexual assault investigations. When a police file landed on her desk, what did it look like? What problems, if any, were Crowns noticing?

"It's a real mix," she told me. Some detectives understood the issues and others didn't. (This Crown, like most Crowns I interviewed, asked not to be quoted by name, since she didn't have authorization from the ministry to speak.) It was apparent to her that some investigators were still being influenced by outdated ideas. Cases where the woman didn't react in a way that might seem logical—maybe she didn't scream for help or fight back or try to run away—weren't always treated as seriously as they should have been, the Crown said. Sometimes the complainant's demeanour during a police interview aroused suspicion in officers. If the individual didn't seem appropriately upset or distressed, or if she couldn't walk the detective through the night's events step by step, some officers saw that as evidence of deception.

"But what the research is telling us is that this is completely normal," she said.

I confessed I had no idea what research she was talking about.

"You really need to speak with Dr. Haskell," she said, referring to a Toronto clinical psychologist who's an expert on the
ways trauma impacts victim behaviour and memory. Lori
Haskell had been conducting seminars with police, prosecutors,
and judges on the topic, and the implications for the justice system were monumental. The Crown believed that such training
should be mandatory for law enforcement officials.

Two weeks later I was sitting on a couch in Dr. Haskell's
home office where she meets her patients. The room was cozy
and exactly what you'd expect of a psychology professor's
office: leather chairs, a cluttered desk, packed book shelves
lining the walls, well-cared-for plants.

I told her about the problems I'd been uncovering in my
research. My data suggested that Canadian police officers were
discarding around 20 percent of sexual assault allegations as
false or baseless, a rate that was much higher than for other
crimes. Dr. Haskell had a good guess about why that was
happening: sexual assault allegations almost always pivot on
consent, not whether a sex act occurred. And since there are
almost never any eyewitnesses, a judge is left to choose between
two versions of an event—the proverbial "he said, she said."
It's a dynamic that gives gut instinct a lot of power, and that's
how misconceptions and stereotypes can sabotage a complaint,
she told me. "Credibility for police is established right away.
If police think, 'This person can't talk about this coherently.
This story doesn't make sense—it's all over the place. I can't
understand this. This is not believable,' I don't think a lot of
cases even get past this point."

If police officers are trying to decide whether a story is
believable, and if the alleged victim is acting in ways that seem

contrary to normal expectations, then it's not surprising that they react with skepticism. And if they have no knowledge of the biological reasons why that complainant may be behaving in ways that seem odd to them, the skepticism will remain.

What the "neurobiology of trauma" does is provide scientific explanations for behaviour that is seemingly counter-intuitive, Haskell said. It comes down to how the brain reacts to threats. If a person feels in imminent danger, the brain's built-in smoke detector—an almond-shaped clump of neurons called the amygdala—sets off an alarm, switching the body into survival mode. When this response is triggered, a primitive system of the brain selected by evolution to save us from being eaten by predators takes over. At the same time, the conscious brain, the part people use to reason, think, and strategize, moves to the back seat. Meanwhile, blood and oxygen reroute to the muscles and adrenalin levels surge as the body prepares to confront a threat, run from it, or, if all else fails, freeze (and hope that the predator will lose interest). Sometimes a traumatized person may report feeling disconnected from his or her body.

Dr. Jim Hopper, an American psychologist who has extensively researched the neurobiology of trauma and who runs training sessions on the topic in the United States, talks about the reaction to trauma using a different framework than fight, flight, or freeze. In times of intense stress, he told me, the brain rapidly shifts to "reflexes and habits." This response is what makes it possible to train soldiers not to run or freeze when they're under attack. It's also where socialization comes into play for sexual assault victims. For example, girls and women are conditioned from an early age to be agreeable and accommodating.

"So they often revert to habits of politely or passively attempting to ward off unwanted advances," Dr. Hopper said.

In either scenario, the point is that if a person feels terrified for their life, their body can react automatically, without them necessarily thinking about it. When these stress hormones hit the part of the brain responsible for filing long-term memories, the hippocampus—a region of the limbic system— begins to function differently. That potent flood of hormones can cause the brain to encode certain images—usually directly related to the threat, for example, a predator's eyes—in vivid detail. But while some central details may be seared into a person's memory, peripheral ones may slip by entirely as a victim focuses all their attention on the present danger.

Dr. Haskell's presentations—I've now watched about five of them—are dense. She takes officials through the basic science, the brain's fear circuitry, and the impact of stress hormones, both during and after an attack. Armed with science, Haskell and others are trying to rewire societal expectations about how "real" victims act. "I'm looking at a lot of rape myths, and I think, Why don't rape myths go away? We do so much education around them. There's been so much written. But I think until people have an explanation that makes sense, they won't give them up," she told me.

Task one is getting police officers and judges to understand why so many victims have memory gaps. In every training session I've watched Dr. Haskell give, she asks the audience to imagine that she's suddenly pulled a gun on them. What are they feeling? Likely afraid and on alert. What are they looking at? Probably the barrel of the weapon. Then she asks everyone to describe the tie worn by the person sitting next to them. Or the colour of the wall. Few can recall. It's common sense that a victim would focus on the central facts of a traumatizing event. And yet police interrogators and courtroom lawyers place a huge value on peripheral details. (There were a hundred reasons why the Jian Ghomeshi trial went poorly for the Crown, but one point that garnered immense media attention was that one of the accusers misstated the make of Ghomeshi's car.)

In general, the way police officers have been taught to investigate crime is the exact opposite approach that should be taken with someone who's gone through a traumatizing event like rape, Haskell said. Traditionally, detectives have been told to ask complainants to tell their story, uninterrupted, from beginning to end and in as much detail as possible. The timing of an interview is important: the sooner after the incident, the better. And once the complainant has given her statement, the officer is expected to ask clarifying questions, probing the statement for inconsistencies. They may even ask her to tell the story again—backwards—on the assumption that if she's lying, it will be harder to keep the facts straight.

The science shows that this approach is setting up the complainant for failure, Haskell told me. A traumatized person may not be able to recount a linear narrative. Some chunks of what happened may be vividly burned into memory while others may not have been captured at all. Some aspects may be stored as sensory fragments—like the smell of a perpetrator's cologne—that are disconnected from time.

So a better way to question complainants is to ask what they *do* remember. What were they feeling? What did they see, smell, and hear? Then work forwards and backwards, slowly filling out the story. This interview should ideally be conducted two sleeps after an incident, since memories are processed during sleep and it can take two full nights for the brain to consolidate them, Haskell said. But instead police have been taught to get as much information as quickly as possible, regardless of whether a victim is tired, overwhelmed, or hungover. An officer might interview a complainant the morning after an incident only for her to remember more information a day or two later. Biologically, that makes sense. But the criminal justice system could view such revisions as inconsistencies—material for defence attorneys during a future cross-examination. (When we spoke, Dr. Hopper cautioned that waiting several days to speak with a complainant has its problems, too. Studies have shown that even more of the fast-fading peripheral details will be lost in this time, he told me. He suggested a middle ground: Police should conduct an initial interview right away that's as stress-free as possible to capture the gist of what happened and any details that could be critical in unearthing key evidence at the crime scene or identifying the perpetrator. Then, after the complainant is well rested, go back for a more in-depth interview.)

A victim's demeanour is also important. In the early 2000s, researchers Linda Light and Gisela Ruebsaat wanted to better understand why sexual assault allegations were being disproportionately dismissed as unfounded compared with other crimes. In a rare arrangement, the pair was given full access to 148 sexual assault files from police jurisdictions in and around British Columbia's Lower Mainland. Light and Ruebsaat examined the cases with an eye to identifying common traits among the complainants who were believed and the ones who weren't. Their findings were groundbreaking in that they confirmed advocates' long-time suspicions: the more a victim conformed to societal expectations of what a person should do when being raped, the more likely it was that her complaint would be taken seriously. If a case file noted that a complainant fought back, said no, or didn't present any mental health or alcohol or drug issues, her allegation was more likely to be treated as a legitimate one. If the reverse was true, the odds were higher that the report would be discarded as unfounded. These results aren't surprising. But Light and Ruebsaat also found that if a complainant seemed insufficiently upset when discussing the incident, their allegation was more likely to be dismissed.

There are many possible explanations as to why a victim may not be distraught when discussing an offence. It could be a result of the trauma itself, especially if she's being questioned shortly after an event. Stress hormones include the natural opiates the body releases to block pain, which can cause a person to seem emotionally flat, Dr. Haskell said. Recounting the attack may also send the victim back to the traumatizing moment, causing them to dissociate—that feeling of being detached from reality. Individual personality, socialization, and nerves can play a role as well. As part of the Unfounded series, I investigated a case where a detective had dismissed a rape complaint in part because the fourteen-year-old victim had giggled when the officer—a middle-aged male officer she'd never met before—asked her to describe the sex acts in detail. "I'm nervous," she explained. After the series ran, the police service reopened the case and obtained DNA evidence that proved the assailant's guilt. The man eventually admitted to having repeatedly abused the girl beginning when she was just twelve years old and he was twenty-six. He was sentenced to five years in prison.

Dr. Haskell thinks progress is being made in recognizing the neurobiological effects of trauma in sexual assault cases. In 2016 she was hired to run about fifty training sessions for Crowns and police—twice as many as the year before. "But it's very inconsistent. I get called in because some officer will see my presentation and say, 'You've got to come do this for us,'" she told me. Five years ago, no one was talking about trauma in this way, she added. That's partly a reflection of changing attitudes and partly because the neuroimaging science is quite new.

EVEN THOUGH POST-TRAUMATIC stress disorder (PTSD) became an official diagnosis in 1980, injuries of the mind remained invisible for another decade. Then, in the early 1990s, advances in physics and computer technology gave scientists a literal window into the brain. Positron emission tomography machines (PET)—which used small amounts of radioactive drugs—and later, magnetic resonance imaging technology (MRI), enabled scientists to see, track, and photograph brain activity. "For the first time we could watch the brain as it processed memories, sensations, and emotions and begin to map the circuits of mind and consciousness," famed psychiatrist Dr. Bessel van der Kolk remarked of this revolution in his bestselling book *The Body Keeps the Score: Brain, Mind, and Body in the Healing of Trauma.*

Not until scientists were able to provide visual evidence that a traumatized brain and a "normal" brain function differently did those in the criminal justice system begin to seriously think about the implications for victims. People needed to see it with their own eyes before they could change their beliefs and behaviour.

My first story in the Unfounded series—a ten-thousand-word piece that ran on February 3, 2017—included a long section about the neurobiology of trauma and the training Dr. Haskell was conducting with police. I summed up the benefits of a trauma-informed approach as follows: "It takes the gut-instinct subjectivity of an officer out of the equation, and instead roots an investigation in non-negotiable science."

It turns out that, like everything else connected to sexual assault reform, not everyone agrees.

CHAPTER 7

NO, IT'S NOT "JUNK SCIENCE"

ON SEPTEMBER 8, 2017—around the same time that dozens of police services across Canada were pledging to implement trauma-informed training—*The Atlantic* published an incendiary article by journalist Emily Yoffe entitled "The Bad Science Behind Campus Response to Sexual Assault." Yoffe argued that, in adjudicating sexual assault cases on campus, school administrations have been unduly influenced by the neurobiology of trauma. "In the past few years, the federal government has required that all institutions of higher education train staff on the effects of 'neurobiological change' in victims of sexual assault, so that officials are able to conduct 'trauma informed' investigations and adjudications," she began. But, she wrote, the research being used to justify these changes is bogus. She called it "junk science."

Yoffe interviewed Justin Dillon, a defence attorney in Washington, D.C., who represents accused students. Dillon said that even a couple of years earlier, trauma responses were barely discussed; now he struggled to remember a case in the past year where the word "frozen" hadn't come up. In paraphrasing his concerns, Yoffe wrote:

> Trauma, he says, is used to explain away all inconsistencies in some complainants' accounts that would otherwise seem to contradict their having been assaulted. Schools do not make public the training materials of those who investigate and adjudicate sexual assault. But through lawsuits, Dillon has obtained some examples, and he says the assertions of the "neurobiology of trauma" that infuse these materials make it almost impossible for the accused to mount a defense. When such assumptions are held by those sitting in judgment, he says, "how do you prove your innocence?"

In the United States—much more than in Canada—a cultural tug of war is being fought over the way universities handle campus sexual assault. Some take the position that schools have an obligation to protect students by taking a hard line against those accused of sexual misconduct. At some universities, this has meant that young men, and occasionally women, have been kicked out of school by internal review committees based on evidence that falls miles short of what would be acceptable in a criminal proceeding. And this in turn has generated intense backlash. Critics like Yoffe argue that the system has become so skewed in favour of the complainant that there's virtually no hope of an accused being accorded due process.

Further inflaming the situation is that the debate has become deeply politicized. In 2011 the Obama administration invoked Title IX—a federal law enacted in 1972 that prohibits discrimination on the basis of sex at any educational program that receives federal funding—to force the country's more than seven thousand post-secondary institutions to adopt new protocols for managing sexual misconduct allegations. Going forward, all students would be entitled to have their complaint investigated by the college—even if police didn't pursue charges. Allegations would be judged based on the civil court standard of a "preponderance of evidence"—what is most likely to have happened—rather than the much higher standard of proof ("beyond a reasonable doubt") used in the criminal courts. To assign a numerical value to this equation: criminal court judges have to be about 98 percent positive about an accused's guilt to convict, whereas university adjudicators had to be only 51 percent sure before expelling a student. (In November 2018, the Trump administration unveiled its plan to rollback the Obama Title IX regulations, including a proposal that would allow schools to raise the threshold for a finding of guilt to the "clear and convincing" evidence standard.)

Supporters have argued that, given colleges' dismal track record in addressing the problem, these were much-needed changes. In the 2015 documentary *The Hunting Ground*, film-maker Kirby Dick makes the case that there's a national epidemic of sexual assault on American campuses, but that schools are more concerned with protecting their reputations—and hence fundraising abilities—than their students.

In Canada, colleges and universities have also struggled to find the right balance between supporting a complainant and being fair to an accused student. Still, it's rare in this country for a student to be expelled. Administrators are more likely to arrange for an accused student to complete classwork off-site or to adjust the two students' class schedules so that they're less likely to cross paths. Even these accommodations have been controversial, as some accused students have complained (and successfully litigated) that in the eyes of their peers, they've been labelled guilty without a trial.

South of the border, the situation is more fraught. If a student makes an allegation of sexual misconduct to the school, it triggers a parallel justice system that's been stacked against the accused.

Three years after the Obama administration issued its order, it complemented the new guidelines with a report outlining best practices. The report mirrors the language of the neurobiology of trauma without actually using the term. "New research has also found that the trauma associated with rape or sexual assault can interfere with parts of the brain that control memory—and, as a result, a victim may have impaired verbal skills, short term memory loss, memory fragmentation, and delayed recall," it reads. One recommendation advised school officials and campus law enforcement to take trauma-informed training. This is the area that has caused controversy in some corners and was the focus of Yoffe's piece in *The Atlantic*.

Much of her article focuses on the work of Dr. Rebecca Campbell, an influential professor of psychology at Michigan

State University and one of the first academics to publicly raise the issue of the neurobiology of trauma in the context of sexual assault. She has been regularly tapped to train campus administrators, military personnel, and law enforcement about the way that fear of imminent death or harm can alter brain function. In 2012 she delivered a presentation at the National Institute of Justice (NIJ) called "The Neurobiology of Sexual Assault" that some schools use in their training. But Dr. Campbell is not a neuroscientist. Like Dr. Haskell, she has extensive research bona fides in the general area of sexual assault from the perspective of a psychologist, but when it comes to the brain, she's largely interpreting the research of others. And unfortunately, she hasn't always been careful with her language.

Dr. Campbell often used an analogy about Post-it Notes to describe how trauma impacts memory. At the NIJ she asked the audience to imagine that they need to take notes about her presentation using tiny Post-it Notes. Only a few words are going to fit on each sheet, Dr. Campbell said. Now think of "the messiest desk ever," because that's really what the human brain is. And envision all of those little squares of information scattered everywhere. All the details are there, perfectly captured. The challenge is putting them back in the right order. "What we know from the research is that the laying-down of that memory is accurate and the recall of it is accurate," she told the conference.

Except that isn't true.

Yes, the research shows that trauma can have a significant impact on memory, but not in the way Dr. Campbell has suggested. Some memories will be retained, but peripheral ones— the wall colour, for example—may never have been captured in the first place. No amount of searching through a desk will turn up those Post-it Notes. Moreover, memory at the best of times is unreliable, as has been proven repeatedly by scholarly studies.

And that wasn't the only thing Campbell got wrong. In that same 2012 presentation she discussed a phenomenon known as "tonic immobility" in which an animal in fear for its life can become paralyzed for an extended period of time. Feigning death is an evolutionary tactic of last resort when an animal is unable to escape or defend itself against a predator. Dr. Campbell asserted at the NIJ conference that "most data suggests" that close to 50 percent of rape victims experience tonic immobility.

But that's also not true.

There is no proof that 50 percent of victims report extended paralysis. Furthermore, tonic immobility hasn't been properly studied in humans. Dr. Campbell acknowledged to Yoffe that she had mistakenly conflated the term "tonic immobility" with a freeze response. (I also contacted Dr. Campbell to discuss the allegations in *The Atlantic* article. In an email, she told me that she no longer conducts training sessions on the neurobiology of trauma as she is focusing on other research projects. She added that the NIJ conference occurred seven years ago and that by the time Yoffe's story appeared in print, the content of her presentations had changed. "The scientific literature on trauma has grown rapidly over the past decade, ideas about how best to talk about these topics with non-scientific audiences have evolved, and so too did my own presentations on this topic until I decided to move on to other projects," she wrote.)

The unfortunate thing is that despite Campbell's mistakes about the science, her recommendations for improved sexual assault investigations are good ones. Like Dr. Haskell, she urges police to understand that sexual assault victims may not be able to spout off a chronological version of events. She warns that trauma can cause people to act in a way that may not make sense. And she advises police to wait two sleep cycles before interviewing a complainant so that their memory has time to consolidate. But in seriously confusing aspects of the science, Campbell handed ammunition to critics. To those looking for a reason not to change, she provided an escape hatch.

Dr. Jim Hopper said two big interest groups are pushing back against these reforms. Some of the resistance comes from those who are generally nervous about #MeToo. These are the "extremists" shouting about the death of due process and the war on men, he said. The other bastion of opposition comes from the libertarian movement, which views this type of mandated training as just more government overreach. In either case, Hopper told me, "this became an issue when it was applied to assaults committed by upper-middle-class white people on college campuses. That's when the backlash really hit." And *The Atlantic* article led the charge. The piece was highly misleading, Hopper said. It was a "selective and harsh characterization of one particular person's past teachings" that ignored decades of extensive and solid science. But that didn't stop it from being widely read and shared. "It was uncritically cited by *The New York Times*. That's the most influential newspaper in our country."

One of the issues critics focus on is psychologists' use of PTSD patients' brain scans—neuroimaging done by neuroscientists—to help explain what happens in the mind of a sexual assault victim at the time of an attack. The question is whether such a comparison is scientifically justified. To find an answer, I approached one of the world's leading experts on neuroscience and trauma—a woman who happened to work two hours outside of Toronto.

THE CENTRE FOR Functional and Metabolic Mapping on the Western University campus in London, Ontario, is a world-class neuroimaging facility that produces some of the field's most substantial research on trauma and the brain. The city's scientists have a long tradition of breaking new ground that extends back to the early 1980s, when researchers at St. Joseph's Health Care London captured many firsts in the field. They were, for example, the first to show that nuclear magnetic imaging could differentiate between normal and diseased tissue and the first centre in Canada to clinically operate an MRI and to capture an MRI scan of a human.

In the summer of 2018 I met Dr. Ruth Lanius, one of the world's most respected experts on the way trauma can physically alter the brain. She is a force, with a combined medical degree and Ph.D. in neuroscience, a background in psychiatry, and a long list of groundbreaking research on her résumé. Perhaps most famously, two decades ago, Dr. Lanius scanned the brains of a husband and wife who'd survived a horrific accident. The couple had been on Highway 401 outside of London en route to Detroit when a thick cloud of fog suddenly overtook the road. The husband, who was driving, hit the brakes. A transport truck slammed into the back of their car. A hundred vehicles were involved in the pile-up. A car slid into the couple's vehicle and caught fire. They watched a teenage girl burn to death. The husband eventually smashed through the front windshield and pulled his wife free. Neither reported any physical injuries, but both began suffering symptoms associated with PTSD.

A month after the accident, the couple agreed to let Dr. Lanius and her team interview them and scan their brains. Each was put in the scanner and read a script that would trigger flashbacks of the incident. With the husband, the front part of his brain lit up. This is an area associated with thinking, planning, and problem solving—such as how to escape from a trapped car. The visual part of his brain was engaged. His heart rate jumped. He was displaying a "hyperarousal response," a reaction that was consistent with other research being done at the time. But then the wife got into the scanner. Dr. Lanius remembers the shocking moment well.

It began the same way. The researchers read her a script designed to conjure intense memories of the accident. She'd been severely traumatized, and Dr. Lanius told me that she and a colleague, researcher Joseph Gati (who was also at the centre on the day of my visit), actually had a bet on how high her heart rate would spike. Instead, it stayed the same. The scans showed a shutdown of brain response. "Joe said, 'God, what the hell, Ruth? Do you think she's kind of gone?' and I said, 'I think you're dead on.' And when we pulled her out of the scanner and interviewed her about her experience, it's the opposite of the fight or flight response. It's that detachment from intense emotional experience." The wife told Dr. Lanius that when she was made to relive the accident in the scanner she felt "numb" and "frozen"—the same way she felt that day on the highway. She had dissociated, and the researchers witnessed it. Dr. Lanius showed me a series of images of both the husband's and wife's brains. The husband's scans are coloured with pockets of yellow and orange, indicating brain activity. The wife's are blank, save for one tiny speck of yellow associated with sight. The paper was published in 2003.

"It was an early breakthrough," Gati told me.

WITH THE SAME technology that Dr. Lanius used to scan the brains of the traumatized couple, scientists are now able to map how thoughts move through the brain. A researcher can show a person an image that triggers a memory and then the scanner can identify what parts of the brain become activated. Experiments have proven that traumatized brains are physically different. Thoughts that may be benign to one person can veer into sections of the brain that trigger stress and anxiety in another. For people suffering from trauma-related symptoms, these scans offer validation, Joseph Gati told me. "If somebody goes into the hospital with a broken leg and you take an X-ray, you go, 'Oh yeah. I see it's broken.' But until you see the brain broken [with these scans], it's very hard to understand."

After a tour of the MRI lab, I headed back to Dr. Lanius's office to ask her the question that had prompted my visit: is it correct to apply PTSD neuroscience to an in-the-moment traumatic experience? The neurobiology of trauma—as it's being used in the context of sexual assault training—relies heavily on research derived from patients remembering horrible experiences. No one has taken a scan of a person's brain while they're being raped, for obvious reasons. I wanted to know what Dr. Lanius thought about her research being used to explain the behaviour of a sexual assault victim. Is PTSD research really applicable?

"Absolutely," she told me. "The whole point of PTSD is that memories are relived. They're not remembered. They're often relived. And so the way people relive the memories is usually in the same form as what happened at the time of the trauma."

It would help, though, she said, if people were more precise with their language. "All of this memory debate, to me, sounds very concerning, because people aren't specifying what type of memory they're talking about." Memory is not monolithic, she explained. There are explicit memories and implicit memories, and the two are diametrically different. An explicit memory is a person remembering the first time they rode a bike. An implicit memory is the body knowing how to ride a bike. The first is rooted in a time. It's connected to a circuitry for autobiographical recall. The second is more procedural; it's not chronological. Dr. Lanius gave me an example involving trauma: imagine a person is stabbed in the neck and the memory that person retains is the sensation of blood dripping down their throat. "This is an example of a person travelling back in time and re-experiencing the bodily sensations that accompanied the trauma—even if they cannot describe the memory in words," she said. "You can't talk about it. You simply feel something warm coming down."

I thought back to a case I'd investigated in which a woman had reported being raped at work by an older, married colleague. He'd been making creepy jokes for weeks and she'd tried to avoid him, but on this occasion, the woman told me, the man cornered her in the break room at the end of their shift. She remembered him kissing her. "And then I froze. I don't remember much after that. My next memory was thirty minutes later," she told me. When I pressed further, she said the only other thing that came to mind when she thought about that day was a feeling of skin slapping against skin, although she couldn't picture this happening. It was just a feeling, she said. When we met, I hadn't heard about the neurobiology of trauma. I didn't know anything about sensory fragments or implicit memory. I hadn't known what to make of her description then. Now it was clicking.

Dr. Lanius said another element of the equation that's often ignored is the fact that people respond to trauma on a continuum. It's not an all-or-nothing reaction. A victim may remember everything. Or nothing. They may recall a mix of explicit and implicit memories. They may experience a fleeting or prolonged freeze—as if they're encased in cement—or feel only partially paralyzed. Perhaps they can move but not speak.

The feeling of tongue-tied terror is a trauma response that's been documented for centuries, but Boston's Dr. Bessel van der Kolk, a pioneer in trauma research, was able to put a picture to that truth more than two decades ago. In one of the first neuroimaging studies he conducted, Dr. van der Kolk scanned the brain of a forty-year-old teacher who'd suffered a horrific trauma. When the woman was seven months pregnant, she was driving with her young daughter when she realized that the girl wasn't properly buckled in. As she turned to adjust her seatbelt, she ran a red light. A car collided with the right side of her vehicle, killing her five-year-old. In the ambulance on the way to the hospital, she also lost the pregnancy.

Dr. van der Kolk scanned the woman's brain while she listened to a script reconstructing the event. Her blood pressure climbed and her heart raced. "Simply hearing the script activated the same physiological responses that had occurred during the accident thirteen years earlier," Dr. van der Kolk wrote of the experiment in *The Body Keeps the Score*. The woman's scans showed large spots of activation in the limbic area, where the amygdala—which helps us detect threats—can be found. None of that was shocking. What did come as a surprise was a white spot on the left frontal cortex in a part of the brain called Broca's area, one of the brain's speech centres. The white colour indicated a marked decrease in activity in the region. "Without a functioning Broca's area, you cannot put your thoughts and feelings into words," Dr. van der Kolk wrote.

I contacted Dr. van der Kolk at his Boston office shortly after visiting Dr. Lanius's lab. I explained that I was investigating the recent push to rethink sexual assault victim behaviour through the lens of trauma, and how it was creating a backlash. Some were arguing that it was built on a foundation of "junk science." I summarized the debate about whether neuroimaging studies done on PTSD patients could be applied to sexual assault victims, and described how critics had pounced on the fact that it was psychologists—not neuroscientists—interpreting that science (sometimes incorrectly). I explained that I was now interviewing scientists who had conducted the original research to see whether they felt PTSD scans could be used to prove that sexual assault victims can exhibit symptoms such as memory changes, freezing, and dissociation during or after an attack.

Dr. van der Kolk seemed annoyed by the premise of my question, "Scans are not the only way to do science. Science is any objective observation that's verified by a bunch of tests . . . I studied traumatic memories before we ever had the capacity to do brain scans," he told me. "The neuroscience is way behind the clinical positions. To the extent that people shut down and don't remember, and have a block against a coherent narrative—[that] is age old. . . . So now we can take pictures of people's brains, and say 'Oh, that explains why people cannot talk.' But we've known this."

The scans are useful in that they can help explain how and why a symptom occurs, he said, but the question of whether trauma victims experience sensations of paralysis, memory issues, or feelings of numbness was answered decades—maybe centuries—ago. The answer is: yes, they do.

Anyone arguing differently, he added, is being wilfully blind to the facts.

TO DATE, IN Canada, the push to use trauma-informed techniques in sex assault investigations has not been politicized in the same way that it has in the United States. Training programs in the neurobiology of trauma have been rolled out in most of the country's police services and many Crown offices without any negative public reaction. Judges are also under pressure from politicians and advocacy groups to take these courses—and many are (although Canadian judges can't be forced to attend specific training modules, as it's regarded as a threat to judicial independence). But behind the scenes, some of the conversations being held in the United States are occurring here. *The Atlantic* article, I'm told, was widely circulated among prominent legal circles.

Part of the reason the debate likely hasn't made waves here is that—as far as I can tell—the country's Crown prosecutors haven't yet tried to introduce this research as expert evidence in a courtroom. (The merits of the neurobiology of trauma is frequently debated during American sexual assault trials.)

It appears only one trial in Canada has referenced the issue of trauma's effect on the brain in the context of sexual assault—and it didn't end well.

The sexual assault trial of Mustafa Ururyar got underway at Toronto's Old City Hall courthouse on February 1, 2016. He stood accused of raping a woman named Mandi Gray when they were both Ph.D. doctoral students at York University. The pair had been in a casual sexual relationship for about two weeks leading up to the night in question.

In Gray's version of events, she and the accused had been out at a bar, drinking with friends. She asked if she could sleep at his place since he lived nearby. On the walk to his apartment, Gray alleged, Ururyar began berating her as "needy" and an embarrassment. Once indoors he grabbed the back of her head and pushed his penis into her mouth. "I don't remember him taking off his clothes or how that happened," she told the court. She said she was afraid he'd be physically violent if she didn't go along with it. "I don't know when that ended or how long that lasted for. I kind of checked out of my physical being," she told the court. "And then I—I don't know, I think he pushed me onto the bed . . . and then he started having sex with me and I just laid there." She couldn't say how long it lasted. In the morning, Gray texted a friend that Ururyar had had sex with her without her explicit approval: "I didn't consent—but I didn't not consent," she wrote. Gray reported the incident to police two days later.

Ururyar presented a very different story to the court.

He testified that there was "no doubt in my mind" that the sex was consensual. In Ururyar's version, Gray sent him a text message earlier in the evening saying, "Come drink and then we can have hot sex." (Gray deleted this text and did not mention it to police when she reported. She explained in court that she'd erased all messages from Ururyar after the incident and forgot about it.) Ururyar testified that Gray began "groping" his inner thigh at the bar and then continued even after he asked her to stop. (Gray told the court she didn't remember doing that, but she did recall Ururyar asking her not to touch him—a statement that she believed came out of nowhere.) That was the reason, he testified, he was angry on the walk home. Inside his apartment Ururyar ended things with Gray but they had sex anyway, with the understanding that it would be the last time, he testified. The next morning Gray left, angry, and he assumed it was because he'd broken it off between them. Later, Gray texted Ururyar, "Last night was really fucked up." He wrote back, "OK." Five days later he sent a final message: "I am sorry things went as they did. I shouldn't have said and done some of the things I did. I was upset and felt wronged by you, but that does not excuse my own mistakes."

When Justice Marvin Zuker came back with his decision, it was a ruling unlike anything anyone had ever heard before. He may as well have been carrying one of the #IBelieveSurvivors placards.

"It doesn't matter if the victim was drinking, out at night alone, sexually exploited, on a date with the perpetrator, or how the victim was dressed. No one asks to be raped," he said. Justice Zuker talked at length about the significance of the neurobiology of trauma. He didn't address the nitty-gritty of the science and didn't use the phrase specifically, but he laid out the findings and implications of the research. Trauma can impact memory function and cause victims to freeze or dissociate. "We are often faced with the dynamics of counter-intuitive victim responses to trauma, memory fragmentation, and delayed recall," Zuker said. Some victims, he continued, "describe a state of 'frozen fright,' in which they become powerless and completely passive." A victim who is experiencing such a freeze or who has been drinking is unlikely to fight back, Zuker added, citing a paper called "False Reports: Moving Beyond the Issue to Successfully Investigate and Prosecute Non-Stranger Sexual Assault," co-authored by Dr. David Lisak, an American psychologist and preeminent voice on the neurobiology of trauma.

Justice Zuker's meaning was clear: the fact that Mandi Gray didn't physically resist and that she couldn't recall some parts of the night did not harm her credibility. The decision, which took the judge two hours to read, referenced a dozen different texts, including a paper co-written by Dr. Rebecca Campbell, the same psychologist who would later be attacked in Emily Yoffe's *Atlantic* article. He also cited *Against Our Will*, journalist Susan Brownmiller's groundbreaking 1975 book that was the first to frame rape as an urgent social and political problem rather than a rare crime committed by sexual deviants.

Justice Zuker showed that he was thinking about all the things that advocates and activists have been demanding judges think about for decades. Reporter Catherine Porter of the *Toronto Star* described the decision this way: "Ontario Court Justice Marvin Zuker changed the landscape of sexual assault and the criminal justice system on Thursday." The headline in *Chatelaine* magazine said the judge's words offered "hope for survivors." Pamela Cross, the legal director of a non-profit organization aimed at helping women navigate the legal system, told the CBC that Judge Zuker had "a profound and almost astonishing understanding of the issue of sexual violence, of women's lack of autonomy in these situations."

But while his impressive feminist reading list played well with progressives, it was perfect grounds for appeal. None of the articles or books referenced in Justice Zuker's ruling were discussed during the trial—a major problem from a legal standpoint. All evidence, whether it's witness testimony or scientific research or books about rape should be presented to both sides for scrutiny. Judges are supposed to reach a decision based solely on the evidence before them, evidence that has been tested and debated. Ururyar's lawyer seized on this in his appeal application. The Superior Court agreed. Judge Michael Dambrot described the verdict as "virtually incomprehensible." He found Justice Zuker to be biased against the accused. A new trial was ordered, but Gray announced that she didn't want to undergo another cross-examination. The Crown concluded that it was not in the interest of justice to try again. Ururyar agreed to a peace bond that included no admission of guilt.

CANADIAN COURTS HAVE historically been cautious in allowing expert evidence, particularly when a jury is involved. This is out of a concern that the testimony of a designated "expert" will be overly persuasive to jurors, who may not understand the limitations of what that expert witness is addressing. And in sexual assault cases, Crown attorneys are likewise proceeding with caution. They're waiting for the right case, with the right set of facts, to mount their possibly precedent-setting argument. (If a judge concludes that evidence on the neurobiology of trauma is inadmissible, it will make it harder for

Crowns to introduce it in future cases.)

In April 2018 a national symposium for Canadian judges, Crowns, and defence counsel was held on the latest developments in sexual assault law and science. Dr. Haskell gave the keynote address. Immediately following her presentation, the organizers scheduled a mock hearing on the admissibility of that evidence. The principals were Crown attorney Meaghan Cunningham, a specialist in sexual assault cases; Toronto criminal defence lawyer Jonathan Shime; and Ontario Superior Court Justice Shaun Nakatsuru. This was the scenario put to the attorneys for argument: A woman had alleged that she'd been raped in a basement bedroom while other people slept on a couch outside the room. Her boyfriend had been asleep upstairs at the time. The accused said the sex was consensual. During the preliminary inquiry, it had emerged that the complainant didn't call out for help. Now that the case was heading to trial, Cunningham had submitted a motion to call Dr. Haskell as an expert witness. She would not be expected to speak to the specific allegations, only to give broad context about the way trauma can impact behaviour.

Jonathan Shime took to the podium first to make the case for the (hypothetical) defence. He opened by saying that he wasn't there to argue against the neurobiology of trauma playing a role in the justice system. A trauma-informed approach could be valuable in the context of a police investigation, for example. But putting Dr. Haskell in front of the jury would taint the process against his client, he argued. The Canadian courts have a sad history of sending innocent people to jail based on expert evidence that was later found to be bogus. Shime cited Dr. Charles Smith, once revered as one of Canada's most talented forensic child pathologists. A 2008 inquiry determined that Dr. Smith had botched twenty cases, resulting in numerous wrongful convictions. More recently, the Motherisk lab at the Hospital for Sick Children made millions of dollars testing hair strands for drug and alcohol remnants. In 2015, Motherisk's tests were found to be unreliable and substandard—although not before that evidence was used in seven criminal trials, six of which ended in convictions. As a result of tragedies such as these, Shime continued, Canadian courts treat the inclusion of expert evidence with great caution. The system recognizes that juries can become "overwhelmed" by the testimony of impressively credentialed professionals who speak in scientific language that is not easy for a layperson to understand. "This evidence is apt to be accepted by the jury as virtually infallible and as having more weight than it deserves," he argued. Shime noted that Dr. Haskell was without question a highly skilled individual, but that the "perils of science and anecdotal evidence" must be a concern.

"The Crown says . . . the jury needs her evidence to combat myths and stereotypes about sex assault victims, notwithstanding that there is no evidence that this jury frankly even holds such stereotypes," Shime told the mock court. "With all due respect to Dr. Haskell . . . what are we going to learn? Sometimes sex assault victims scream. Sometimes they don't. Sometimes sex assault victims fight. Sometimes they don't." These were all things that the trial judge could simply instruct the jury to be aware of, he concluded. (For the purposes of this friendly admissibility exercise, both lawyers agreed that they would not spend time debating the validity of the science itself. But afterwards, Shime told me that had it been a real trial, he—like any defence attorney—would have challenged the scientific claims attached to the neurobiology of trauma. Shime regards it as a catch-all phrase that has come to represent a cluster of disconnected studies all being used to interpret the behaviour of alleged sexual assault victims.)

Crown Meaghan Cunningham was up next. Because this (hypothetical) case centres on consent, the victim's credibility will be the central question of this trial, she began. Judges instruct juries to use their common sense to assess a witness's credibility, but "common sense is the byproduct of our experiences and also the beliefs and values that we're raised with. And sometimes those beliefs and values are not based on reality, but are based instead on stereotype or inaccurate or incomplete understanding." When common sense is rooted in archaic ideas, how can an accurate assessment of the victim's actions be made?

Although she didn't use those words, Cunningham was talking about rape culture. Because of its pervasiveness, people may not notice that they're basing an opinion on a myth. That's why you need an expert like Dr. Haskell to lay out the facts. Dr. Haskell's evidence would be essential in helping the jury understand the normal range of reactions that traumatized people experience, Cunningham argued. Simply being told that a person may not always call out for help is not enough. They need to understand the biological reasons why that can occur. "The purpose of this evidence is not to offer an opinion about why this victim behaved this way in this case. It is simply to undo the unfair and inaccurate expectations that many people have about how a victim of sexual assault should react to being assaulted." (Later I asked Cunningham about the fact that in a real trial, the defence's first move would have been to challenge the science. "That's something the Crown would expect. They would try to argue this is novel science. We would argue the science is not novel, its use in the criminal trial context is novel.")

After about forty minutes of arguments, Justice Shaun Nakatsuru offered some analysis. He said he couldn't rule on the admissibility one way or the other, because he may one day have to decide that very issue in a real courtroom, but he could make some general observations. Justice Nakatsuru said he found it helpful that Cunningham had laid out specific areas that she hoped Haskell would address. This way, a trial judge wasn't being asked to green-light every sweeping position associated with the neurobiology of trauma. It's important to remember that "it's never an 'all or nothing' [thing] on admissibility," he said.

IN EARLY 2019, I asked Emily Yoffe to talk about her piece in *The Atlantic*. Yoffe said that some who are championing the "neurobiology of trauma" are wildly overstating how much has been proven. "People who promote the 'neurobiology of trauma,' especially urging its adoption in criminal and administrative settings, will conduct police trainings or advise campus administrators, and they will assert everything they are saying is established science." Yes, Yoffe continued, some of what they're saying is generally agreed upon neuroscience, but some is not rooted in established science. Other parts actually contradict accepted science or are grossly simplified or overstated. Moreover, Yoffe continued, this mish-mash of research is being used as evidence that trauma occurred. "So if someone can't tell a coherent story, it means she experienced a possibly life-threatening trauma. If she changes her story multiple times, it means she was traumatized. If she has a flat affect when telling her story, it proves she was traumatized. The so-called science essentially says any behaviour by the accuser should be considered as confirmation of a trauma. That is a serious corruption of science and it leads to unjust outcomes." I agree with Yoffe that trying to use symptoms like a victim's memory loss as evidence against an accused is dangerous. I also agree that many questions about how trauma impacts the brain and body remain unanswered.

That said, to me there is no question: The neurobiology of trauma is not junk science. Through centuries of clinical observations and, more recently, cutting-edge neuroimaging technology, researchers have identified ways that trauma alters brain function and can impact an individual's actions and memory. For the criminal justice system, this research is a game-changer. It shows that the old approach to assessing a complainant's credibility is deeply flawed.

The jury is still out on whether it will ever become a fixture of the evidence in a sexual assault trial. But that's almost beside the point. I think the arena where knowledge of trauma stands to do the most good is at the entry point to the justice system: the police. It's crucial that officers tasked with investigating sexual violence undergo this training. It's reasonable to assume that, in the past, sexual assault complaints went nowhere, or were improperly categorized as "unfounded" because the investigating officer misread a symptom of trauma as evidence that the person was lying. The goal of teaching police officers about trauma is to generate better investigations, which will in turn produce better evidence that a Crown can use in a prosecution and that a judge or jury can use to assess guilt or innocence.

A trauma-informed approach doesn't mean that a complainant who is struggling to communicate details of an incident should automatically be believed. It does mean, however, that she shouldn't automatically be labelled a liar.

CHAPTER 8

THE MYTH OF FALSE ALLEGATIONS

THE DETECTIVES THOUGHT she was making it up.

The woman, a twenty-eight-year-old artist living in Philadelphia's upscale Rittenhouse Square neighbourhood, told police that around four a.m. a man broke into her studio apartment, covered her face with a T-shirt, pulled down his pants and underwear, and fondled her breasts. She had been asleep at the time. The woman theorized that the intruder—who was rail-thin and looked to be around 145 pounds—likely squeezed through a seven-inch gap in the bars on her window. Within days the case was stamped as "inactive" and down-graded to a non-criminal classification. The investigation was over. In a later interview with *The Philadelphia Inquirer*, one of the first responding patrol officers said the complainant seemed like "a nice lady," but that she also appeared to be a person who thrived on drama. "She looked like a woman who thought every man should want her," the officer said.

That happened in June 1997.

A month later, a twenty-five-year-old office worker who worked in the same area went out for drinks with a friend a few blocks west of Rittenhouse Square. Around four a.m. she woke up naked and confused at the foot of her bed. She noticed the window to her ground-floor apartment was open and her front door was locked. The telephone had been disconnected. Her neck felt swollen and raw. The woman staggered to the washroom and found the water running in the tub and towels scattered around the room. The whites of her eyes were red with popped blood vessels. She had no memory of what had happened. The woman, who can only be identified as M.M., called a friend, who phoned 911. The officer barely investigated before closing the file, even though police documents later showed that investigators were aware that someone had ejaculated at the scene. The detective told the woman he was sure she was going to "end up remembering it was a boyfriend" who assaulted her.

These ignored complaints were added to the stack of thousands of sexual assault and rape reports that the Philadelphia Police Department had been improperly dismissing or downgrading for more than a decade.

Everything changed in May 1998, when that same assailant killed a young doctoral student. Like the other times, the man targeted an apartment in the Rittenhouse Square area and broke in through the balcony. But this time, after he sexually assaulted the woman—a twenty-three-year-old named Shannon Schieber—he strangled her. It was only then, after reporters from *The Philadelphia Inquirer* noticed similarities between the latest attack and the dismissed allegation from the office worker that police made the connection. Investigators themselves unearthed the second discarded file. DNA from both scenes matched Schieber's killer. The suspect was later identified as Troy Graves and connected to six sexual assaults.

The scandal enraged the citizens of Philadelphia. If only the earlier complaints had been taken seriously, Schieber would likely still be alive. An internal investigation ordered by the police commissioner found that thousands of allegations had been improperly shelved in the non-criminal "investigation of a person" category. In the years before Schieber's murder, the sex crimes unit had discarded about a third of all cases it was assigned—triple the rate at which other crimes were downgraded, the *Inquirer* reported. Over and above that, the department was classifying 18 percent of all rape complaints as "unfounded." It was the highest average among the ten largest cities in the United States at the time, the paper wrote.

The newspaper's multi-year investigation into the Philadelphia Police Department revealed that within the unit in charge of investigating sexual assault, the prevailing attitude was one of disbelief. Among the many troubling details to emerge was the revelation that one of the unit's longtime officers jokingly referred to his department as the "lying bitches unit." The department's head of detectives told the *Inquirer* that women were making false accusations to qualify for state-funded abortions. (The *Inquirer* found that only ten women had obtained a Medicaid abortion on the grounds of rape in 1993— the last year that a police report was required to qualify.)

Social scientists believe that there is strong evidence that only 2 to 8 percent of sexual assault allegations are false. This range encompasses the findings of respected studies in North America, the United Kingdom, and Australia. And while some voices suggest that as many as 40 percent of sexual assault claims are fabricated, most academics agree that the false-reporting rate for sexual assault is in line with the false-reporting rate for other types of crime. In fact, people are more likely to make up stories of car theft than rape, if auto insurance industry estimates are correct that 10 percent of all claims are fraudulent. Yet for a lot of people, the statistics seem to carry little weight.

The threat of the lying woman looms large in our culture.

Days after police charged basketball all-star Kobe Bryant with the rape of a nineteen-year-old hotel staffer, *Miami Herald* columnist Leonard Pitts declared, based on nothing more than gut instinct, "No way in hell." In a later column he opined that people need to acknowledge that "sometimes women lie too, and that if it is humiliating to be raped, it is no picnic to be falsely accused of rape." While it's no longer politically correct to be outwardly skeptical of rape complainants, the suspicion isn't gone. Why else did I find that nearly twice as many sexual assault complaints were dismissed as unfounded compared with common physical assault?

SOCIETY'S DEEP MISTRUST of women has been woven into the fabric of civilization over thousands of years, cultivated and encouraged by the two most dominant forces in people's lives: the church and the state.

The girl-who-cried-rape trope appears in Genesis. In one story, Potiphar, an Egyptian and the captain of the Pharaoh's bodyguards, buys a slave named Joseph and puts him in charge of the household. Joseph is strong and handsome and catches the eye of Potiphar's wife, who repeatedly tries to seduce him. He always refuses. One day she finds herself alone in the house with Joseph and again propositions him—"Lie with me!"—and again he declines. She grabs him by the cloak, but Joseph runs out of the house without it. Potiphar's wife then claims that Joseph tried to rape her but fled when she screamed, leaving his cloak behind. Joseph is sent to prison.

In 1484, Pope Innocent VIII decried the spread of witchcraft and issued a papal bull authorizing the German clergymen Heinrich Kramer and Jacob Sprenger to stamp it out. Two years later the pair published their infamous *Malleus Maleficarum*, a guidebook on how to locate, investigate, and punish witches that would help to incite two blood-soaked centuries of witch-hunting. Women, the men declared, were defective creatures with unreliable memories. They were forged from a bent rib bone "and from this weakness one concludes that, since she is an unfinished animal, she is always being deceptive." It states that women are prone to emotional excess, which is why they seek out retribution through magic. "It is not a matter for astonishment that there is such a great number of witches in this sex."

As society's institutions developed, doubt of a woman's word was baked into the legal system. In the 1600s, Sir Matthew Hale, an English judge, wrote a massive two-part treatise of criminal law in England called *The History of the Pleas of the Crown*. The text, which was published posthumously, warned that rape was "an accusation easily to be made and hard to be proved, and harder to be defended by the party accused, tho never so innocent." Translation: women lie and destroy men's reputations.

Hale levelled this claim without sociological or statistical evidence, but it still went on to shape the criminal justice system in Canada and the United States for centuries. This type of thinking is why for so many years rape complainants were legally required to produce physical evidence of their victimization—torn clothing, bloodied bruises—if they expected the case to go to court. In fact, until the legal reforms of the 1980s, a person could not be convicted of rape without outside corroboration. When Sir Matthew Hale walked the earth, people believed that swallowing spiders could cure a fever, yet his opinions of women went unquestioned well into the twentieth century. In his book Hale asserted that a "ravished" woman must "make fresh discovery and pursuit" of the offender—meaning she was expected to scream for help and report the attack as soon as possible—"otherwise it carries a presumption that her suit is but malicious and feigned." Amazingly, this remained the law of the land in Canada until 1983, when Bill C-127 abrogated the doctrine of "recent complaint" from the Criminal Code. Up until three decades ago, if a sexual assault complainant didn't immediately report an incident, judges and juries were required to question her credibility.

In the United States, judges echoed Hale's warnings in their jury instructions well into the 1970s. Many juries were cautioned that rape is an allegation easily made, difficult to disprove, and that a victim's version of events should be more carefully scrutinized than the testimony of other witnesses.

The history books reveal a pattern of misogynist beliefs underlying our criminal justice system. Celebrated American legal mind John Wigmore, whose foundational 1904 legal encyclopedia *Wigmore on Evidence* established evidentiary principles that are still in use today on both sides of the border, shared Sir Hale's deep distrust of rape complainants. He infamously advised, "No judge should ever let a sex-offence charge go to the jury, unless the female complainant's social history and mental makeup have been examined and testified [to] by a qualified physician." It was also Wigmore's opinion that "the failure to complain speedily of a rape is universally conceded to be a damaging circumstance against the woman making the charge."

THOSE WHO SUBSCRIBE to the belief that false reports of sexual assault are a pressing threat to society seem divided into two camps. One group accepts that fabricated claims of rape are rare, but given the potentially ruinous consequences that even an accusation of sexual misconduct can have on a person's life, they maintain that the issue deserves amplified attention. The other group disputes outright the 2 to 8 percent figure as feminist propaganda and points to other studies that suggest rape hoaxes are actually common occurrences.

During my Unfounded reporting, I interviewed numerous officers who said they believed that as many as half of sexual assault claims aren't true. "Statistically, I've heard up to 60 percent are false allegations," one Ontario-based sex crimes unit investigator told me. "Do I think 60 percent are made up? No, I don't believe that. Do I think a large majority of them are altered or maybe the perception is off? I do. But I don't think people are intentionally lying." Several officers I spoke to— men and women—offered similar sentiments. Other officials were less diplomatic.

"People lie about having been sexually assaulted. It happens all the time. It doesn't matter how often it happens. That's a red herring. What matters is that it can happen," forensic scientist Brent Turvey told me. Turvey is the co-author of an influential police textbook called the *Rape Investigation Handbook*, which he wrote with retired NYPD detective John Savino. One Canadian academic told me that this book was regarded as "the bible" among some law enforcement agencies. (Anecdotally, I spoke with officers who were aware of the handbook, but police services refused to disclose any information about training materials to me.)

In Turvey and Savino's book they declare that as many as 41 percent of sexual assault claims are false. "There is no shortage of politicians, victims' advocates and news articles claiming that the nationwide false report rate for rape and sexual assault is almost nonexistent, presenting a figure of around 2 per cent. This figure is not only inaccurate; it has no basis in reality," they assert. The "2 per cent myth," they write, goes back to Susan Brownmiller's influential 1975 book, *Against Our Will*, in which she reported that after New York City police began using female officers to interview complainants, unfounded rates plummeted to 2 percent. She attributed this statistic to an appeals court judge named Lawrence H. Cooke, who made the remark at a New York bar association event in 1974. But Turvey has written that he's never been able to track down the source of Cooke's information.

When I spoke with Turvey by phone, I asked him how many people he believes make up rape. He told me that I was asking the wrong question. "I don't care how many people lie," Turvey said. "The real issue is, Do people lie about having been sexually assaulted? That's a binary question. Either they do or they

don't. Does that potential or capacity exist? And the answer is
yes. Overwhelmingly yes." In their book, Turvey and Savino
highlight a number of papers that cast doubt on the oft-cited 2
to 8 percent false-reporting rate. These include a 2002 study by
the Crown prosecutor's office and Inspectorate of Constabulary
in the United Kingdom that found 11.8 percent of reported
sexual assaults didn't happen; a 1973 paper that showed 25 percent of the rape complaints made to police in Denver, Colorado,
were actually false accusations; and a famous 1994 report by
Purdue University's Dr. Eugene J. Kanin, which concluded that
41 percent of rape claims were bogus. Kanin looked at 109 allegations investigated by an unnamed Midwestern American city
between 1978 and 1987. That city had a population of about
about seventy thousand. In each instance, Kanin said, the supposed victim had recanted and, almost always, the false accusations had been made for one of three reasons: "providing an
alibi, a means of gaining revenge, and a platform for seeking
attention/sympathy." A study published in 2000 that attempted
to replicate Kanin's findings found that 32 percent of rapes
reported to a police service in a suburb of Detroit were fake, the
authors noted in their book. Other researchers have taken issue
with the methodology of Kanin's study.

DAVID LISAK, AN American psychologist who has researched
and written extensively on the myriad of false-reporting
studies, told me that not all studies are created equal. He estimates that a majority of the papers that put the false-reporting
rate higher than 8 percent come from reviews of a police service's internal statistics. "Here's your problem," he said. "Police
departments routinely misclassify these cases. It's been

demonstrated so often, with such detail, that there's no way as a researcher you can publish results like that with a straight face. It's completely misleading. That's where you get so many of these [incorrect] figures, the 20 and 30 percent numbers." The Kanin study, for example, was conducted that way, he said. Kanin was told that 41 percent of the rape accusations reported to police were false and that in each of those cases the victim recanted. However, Lisak said, Kanin didn't get a full picture of what had happened during those investigations. Furthermore, the police force in question was threatening alleged victims with lie detector tests, which could intimidate someone into a false recantation. "Kanin's study is literally not research. It's the opinion of a police chief."

Police officers have also told me that the most common reason they designate a complaint as false is that the victim has recanted. But experts in victim behaviour warn that there are plenty of reasons why a person may want to back out of a legitimate complaint.

"We absolutely know that if women feel discouraged in the process of the investigation, or if they feel disbelieved in the process of the investigation, they're more likely to say 'Fine, I made it up. Just let me go home,'" Sunny Marriner, the executive director of the Ottawa Rape Crisis Centre, told me. "Recantation can be the result of pressure or subtle warnings. We certainly see women hearing the officer saying, 'We can go forward with this, but I do need to let you know that if you're found to be lying, you could be charged yourself.'" If an individual is already worried that the officer doesn't believe her, this threat can lead to a recantation that simply isn't true, she said.

For the better part of the last decade, Marriner has led a crusade to bring a civilian-led sexual assault case review model to Canada. It would be based on the same oversight program that was implemented by the Philadelphia Police Department following Shannon Schieber's murder. Back in the late 1990s, with his sex crimes unit under siege, then commissioner John Timoney did something revolutionary. He didn't get defensive and make excuses—he blew the unit up. After cleaning house, he ordered an audit of every sexual assault complaint that had been dropped as unfounded or downgraded to a non-criminal offence in the past five years (as far back as the statute of limitations allowed). That review determined that more than two thousand offences had been misclassified and not properly investigated. And Timoney didn't stop there. He partnered with officials at the Women's Law Project, a Philadelphia legal centre devoted to protecting the rights of women and girls. Front-line advocates are now invited into police headquarters each year to look through raw case files for signs of bias and investigative missteps. The new oversight measures were implemented in tandem with modern training for officers. The result is that Philadelphia's unfounded rate has plummeted to around 4 percent. I wrote about this model in my Unfounded series, and to date, dozens of police services, collectively responsible for about half the Canadian population, are instituting a similar type of civilian-led case review.

In early 2017, Thomas McDevitt, a retired lieutenant with the Philadelphia Police Department's special victims unit, spoke about Philadelphia's much-lauded oversight model at a legal conference in Gatineau, Quebec. During the question period, a Canadian officer in attendance asked McDevitt about the false report case files. "It was mostly recants by the victim, but then later on, we realized, 'Was that recant because it didn't happen or because of the way they were treated by the police officer or the way they were treated by the system?'" McDevitt replied. In the rare instances of an actual false complaint, he said, it was usually obvious very early on. McDevitt told the audience of lawyers and police officers that he believes as many as 90 percent of recantations are legitimate victims who don't want to bother—potentially because of their experience with police.

For David Lisak, the challenge of trying to academically pinpoint the prevalence of false rape reports is that it's a notoriously hard issue to study. Researchers need access to the actual case files so that they can evaluate the facts themselves in order to, for example, examine the circumstances around a recantation. But such an effort requires the cooperation of a local police service and the district attorney—and in the United States, the justice system is more fragmented. The landscape changes from county to county. It's also more politicized. The district attorney position is an elected one, often held by a person with greater political ambitions, Lisak pointed out. "So why would a DA decide to open their books to the scrutiny of an independent investigator?" he asked. This is why the most respected studies of false reports have been conducted in Commonwealth countries, such as the United Kingdom, where the Home Office can simply order a review and all the jurisdictions are required to cooperate, he told me.

Perhaps the most rigorous study ever completed on the issue was commissioned by the British Home Office. It reviewed 2643 cases reported to British police over a fifteen-year period.

In an initial pass on the results, three researchers from London Metropolitan University determined that the false-reporting rate was 8 percent, but this was based solely on the police officers' judgment. Upon closer inspection, the researchers concluded that the number was closer to 3 percent. They found a pattern of cases being deemed false among complainants with mental health problems, individuals who'd previously reported an assault, those whose statements contained inconsistencies, and complainants who'd been using alcohol or drugs at the time.

In a paper Lisak co-authored on the false-reporting issue, he singled out other studies that put the number in the low single digits: a 2006 study from Australia involving 850 rape cases (2.1 percent), a review of 116 rapes reported to the Toronto Metropolitan Police Department published in 1977 (6 percent), and another one of 348 allegations from England completed in 1992 (8.3 percent). The pattern is obvious, Lisak told me: the bigger and more comprehensive the study, the more likely the results will show the false-reporting rate to be low. It's for that reason that most researchers put the range at between 2 and 8 percent.

Janine Benedet, a law professor at the University of British Columbia whose research focuses on sexual assault law, told me that even 8 percent seems excessively high to her. Much of Dr. Benedet's recent work has focused on how the justice system handles incapacity cases. She has also looked at the ways in which stereotypes about women also depend on factors such as age and disability. In two decades of studying those areas, she can think of only a handful of cases where there was evidence that the event didn't happen or that the wrong person had been accused. But even in the face of mountains of research that suggest fabricated sexual assaults are extremely rare, it's the complainant—not the accused—who bears the brunt of suspicion, she said. This is not the case with other crimes.

"Think of a man being caught driving a stolen van," Dr. Benedet told me. He may try to tell police that some random person just gave him the vehicle and he had no idea it was stolen, "but [he's] going to be viewed with a measure of skepticism," she said. Sexual assault cases should be treated the same. "Absolutely, there needs to be space in a justice system that has a presumption of innocence for people to argue that a sexual assault allegation against them is false, but it ought to be viewed with the same level of skepticism that that claim would be met with for other offences."

The system has tried to make that happen. The legislative reforms of the 1980s and 1990s dismantled the obvious structures that propped up the most pervasive rape myths—that women lie, that women want to be taken by force, that a woman's previous sexual history is an indication of consent. The corroboration requirement and the rule of recent complaint were abolished. Restrictions were put in place around the use of complainants' previous sexual history. The definition of consent was amended. "We worked hard to remove all those formal markers of that way of thinking in the criminal law, but we didn't necessarily do a lot to change the underlying attitudes," Benedet told me. "At the end of the day, you still have an individual decision-maker who has to make findings of credibility. . . . There's a tremendous amount of discretion. You can rewrite the rules all you want, but you still need a judge who is prepared to believe women."

That goal gets further away every time a person fabricates an allegation, because these outliers dominate so much space in our culture's consciousness. False allegations—rare though they may be—reinforce the ingrained suspicion that women lie about rape. They make it exponentially harder for real victims to find justice.

THE STORY WAS as disturbing as its teller had intended. An eighteen-year-old freshman was gang-raped by seven male students at the University of Virginia, apparently as part of a fraternity's sick pledge ritual. "Jackie" had been invited to a party at Phi Kappa Psi by a handsome third-year she worked with at the university's pool. He also belonged to the fraternity. She thought they were going on a date. But at the party, he lured her to an upstairs bedroom, where the pledges were waiting. Jackie screamed. A man charged at her and they both crashed through a glass coffee table. Jackie's date was one of the ringleaders. One by one he directed the others in their horrible task while shards of glass shredded her back. "Don't you want to be a brother?" the men taunted when one struggled to hold an erection. "We all had to do it, so you do, too." That man—whom Jackie recognized from her anthropology discussion groups—thrust a beer bottle inside of her. This vicious attack lasted three hours. When Jackie finally emerged from the fraternity after three a.m., she was barefoot and dishevelled. Her red dress was stained with blood, her face beaten. *Rolling Stone* published "A Rape on Campus: A Brutal Assault and Struggle for Justice at UVA" on November 19, 2014. Within months the online version was viewed more than 2.7 million times—more than any other feature the magazine had published that wasn't about a celebrity. Outrage ensued.

But the attack never happened.

The central narrative of "A Rape on Campus" was fiction, invented by "Jackie," uncorroborated by the journalist who reported her story, and retracted by the revered magazine five months after its publication. It was a black day for journalism, but a worse one for those who want the public and institutions to take sexual violence more seriously.

Journalist Richard Bradley was among the first to raise serious doubts about *Rolling Stone*'s campus rape story. Bradley had been an editor at *George* magazine, where he handled pieces by the now notorious Stephen Glass. Glass, once one of the most sought after young writers in the United States, was unmasked as a serial fabulist, having invented in whole or in part dozens of articles in his years writing for *George*, *Harper's*, and, most famously, *The New Republic*. Bradley, like so many of Glass's former editors, had been forced to look at his own actions critically. How had he—along with other professional, seasoned journalists—been fooled? It was through this experience that Bradley spotted holes in writer Sabrina Rubin Erdely's reporting, as he explained in a blog post on November 24, 2014, less than a week after *Rolling Stone* published its piece. "Something about this story doesn't feel right," he wrote.

In her story Erdely mentioned that Jackie had been with three friends that night, but none was named or interviewed. "So the three people who could allegedly corroborate the assault don't," he noted. Then there was the fact that Jackie apparently knew the names of two of her attackers, yet it appeared that Erdely either wasn't aware of their identities or didn't reach out for their side of the story—"a cardinal rule of journalism." And what about the detail that after three hours of being brutally raped, Jackie reappeared at the party, her dress covered in blood from the broken glass table, dishevelled and traumatized, yet it seemed not a single person took notice?

The implication from *Rolling Stone*'s piece, Bradley continued, is that at the University of Virginia, young men are expected to commit gang rape if they want to join a fraternity. "It's possible," he wrote. Although "one would think that we'd have heard of this before—gang rape as a fraternity initiation is hard to keep secret—but it's possible."

Around this time Erdely herself began having doubts. With the story out, Jackie finally told her the lifeguard's name, except she wasn't sure how to spell it, which Erdely found suspicious given how terrified Jackie supposedly was of this man. Erdely began looking into him, but couldn't confirm that he worked at the pool or was a member of Phi Kappa Psi.

Then, on December 5, 2014, *The Washington Post* delivered the final blow. Reporter T. Rees Shapiro had tracked down one of the people who'd attended to Jackie after the supposed attack. According to that student, Jackie didn't appear physically injured, although she seemed shaken and claimed she'd been forced to perform oral sex on a group of men. Her story had changed several times, the individual said. The *Post* also tracked down the lifeguard, who was indeed not a member of the fraternity. He said that he'd worked at the pool and was aware of Jackie, but that they'd never met before. Furthermore, the fraternity told the *Post* that it hadn't hosted a party or social event on the weekend of September 28, 2012, when Jackie claimed she'd been raped. Hours before the *Post* ran its story, *Rolling Stone* published an editor's note on its website declaring that it no longer had confidence in its reporting. Several weeks after the *Post* article further undermined the plausibility of the piece, *Rolling Stone* managing editor Will Dana asked the prestigious Columbia School of Journalism to probe its errors. *Rolling Stone* staff agreed to participate fully with Columbia's investigation. The finished product was comprehensive, fair— and scathing. Every blunder, misstep, and consequence was laid bare.

"[Writer Sabrina Rubin] Erdely and her editors had hoped their investigation would sound an alarm about campus sexual assault and would challenge Virginia and other universities to do better. Instead, the magazine's failure may have spread the idea that many women invent rape allegations," the Columbia report summarized.

The thing is, society *wants* to believe that false reports are common. And so every time one of these rare events occurs, it undermines the statistics in the eyes of the public. This, as the Columbia piece underscored, was the real damage done by "A Rape on Campus."

In interviews with Columbia's journalists, Erdely and her editors said they had shied away from pressing Jackie for supporting evidence in the way they might have in another story, citing their concern that it might retraumatize her. It's why the reporter never attempted to locate the very locatable alleged assailants, and why she decided not to track down the three friends Jackie had been with that night.

The Charlottesville police service spent four months investigating the allegations raised in the piece. In late March, after interviewing about seventy individuals and obtaining records from the fraternity and the University of Virginia, the police concluded that there was "no substantive basis to support the account alleged in the *Rolling Stone* article." Charlottesville police chief Timothy Longo noted that this conclusion "doesn't mean that something terrible didn't happen to Jackie" that night.

Rolling Stone was hit with defamation lawsuits from both the fraternity and one of the university's associate deans, Nicole Eramo, who argued that she'd been unfairly smeared in the piece. The magazine ended up paying out more than $4.6 million US in settlements. It was during one of those court proceedings that Jackie offered an explanation. In a taped deposition that was played in court, Jackie testified that she believed the story she'd recounted to the *Rolling Stone* reporter was "true at the time," although she could no longer be sure about the specifics. She couldn't remember if she told the magazine writer that the party had been on September 28; she couldn't remember if she told Erdely that she met the lifeguard—her date and the one who orchestrated the attack—on a shared shift; and she couldn't remember if she told *Rolling Stone* she left the party splattered in blood. "I believe that I was assaulted, but some of the details of my assault—um, I have PTSD and some of them are foggy. I can't remember everything," she said.

It was an ending not unlike that of the infamous Duke lacrosse case.

In that instance, news broke in March 2006 that police had collected DNA samples from forty-six members of the Duke University lacrosse team. Investigators were looking to identify three players in connection with the alleged gang rape and assault of an exotic dancer who'd been hired to dance at a house party. The twenty-seven-year-old woman, a student at the nearby North Carolina Central University, alleged that the players pulled her into a bathroom, choked her, and took turns brutally raping her. That the woman was black and the players were wealthy white athletes further inflamed the situation. This national scandal entwined gender, race, class, and power. The stakes could not have been higher. And then her story began to unravel. A second dancer at the party, for example, disputed key details of her account. The complainant's own version of events seemed to evolve with each telling. The chronology shifted as did the actions of the players involved. But the turning point came with the DNA test results. The woman had told detectives and medical staff that the men hadn't used condoms. But there was no trace of any of the players' DNA. Confronted with this, she changed her story again, saying that she wasn't sure what the men had penetrated her with. It increasingly appeared that the investigation was being driven by an overzealous district attorney, Michael B. Nifong, looking to score political points. Nifong was later disbarred over his handling of the case, after being found to have committed two dozen ethical and professional breaches, including withholding vital evidence from the defence.

The complainant, whose name is Crystal Mangum, has maintained that she was sexually assaulted. (In 2013 Mangum was convicted of second-degree murder after fatally stabbing her boyfriend.)

Recently retired police inspector Monique Rollin told me that the damage stories like the *Rolling Stone* piece and the Duke lacrosse case do to victims is immeasurable. It's not just that these stories provide fodder to those peddling the idea that false rape allegations are common; it's also that victims—and police for that matter—understand that these scandals sow doubt in the public's mind. And if victims are already worried about being believed, the blowback from a high-profile false allegation may shake their confidence even further, causing them not to report, she told me. Or the victims may alter their stories, leaving out unflattering details or filling in gaps in their memory, because they think it will sound more plausible. "We do see this happening. And then it ultimately hurts their credibility. . . . The allegation isn't false, but the victim has lied out of fear of not being believed."

For the most part, Rollin said, police officers know that false reports are rare. "What you do see happening is officers looking at the evidence and thinking 'This isn't going anywhere.'" It's not that the officer doesn't believe the complainant; it's that he or she thinks a jury might not, or that a Crown wouldn't be able to prosecute, or that a defence attorney would rip the victim apart on the stand. This instinct is coming from a good place, Rollin told me, but it's still improper, because it's not the job of a police officer to think about prosecution.

For two years, before she retired from the Sault Ste. Marie Police Service in January 2019, Rollin was one of a pair of officers leading the Ontario Association of Chiefs of Police response to my Unfounded series. She was involved in reforming how sexual assault investigations are undertaken and she helped to develop a case audit framework for all Ontario police services.

In the cases she's seen, Rollin said one of the biggest problems is that patrol officers—often the first point of contact for complainants—haven't been taught the ways trauma can alter a person's behaviour and memory. Without this training, a legitimate victim may appear difficult to believe. "Here's the problem: victims who've been exposed to tremendous trauma don't present well [in an interview]. And people who are lying don't present well," she told me. Even for investigators who have the specialized knowledge, it can be difficult to assess. "That's why we tell officers the only way to proceed on these cases is full due diligence. No stone left unturned."

IN MID-SEPTEMBER 2018, during the final days of confirmation hearings for Brett Kavanaugh, President Trump's Supreme Court nominee, news broke that Kavanaugh had been involved in a possible incident of sexual misconduct with a woman back when they were in high school. That woman, Dr. Christine Blasey Ford, now a psychology professor at Palo Alto University, had quietly approached Democratic lawmakers in the summer after learning that Kavanaugh's name was on the short list of Trump's Supreme Court picks. Ford, a registered Democrat who had made small political donations to the party in the past, never intended to come forward, but when news about her allegations started to spread around Washington— and after reporters showed up at her home and at her job and began contacting colleagues—she decided to go public in *The Washington Post*. Ford told the *Post* that when she was in high school, she attended a small gathering with a friend. Kavanaugh, whom she did not know well, was also there, and he was "stumbling drunk." At one point he and a friend cornered her in a bedroom, and Kavanaugh pinned her down and groped her. She tried to scream but he covered her mouth, the now fifty-one-year-old Ford told the *Post*. "I thought he might inadvertently kill me," she said. "He was trying to attack me and remove my clothing." When Kavanaugh's friend jumped on the bed, the three of them rolled off and Ford was able to escape. She described the incident as a "rape attempt."

Brett Kavanaugh didn't hedge his response: "This is a completely false allegation. I have never done anything like what the accuser describes—to her or to anyone." Kavanaugh's confirmation hearings had already stirred up Washington. If approved, Republicans believed he would be the long-sought conservative judge who would finally and definitively swing the country's highest judiciary body to the right. Ford's allegations, coming so late in the process and against the backdrop of the #MeToo movement and all the cultural tensions that came with it, was a bombshell.

One side raised the #IBelieveSurvivors banner. The other side broadcasted warnings of false accusations.

"Given what we know of the accuser's political inclination and her support of left-wing causes, it's not unreasonable to believe that she has a political axe to grind. The hyperbolic overheated reaction to these charges is somewhat reminiscent of what happened to the Duke lacrosse team more than a decade ago," charged Fox TV host Laura Ingraham. "The media seized on the story, spinning the stripper's credible accusation into a tale of white privilege, misogyny, and just pure evil. A media swarm and rush to judgment follows."

In a column in the *Chicago Sun-Times*, Mona Charen wrote, "Why would a woman lie about something like that, knowing that her character is likely to be sullied? Well, most women don't lie about rape, but some do. The student accuser in the *Rolling Stone* account of a rape at the University of Virginia fabricated the whole story."

An editorial in the *Las Vegas Review-Journal* warned, "Allegations of sexual misconduct have led to the downfall of Harvey Weinstein, Alabama Senate candidate Roy Moore, former Sen. Al Franken and Steve Wynn. Yet there are also prominent cases of women wrongly accusing men. A woman falsely accused members of the Duke lacrosse team of raping her. . . . Each accusation must be evaluated on its own merits."

On that last point, I don't disagree. The real issue is that for years, centuries, millennia, sexual assault accusations made by women have not been evaluated on their merits. They've been ignored or dismissed because of cultural biases. That's why we've seen movements like #IBelieveSurvivors in recent years; they're intended to draw attention to this imbalance. But as an inviolable position, I think it poses dangers.

As a journalist, I'm supposed to uncover facts. When I investigated those fifty-four claims of sexual assault for the Unfounded series, in each case I made it clear to the complainant that to do my job properly, I'd need to thoroughly check the details of her allegation. I was going to need her police file—the good and the bad. Health records. Emails. Text messages. I needed to talk to the people involved. I explained that if I didn't approach the story with the same skepticism with which I'd treat any other piece of reporting, I'd be doing her a disservice. The more ironclad the reporting, the more believable the story would be. Every single one of the complainants understood completely.

The fact is, there is no pandemic of rape hoaxes sending people to jail. While it's true that even an accusation of sexual misconduct carries a deeply damaging stigma, my takeaway from the *Rolling Stone* and Duke University stories is that when the facts don't add up, a little digging unearths the truth pretty quickly.

This was the case in 2018 when Canadian broadcast journalist Steve Paikin was accused of trying to extort sex from would-be guests in exchange for air time on his program. Many have made the argument that the saga is proof that men can get a fair hearing in the age of #MeToo, even in the court of public opinion.

CHAPTER 9

"AM I GOING TO SURVIVE THIS?"

STEVE PAIKIN IS the host of a current affairs show called *The Agenda* on TVO, the public broadcaster in Ontario. Sarah Thomson is the publisher of an online women's magazine and a former politician, having run in Toronto's mayoral election as well as for a seat in the provincial legislature. In February 2018 Paikin received an unexpected email from Thomson— the two did not regularly speak—warning him that if he didn't resign from his job, there would be consequences. She alleged that years earlier he had pressured her for sex and then blocked her from appearing on his show when she refused. Paikin immediately forwarded the email to his superiors, expressing his bewilderment and disputing her claim. Thomson had repeated the accusation in more detail in a post on her website, the Women's Post. Although she didn't name the host, it was clear who she was talking about to anyone familiar with Toronto's media scene.

This was unfolding at a time when every week seemed to bring news that another powerful man was losing his job over a "#MeToo" issue. So while the plot may sound familiar, what happened next was not.

This was the #MeToo controversy that bucked the script. Reporters covering the story treated Thomson's claim with a measure of skepticism reminiscent of a different era—and readers didn't complain. At least in Toronto, Paikin and Thomson were both well-known figures, so the public had already formed opinions about them. Paikin was beloved. Thomson was complicated, and the specifics of her accusation were suspicious. Journalists found holes in her story. TVO issued a statement. Paikin would remain on air while an independent investigator looked into the complaint. The network would wait for the result of that investigation before making any decisions about his future employment. To those worried that the #MeToo movement had destroyed due process, this approach seemed like a return to sanity. The third-party probe eventually exonerated Paikin and the public accepted that outcome. Today he is not thought of as a #MeToo offender.

The story is a fascinating case study in that it seemed to unfold exactly as it should. A woman had spoken out about harassment she'd allegedly experienced. She was taken seriously. The man she accused was given the opportunity to present his version of events. His employer didn't rush to judgment. An independent investigator examined the evidence and concluded that the incident likely didn't happen. Everyone moved on.

But since its conclusion, I've thought about the case often. I was curious to know whether Paikin felt himself to be exonerated. And what had it been like going through that process? Was he scared? Was he angry? What about Thomson? What did she think about the investigation's outcome? I wanted to know what had motivated her to send that email when she did—she stands by her story, by the way—and if she regretted anything. What was it like to be branded a liar? To my surprise, both agreed to speak with me about the experience.

What follows is the anatomy of a "false" accusation.

STEVE PAIKIN WAS sitting alone in his family room that Saturday afternoon, watching an hour-long special about the 1979 Major League Baseball season, when he glanced at his phone during a commercial break and noticed an email from Sarah Thomson. The subject line was "Do the right thing."

The then fifty-seven-year-old broadcaster was surprised. Thomson had run for mayor of Toronto in 2010 and 2014. Paikin hadn't seen or spoken to her in years. Perplexed, he clicked it open.

"Steve," the message began, "I am sorry but I could not let you carry on—what you did to me wasn't fair—and with the elections this year, I don't want you doing it to other women candidates." Thomson went on to say that during her campaign for mayor, they'd gone for lunch to talk about her appearing as a guest on his show, except that "you weren't interested in discussing the show, but instead wanted to sleep with me." She said her executive assistant had been at the table when Paikin propositioned her and had recounted the episode to her entire campaign team afterwards. A few weeks later,

Thomson continued, she noticed that one of her male competitors had been invited on the show. "Not an easy thing for a woman running for mayor to have to deal with. Using your position to try to get women to have sex with you is wrong on EVERY level—and you should not have that kind of power over women," she wrote. Thomson said that she was collecting statements from other women who'd had similar experiences. She said she would forward all of them—along with a statement from her executive assistant—to TVO's CEO and board. But, she offered, he could get ahead of this and avoid the public shaming. "My advice to you is to step down now, before this blows up. That is the right thing to do. Do the right thing. Sarah."

Paikin stared at the words. He reread the email. Then read it again. Slowly, the gravity of the situation descended upon him: Sarah Thomson was threatening to publicly accuse him of sexual misconduct if he didn't immediately resign as the host of *The Agenda*, a show he had helmed for twelve seasons. Paikin was positive he had never engaged in that type of behaviour in his life, but given the timing of Thomson's allegation, he worried that might not matter.

It was February 3, 2018, three and a half months into the #MeToo movement, and outside of Hollywood, the group most visibly targeted by accusations of sexual misconduct seemed to be powerful players in journalism. The list of fallen media men was extensive, and included American news anchor Charlie Rose, NBC host Matt Lauer, Vice Media executives Andrew Creighton and Mike Germano, *The New Yorker* magazine's Ryan Lizza, *The New York Times* White House correspondent Glenn Thrush, MSNBC political analyst Mark Halperin, NPR's senior vice president of news Michael Oreskes, and, of course,

Fox News' Bill O'Reilly, whose 2017 firing over allegations of
sexual harassment laid the groundwork for *The New York Times'*
Weinstein reporting. These men's alleged offences ranged
from unwanted kissing to groping and rape. With the excep-
tion of Thrush, who was allowed to stay at the *Times* following
a suspension, albeit in a less prestigious reporting beat, all of
these men were forced out of their jobs.

Paikin found his wife, Francesca, in the living room and
passed her his BlackBerry—he's the kind of person who still
uses a BlackBerry in 2018. "Read this," he said. She scanned
the email several times and then they stared at each other in
silence. "This is ridiculous," she said. They'd been happily
married for seventeen years and she never entertained the
notion that it could be true, but given the climate, she also
recognized the precariousness of the situation. "Things were
at a fever pitch with the #MeToo movement," she told me. "I'll
be honest with you. I kind of assumed that that was going to
be it. [That TVO] was going to say 'Look, Bub, we believe you,
sorry, but there's really not much we can do about it. The
optics are too bad.'"

Paikin forwarded the email to his executive producer, who
alerted the top brass at TVO. His boss told him to come in the
next day for a meeting.

At eleven-thirty on the Sunday morning, Paikin arrived at
the fifth-floor boardroom. The CEO, the vice president of current affairs, the executive producer, someone from public
relations, and TVO's lawyer were all in the room. They grilled
him for two hours about the specific allegations, every detail
he could remember from that lunch, and every interaction he'd
ever had with Thomson.

Any chance he'd said something that could have been misinterpreted?

No.

Maybe he was joking?

No. He doesn't joke with political candidates about having sex with them in exchange for access to the show, he told them.

Was any alcohol consumed at the lunch?

No. He never drank alcohol at business lunches. Ever.

Was he sure that there was someone else at the table with him at all times?

Yes. Her executive assistant.

Did he have any negative history with her?

Absolutely not.

At the meeting's end, chief executive Lisa de Wilde turned to Paikin. "I wanted to look you in the eye when you told us what happened," he recalls her saying. "Here's what's going to happen. You're going to stay on the air. You're going to stay in your job. We're going to hire an independent investigator. We're going to be very transparent."

The following morning, Monday, February 5, TVO issued a press release: "Over the weekend, an allegation of sexual harassment has come to the attention of TVO that we believe we have a responsibility to disclose. TVO became aware of this allegation on Feb. 3 when an email from former Toronto mayoral candidate Sarah Thomson was sent to Steve Paikin," it read. "TVO does not tolerate sexual harassment. We believe it is important that allegations be fully heard and investigated."

Reporters began chasing down details of Thomson's accusation. Although TVO's statement had been brief, Thomson had posted a full recounting of the alleged incident in an article for the Women's Post the day before she emailed Paikin. Under the headline "Media Personality Uses His Position to Gain Sex," Thomson wrote that when she was running to be mayor of Toronto in 2010, she appeared on a political talk show with four other candidates. After the segment aired she saw a bump in her polling numbers, so the next time she ran into "the host," she asked about coming back on as a guest. "Always kind and friendly, he suggested we meet over lunch to discuss. My assistant and I met him at Grano's on Yonge Street"—a restaurant down the street from TVO—"and the three of us ordered our lunch."

But then, she continued, "not five minutes into the lunch the host asked me if I would sleep with him." Her assistant nearly spit out his drink, she said. Thomson wrote that she politely told Paikin that she loved her husband and would never do that. Then she immediately excused herself and called her campaign manager, who advised her to leave, which she did. She said that while she was on the call, her assistant asked the "host" if asking for sex so directly ever worked. "The host said that it worked 50 percent of the time. I hope he was just bragging, but I've always wondered if the women who are frequent guests on his show have slept with him," Thomson wrote.

After that lunch, Thomson said she was never invited back on the show, although Paikin had continued to proposition her for sex when they bumped into each other at events. "In 2010, the host made it harder for me to compete with the men I was up against, because they were invited to appear on his show while I wasn't. He didn't give a damn about how he impacted my future," Thomson alleged.

Most of the major Toronto dailies carried the story on the front page that week. Paikin's photo ran on A1 of the *Toronto*

Star alongside a seventy-two-point headline "TVO Investigates Paikin Over Harassment Allegation." Paikin, who subscribes to all the papers, forced himself not to look as he collected the pile from his doorstop each morning. He was humiliated in ways he had never imagined, he told me.

Thomson's allegation landed within weeks of another high-profile Ontario #MeToo controversy. During the last week of January, CTV News reported that two women were accusing the thirty-nine-year-old leader of the Ontario Progressive Conservative party, Patrick Brown, of sexual misconduct. The alleged incidents had taken place about ten and five years earlier, when Brown was a federal member of Parliament. One woman said she was still in high school and drunk when the politician asked her to perform oral sex on him, although she later revised the timeline to say she had graduated and was of legal age. The other was a university student working in Brown's constituency office. She alleged that Brown sexually assaulted her while she was intoxicated at his home in Barrie, about an hour north of Toronto. Brown vehemently denied the allegations, but he was forced to resign the leadership of the party just months ahead of a provincial election that the polls suggested he would win. His replacement, Doug Ford, won in a landslide. (Brown has since launched an $8 million defamation lawsuit against CTV.)

The Brown scandal, which unfolded over many weeks, amplified the attention on the Paikin allegations. Articles and think pieces on each made mention of the other big Made-in-Ontario #MeToo allegation, although the media treated the stories quite differently.

From the outset the tone was sympathetic towards Paikin,

which was a notable departure from other #MeToo reporting. This dynamic spoke to a unique layer of this particular accusation. Toronto journalists knew both Steve Paikin and Sarah Thomson. Thomson was regarded by most as someone who too often gravitated towards publicity stunts. She wasn't—in my opinion—viewed as a source whose word could be fully trusted. By the second day of media coverage, questions began to surface about her version of events. The *Toronto Star*'s Samantha Beattie tracked down five individuals who worked on Thomson's campaign in 2010, including the campaign manager. Each said they had no knowledge of any such incident—a significant detail given that Thomson claimed her assistant had immediately told the "entire campaign" about what had happened at the Grano lunch.

By contrast, Steve Paikin came across as the consummate straight arrow. On the day of our interview, he greeted me in TVO's reception area looking exactly as he had the previous two times we'd met: perfectly starched white shirt, neutral tie, no-nonsense dark slacks. He's tall, more than six feet, and with an oversized chin and a perennial half-smile, almost looks like a caricature of a news anchor. He's also exceedingly polite, the kind of person who doesn't swear in public.

As a reporter, I've often heard the adage that if everyone is mad at you, you're doing your job. But perhaps it's also true that you're doing a good job if everyone likes and respects you. That is Paikin. He has a way of conducting a tough interview without coming across as snarky or superior. He has moderated federal and provincial leadership debates seven times since 2006. He seems completely enthralled with the most boring topics, but that earnest enthusiasm is what makes *The Agenda* fun to watch.

When my *Globe* colleague Zosia Bielski wrote a profile of him in 2011, she described him as follows: "Beyond being brainy, Mr. Paikin has a reputation for being exceptionally even-keeled. 'I like everybody,' he offers when asked about the Bush/Cheney campaign sign that hangs next to one for Clinton/Gore on his busy office wall." Before being accused of extorting sexual favours from potential *Agenda* guests, the most controversial thing about Paikin was his fanatical devotion to the Boston Red Sox, despite living in Blue Jays country. But even for this, he has a reasonable explanation: he fell in love with the Sox as a child growing up in Hamilton, Ontario, before the Toronto Blue Jays existed and long before he moved to Boston to earn a master's degree in broadcast journalism.

Here's the other thing: women look out for each other. When I started working in newsrooms in my early twenties, female colleagues pulled me aside to warn me about the creeps—editors who expected you to flirt with them and who would otherwise treat you like dirt, men whose invitation to after-work drinks you should never accept, male reporters you should avoid working with if possible. These conversations happen in every newsroom—let's be real, every workplace—and the information gets shared between outlets. I have friends or acquaintances at almost every major media company in the country, including at TVO. I had never heard a whisper against Paikin. That's not to say Thomson's allegation couldn't have happened. #MeToo has shown that outwardly upstanding people are capable of surprisingly awful behaviour. But given the specifics of her claim—systematic sexual extortion—the silence seemed relevant to me and, I suspect, to TVO bosses.

Ontario's public broadcaster was widely praised for its decision to defer judgment on Paikin's future until after the results of the third-party investigation. "I don't know who's telling the truth and who's lying," wrote *Toronto Star* columnist Rosie DiManno. "But I do know that, amidst the tsunami of allegations of sexual impropriety against high-profile individuals, at least one employer has not taken shelter from the storm by pre-emptively firing or suspending or cutting off at the knees the alleged perpetrator." That probe would be carried out by Toronto lawyer Rachel Turnpenney, a specialist in workplace misconduct investigations.

For Paikin, all he could do was wait. He gave no interviews. He carried on at work as if nothing had happened. He made his one and only statement on Facebook after TVO announced he was under investigation: "I've spent 35 years building my reputation. In one fell swoop, these lies have prompted outrageous headlines and connected me to a story to which I have no business being connected. Well, all that ends today," he wrote. "I mean no harm to Sarah Thomson. But Sarah, you and I both know the incident you described never happened. . . . You've defamed me Sarah. I have no idea why, but you have. And I simply can't allow that to stand. The quest to reclaim my reputation, which you've tried to destroy, begins now. I look forward to vindication."

His words were defiant, but privately, he was consumed with worry.

"I didn't sleep through the night once for the next three months—between that moment [writing his statement] until the investigator finally released her report," he told me. No matter what the investigator came back with, he figured some people were always going to wonder if it was true. He had once walked down the street with a presumption of innocence. Now, Paikin said he felt permanently stained. He told me he would wake up at two a.m. and his mind would spiral.

"What would you think about?" I asked.

"Am I going to survive this? Am I going to get fired? If I do get fired, am I ever going to work again?" he said.

Paikin had been a journalist for thirty-six years. It was all he'd ever known, all he'd ever wanted to do. And if he couldn't be a journalist, who was he? "You start thinking some fairly existential thoughts about your life."

Two weeks after Thomson's email, it was the Family Day long weekend in Ontario. Around that time every year, Paikin and his family head to Florida to visit Paikin's parents. On that day he was one of the last to board the flight, and he happened to be sitting near the back.

"It is not an unfamiliar experience for people to look at me. Usually it's a nice look, a look of recognition," he said. "I'm accustomed to having interactions with the public . . . this was one of those moments that did not feel pleasant. And I don't know why, but I just started to say to people, as I walked down the aisle: 'I didn't do it. I didn't do it. I didn't do it.'"

SARAH THOMSON FIRST stepped into the public sphere in 2010, in a plucky long-shot bid for mayor. She withdrew a month before the election with low poll numbers, but her common-sense ideas about transit—tolling major highways to pay for service expansions, for example—helped shape the election discussion. The following year she made a second attempt at political office by running as a Liberal in the provincial election. Just as she did while running for mayor, Thomson stumped in sharply tailored dresses and rarely deviated from her talking points. She presented as a seasoned, polished politician. But after losing the provincial campaign, she very publicly ditched her heels for Birkenstocks and her updos for dreadlocks. Thomson, a middle-aged white woman, brushed off concerns about cultural appropriation with "Shut up, girl! Really?" and explained that her handlers had been keeping the real Sarah hidden. She transitioned to transit activist and took on the role of chair of the Toronto Transit Alliance, but she mostly kept a low profile—that is, until she publicly accused the city's mayor, Rob Ford, of groping her at an event.

On March 7, 2013, Thomson casually posted the following on her Facebook page: "Thought it was a friendly hello to Toronto Mayor Rob Ford at the [Canadian Jewish Political Affairs Committee] Action Party tonight until he suggested I should have been in Florida with him last week because his wife wasn't there." She included a blurry photo of the two of them at the event. Ford's mouth was gaping and he appeared very drunk. As the days went by, the story worsened. Thomson elaborated to the *Toronto Star*, "We posed to get our picture taken and he grabbed my ass." She then told a local radio host that she believed Ford had been high on cocaine—and this was before the crack scandal became public.

Thomson faced considerable blowback. Things took an even messier turn when a councillor from Richmond Hill came forward to say he'd been at the event and had overheard Thomson tell her female assistant, "We need to get a picture with Rob Ford's hand near your butt; it would be good for [the] campaign." Thomson told CBC News that this conversation happened after Ford had groped her. She said she'd hoped that if the mayor did the same to her assistant, it would bolster her own claim.

I was working as a municipal politics reporter at the *Toronto Star* during this period and had spent the preceding year and a half investigating Mayor Ford's substance abuse. My editors were nervous about publishing what I'd uncovered because my most well-placed sources were anonymous. The story had essentially been shelved. Thomson's claim helped revive interest. I dug into her allegation, interviewing people who'd attended the event and people whose job it was to cover up Ford's bad behaviour. I found nothing. But I did learn about an unrelated incident where a deeply intoxicated Ford had been asked to leave a military ball, and that enabled the *Star* to print my story, which eventually led to the discovery of the video showing Ford smoking crack. When it came time to write about "#Assgate" in my book *Crazy Town: The Rob Ford Story*, I struggled with how to handle it. Thomson's penchant for spectacle—she'd once shown up at city hall in a horse-drawn red wagon to make a point about outdated transit—along with the flip wording of her original Facebook post and the way her story had changed, made me hesitate. Ultimately, I summed it up by noting that although Thomson had once been regarded as a serious political contender, she seemed to have gone "a bit loopy" after her last election loss.

At the book launch for *Crazy Town*, Thomson stood in line for me to sign her book. When she got to the front she blasted me for what I'd written (fair) and then asked me to autograph her book where the "loopy" paragraph appeared. I, of course, felt awkward, but signed the book and made a comment to try to defuse the situation. Later that night I noticed that Thomson had written a Facebook post claiming that she'd just arrived home, finally opened my book, and was crushed to see how I'd described her. There were "a few tears," she wrote. It was a small fib, but puzzling. She would have realized I would know that wasn't how it had happened. I thought of it when I heard her claim against Steve Paikin. It was that type of misrepresentation that concerned the independent investigator, lawyer Rachel Turnpenney, as well.

TVO announced the results of its third-party probe on April 27, 2018. The network posted the full twenty-seven-page report online. In conducting her investigation, Turnpenney questioned Paikin on three occasions, Thomson twice with her lawyer present, and twenty-one other witnesses. She also examined documentation provided by each of the parties, including emails, text messages, and Facebook conversations. All in, the review took two and a half months.

"There is little doubt that Thomson genuinely believes that Paikin made a sexual advance and/or sexually propositioned her at the 2010 Grano lunch," Turnpenney wrote. However, she could not substantiate the allegation. Witnesses with direct involvement in the incident could not support Thomson's claim. Turnpenney also found Thomson to have credibility issues.

Although overall the lawyer found her to be "forthright and unguarded," she also had "doubts surrounding Thomson's ability to accurately observe and recount the events in question. For example, she tended to make leaps without sufficient evidence. . . . Thomson's evidence also veered towards being exaggerated and untrue."

Thomson claimed, for example, that after turning Paikin down, she was never allowed on *The Agenda* again, but in fact she appeared on the show in September 2011, ahead of the provincial election. (Thomson said she forgot about this, but noted that it had been arranged by the Liberal Party.) Also, Thomson suggested that Paikin had hurt her chances of winning the election by blocking her from the show while hosting her male competitors. She wrote in the Women's Post that Paikin "made it harder for me to compete with the men I was up against, because they were invited to appear on his show while I wasn't." But Turnpenney's report pointed out that the Grano lunch occurred after the October municipal election, on November 5, 2010. And with respect to the subsequent incidents that Thomson referenced in her Women's Post article— where Paikin approached her at events and suggested they sleep together—the investigator zeroed in on one alleged experience at a political event, which Thomson said occurred sometime in 2012. Thomson couldn't be sure of the timing or location. First she said Ottawa, then changed it to Sudbury. The investigator asked if she could provide any receipts or records of the visit, but Thomson never did. Another witness who was at the convention couldn't recall seeing her there. Paikin confirmed that he hadn't attended any Liberal event in Sudbury during that time period.

Turnpenney did interview seven witnesses who said that at some point before 2018, Thomson had told them about Paikin asking her for sex at Grano. But this proved only that the allegation wasn't new.

Perhaps the most damaging piece of corroborating evidence against Paikin was an email that Thomson's assistant sent immediately after the Grano lunch: "I'll never understand men who chase married women . . . he seemed so focused on trying to get you into bed with him that he didn't give a shit that I was there." But when Turnpenney interviewed that assistant, the individual said none of what Thomson alleged occurred. He also couldn't recall sending the email. Thomson gave the investigator a copy of a Facebook Messenger conversation she had with that assistant a few days before she emailed Paikin. In that exchange, the assistant told Thomson that his "recollections are tainted through time" but that he remembered joking about Paikin hitting on her. "What the come-on consisted of I can't be relied upon to repeat now. I know we were shaking our heads," he wrote to her. Turnpenney referred to this assistant as Witness J in her report. During their interview, the lawyer wrote that she found Witness J to be "evasive." The former assistant told Turnpenney that he'd decided to "play along" with Thomson in their recent Facebook exchange, which he regretted. Turnpenney also reviewed a text message conversation between Witness J and another individual that occurred after Thomson made her allegation in February 2018. "Yeah I'm the Assistant to the woman with the false memory syndrome. Ignoring it all. She fucking texted me 20 times yesterday," Witness J wrote.

As for Paikin, Turnpenney found him to be consistent, credible, and forthright.

With all the evidence taken together, Turnpenney concluded the allegations were unsubstantiated. And while that may not sound like vindication, when read with the report, it was as close to it as possible under the circumstances.

Thomson shot back at the report's findings in a Women's Post article. "I was warned by many PR experts not to take part in an investigation that was controlled and paid for by TVO as the scope of the investigation could change and eliminate evidence that could damage Mr. Paikin." She said her former assistant's decision to "back-peddle" was "devastating." She also lambasted Turnpenney for not mentioning the reason she'd decided to act in the first place: Thomson believed Paikin was having an affair with her friend's wife. "The wife had also appeared on the Agenda. I realized that my inaction eight years ago had enabled Paikin."

When I asked Paikin about this, he shook his head in exasperation: "No."

SARAH THOMSON CONTACTED me at the end of May 2018 to ask if I'd meet her for a lunch. She was moving out of the country and wanted to connect. She mentioned my recent work in the *Globe* and the Paikin allegation. The timing was odd, since we hadn't spoken in at least four years. I told her I was writing a book and coincidentally had been planning to get in touch with her to ask some questions about the Paikin allegation. In the interest of fairness, I told her I had doubts about her version of events. She agreed to meet anyway.

Several weeks later I arrived at the café where we'd arranged to meet. Thomson was sitting by the window, wearing a stylish navy blazer and white linen top. The dreadlocks were gone. It was the first time we'd seen each other since my book launch. We shared an awkward hug and I thanked her for agreeing to talk about the Paikin allegation, something she repeatedly told me she was reluctant to do. Despite what people may think, Thomson said, she was uncomfortable in the spotlight. She preferred to work behind the scenes. With Paikin, it was never her intention to speak out publicly. She thought her email would either prompt him to resign or force a quiet internal review. It didn't occur to her that TVO wouldn't keep her allegation confidential. She couldn't believe they'd named her in a press release. It was the network, not her, she told me, that made the allegation public.

"But you wrote that blog post," I said. "Even though you didn't name him, it would have been pretty apparent you were talking about Paikin once TVO announced its investigation." And how could she not expect him to tell his superiors about the email?

"I did not handle it correctly," Thomson said. If she could do it again, rather than email Paikin directly, she would have gone to the Ontario Human Rights Tribunal or had a lawyer contact TVO management. She'd let her emotions over her friend's failing marriage cloud her judgment, she said.

Thomson told me she still felt mistreated by the process and believed that the third-party probe was set up to exonerate Paikin. She outlined a number of would-be corroborating threads that the investigator supposedly didn't pursue. For example, Thomson asked whether I was aware that Paikin had done the same thing to a colleague of mine at *The Globe and Mail*. I told her I hadn't heard about this but would certainly be interested in speaking with the woman. Thomson encouraged me to do so, but said she couldn't disclose her identity. Perhaps she could give me a hint? She pursed her lips, sighed, and shook her head. That night Thomson emailed me a link to an article in *Frank*, a Canadian gossip site that reports on politicians and media personalities. After her Paikin allegation, the site posted a rumour that a *Globe* reporter had interviewed a woman who'd had a similar experience with the TVO host. In her follow-up email to me, Thomson glossed over the fact that this was a very different scenario from what she had presented to me over coffee: not only was it unsubstantiated gossip (and by the way, I did ask around and no one had heard this), but the woman in question wasn't even a reporter. In an email, I asked her to clarify. "One of my friends had mentioned [the article] and told me he thought it was a reporter at the *Globe* but the piece doesn't actually say that," she wrote back.

This was typical of Thomson. And it makes it hard to believe her. Even as I type these words, I realize how problematic this is, because what I know from my own reporting and from numerous studies is that the women most likely to be victimized are the ones who don't conform to societal expectations. Thomson seemed aware of this.

"I could be discredited easily because I'm quirky. 'Oh, she rode a horse, she must be lying,'" she'd said at the coffee shop.

But what's the alternative? Thomson made a serious accusation and demanded Paikin's job. A reporter or a police investigator can't ignore the contradictions and red flags in her account; doing so would hurt all women's credibility.

As I learned in my Unfounded reporting, a memory isn't a video recording. It's notoriously faulty. Every time a person thinks back to an event, there is the potential to taint that memory and leave it altered. I've heard it compared to the broken telephone game. And what's really dangerous is that people aren't aware if their memory is shifting. In one famous study, researchers interviewed thousands of people living in the United States about the moment they learned that the World Trade Center had been attacked. Memories generated from big, highly emotional events such as those are some-times referred to as "flashbulb memories." And the generally accepted belief was that something like 9/11 would be vividly seared into a person's memory. The researchers followed up with the respondents at one- and three-year intervals and then a decade later. At each interval, most people were very confident about the accuracy of their recollections. But as the findings showed, they shouldn't have been. In total, about 40 percent of the respondents' stories about that day had changed. (Dr. William Hirst, one of the study's lead authors, told me that it's important to note that the errors were often not substantial. A person may have initially said they learned about the attack on the train to work, but later recalled hear-ing the news in the office. "Participants did not, for instance, say they were in Paris when they were in Toronto." That point is relevant to such instances as the Brett Kavanaugh hearings, he said. A person can confuse details of an event, such as the time, but typically they are unlikely to invent a memory that would be outside the scope of what they might realistically have experienced.

I talked about all of this with Thomson.

The third-party investigator wrote that she felt Thomson truly believed the incident happened, even though the evi-dence did not support it. I had a similar impression. My guess is that if you gave Thomson a lie detector test, she'd pass it—but I also don't think Paikin propositioned her. I asked Thomson if she thought it was possible that she had misremembered the event. Was it possible that whatever happened had become exaggerated in her mind through the years? Maybe she heard him wrong?

"I remember being totally shocked and I don't shock easily," Thomson said. "Did he say sex or sleep with—I'm not sure. The innuendo was that I had to sleep with him. It was so thick you could cut it with a knife."

WHEN DR. CHRISTINE Blasey Ford's allegations against Supreme Court nominee Brett Kavanaugh became public in September 2018, Republicans initially shied away from calling her a liar. Instead, they honed in on the gaps in her memory. The alleged attack took place decades earlier, when Ford was a teenager in high school at a home in suburban Maryland. She couldn't recall exactly where or when it had happened. She wasn't sure how she got home afterwards. At various points her recollection shifted slightly. At first she thought the incident took place in the mid-1980s, but later concluded it was 1982.

Moreover, given how unreliable memory is known to be, supporters of the nominee questioned whether the things Dr. Ford did remember—Kavanaugh putting his hand over her mouth when she tried to scream; the "uproarious laughter" coming from Kavanaugh and his friend as the former pinned her to the bed; hiding in the bathroom and locking the door after escaping the bedroom—could be trusted. "Read about false memories. Read about people who have actually confessed to crimes and then later proven totally innocent," Senator Ron Johnson told a local filmmaker at Mitchell International Airport in Milwaukee. "She seems sincere. She's being used and abused by the Democrats." Senator Lindsey Graham wondered if it was a case of "mistaken identity." And in the opinion of Senator Joe Manchin III, the only Democrat to support the nominee,

"Something happened to Dr. Ford; I don't believe the facts show it was Brett Kavanaugh."

This political tactic inspired dozens of articles about memory and trauma. They explained how periods of intense stress alter the way memory is encoded, capturing central details while less important pieces of information can be lost. As Richard McNally, a psychologist at Harvard University and author of *Remembering Trauma*, told NPR, "The most meaningful aspects of the experience for the victim" will be remembered best. In an interview with *Time* magazine, Charan Ranganath, director of the Memory and Plasticity program at the University of California Davis, explained that people tend to think about memory as an "all-or-none" thing—we can either recall everything perfectly or the entire memory is flawed—but that's not how it works. Some events will be prioritized over others. "The way we remember things is that we make narratives out of them," Ranganath said. "The fact that someone was [uproariously] laughing during this traumatic event would be something that really sticks out."

For all these reasons, the experts agreed, Ford's version of events was in line with the science of memory. It didn't necessarily mean that the events happened as she described, but the holes in her testimony weren't reason to dismiss it outright.

In light of what had happened to him, I was curious to know what Steve Paikin thought about the Kavanaugh situation. Coincidentally, the day I was scheduled to interview Paikin—a day we'd set more than a month earlier—was September 27, 2018, the day that Ford faced the Senate Judiciary Committee.

When I walked into Paikin's office late that afternoon, the hearing was playing on the little flat-screen television on his desk. Kavanaugh was nearing the end of his testimony.

I'd watched Ford that morning and been listening to Kavanaugh in my car on the drive to TVO. When she finished her opening statement, I thought Kavanaugh was in deep trouble. It was plain to see that she didn't want to be there, explaining that, since Kavanaugh was on the verge of receiving a lifetime appointment to the highest court in the land, she felt it was her "civic duty" to let decision-makers know what he'd done. She had already passed a lie detector test. Throughout her testimony, Ford seemed to teeter on the edge of tears, but she was measured, immensely likable, and provided compelling details.

> I was pushed from behind into a bedroom across from the bathroom. I couldn't see who pushed me. Brett and [his friend] Mark came into the bedroom and locked the door behind them. There was music playing in the bedroom. . . . I was pushed onto the bed and Brett got on top of me. . . . Brett groped me and tried to take off my clothes. He had a hard time because he was very inebriated, and because I was wearing a one-piece bathing suit underneath my clothing. I believed he was going to rape me. I tried to yell for help. When I did, Brett put his hand over my mouth to stop me from yelling. This is what terrified me the most, and has had the most lasting impact on my life. It was hard for me to breathe, and I thought that Brett was accidentally going to kill me.

She remembered Brett and Mark laughing at her expense. She was 100 percent certain that Kavanaugh had been her attacker. For years she tried to forget what had happened. She told her husband before they were married that she'd been sexually assaulted, but did not elaborate. The full details came out in a couples counselling session many years later, in May 2012. She and her husband had been renovating their home and she had insisted on adding a second front door, an idea that no one understood at the time. It was only by explaining her trauma that the need for a backup escape route made sense.

"It is not my responsibility to determine whether Mr. Kavanaugh deserves to sit on the Supreme Court. My responsibility is to tell you the truth," Ford told the committee.

When it was Kavanaugh's turn, he appeared to be vibrating with fury. And although his rage was mocked endlessly online, it was effective. It looked like the raw anger of a person who thought he'd been falsely accused. "This confirmation process has become a national disgrace," he hollered. "This is a circus. The consequences will extend long past my nomination. . . . This grotesque and coordinated character assassination will dissuade competent and good people of all political persuasions from serving our country." He told the committee that all the evidence pointed to his innocence. Mark Judge, the man Ford had said was in the room during the incident, had told the committee in a letter that he could not recall the party in question and had "never [seen] Brett act in the manner Dr. Ford describes." The friend that Ford said she went to the party with, Leland Keyser, released a statement that she did not know Kavanaugh and couldn't recall being at a party with him. "My family and my name have been totally and permanently destroyed by vicious and false additional accusations," Kavanaugh went on, referring to the fact that two other women had come forward in the media with allegations of impropriety. Sexual assault allegations must always be taken seriously, he said, but an accused person also deserves to be heard. "Due process is a foundation of the American rule of law."

One plausible explanation for how both Ford and Kavanaugh could appear so believable and so sure of their diametrically opposite version of events was that Kavanaugh had been too drunk to remember the incident. After the allegations broke, reporters interviewed former classmates of the nominee who said that Kavanaugh had been an extremely heavy drinker as a young man. People wondered whether Kavanaugh had attacked Ford while in a blackout. Under questioning from the committee, Kavanaugh acknowledged liking beer, but denied ever being drunk enough to forget parts of a night.

"So?" I asked Paikin, gesturing to the television where Kavanaugh's testimony continued. "What do you think?"

Paikin told me that he too had been following the hearing throughout the day. "She comes across as utterly convincing and credible and he comes across as absolutely convinced in his own mind that this didn't happen. So, what do you do with that?" he said. "You'd think that after having gone through all this, I'd have a much better sense or answer for 'How do we handle these things now?' And I don't know if I do."

Paikin's office at TVO looks out onto the newsroom. Its light blue walls are cluttered from ceiling to carpet with mementos. There are dozens of photos of the host alongside politicians—prime ministers, a premier, President Bill Clinton. There's a corkboard covered with campaign memorabilia—a Trump leaflet, buttons for Hillary, Obama, and Ted Cruz, a Bush-Quayle bumper sticker. Behind his messy desk are family portraits. On one wall is a sports shrine—a collage of baseball cards, a giant photo of famous Red Sox left-fielder Ted Williams, a collection of pictures of Paikin with his family at various games. Pinned beside his computer is a list of Canadian journalist John Sawatsky's sacred principles for conducting a good interview. To journalism nerds, Sawatsky—an internationally recognized expert on the art of interviewing—is a legend. Paikin is definitely a journalism nerd.

"I wouldn't say it was my plan right out of the womb, but shortly thereafter," he told me. Paikin landed his first full-time job in 1982 as a reporter covering city hall for a local Toronto radio station, then he turned to television with the CBC for seven years, and in 1992 finally came to settle at TVO. He is the face of the network and its highest paid star, earning $337,201.03 in 2018.

At least within Ontario, he's one of the few journalists who may get recognized at the grocery store. Before Sarah Thomson accused him of sexual misconduct, people used to stop him to talk about a guest on his show or to chat about baseball.

"Since all this happened, people still stop me on the street, but they want to talk about this [the allegation]. . . . Even before the report came out, they would say, 'We don't believe this. We believe you.' That was incredibly sustaining during some bleak moments," he told me. In that respect, Paikin realizes he's lucky. He wasn't inundated with hate mail. He received hundreds of emails, tweets, and messages of support. Still, the experience of being accused of something so horrible capsized his world. Even though he was cleared, even though the public believed him, it's still the first thing that comes to mind when people hear his name now.

"I hope eventually it will recede in people's memory and the stuff that I actually do for a living will be more present. But who knows?" he said. "There may always be people out there who will wonder if it's true." He worries his reputation is permanently tainted.

In light of all that, I asked, what did he think about #MeToo? Had things gone too far?

"My views on #MeToo haven't changed at all," he said. "My default position is to believe women when they come forward. To the extent that my example shows anything, it's that we still need due process, and that's one part of the equation that cannot be forgotten."

The concept of "due process" has become one of the most polarizing subjects in the #MeToo era. The term refers to an accused person's right to a formal hearing (usually in the legal context), but lately it's taken on a new meaning for some. Critics of the movement talk about the "death of due process" as a way to complain about the practice of publicly calling out a person's bad behaviour. They argue that it's not fair to openly accuse someone of wrongdoing, because even an unproven allegation can tarnish a person's reputation. Allegations should be lodged through proper channels, like a police service. Others contend that speaking out about sexual impropriety was the whole point of #MeToo. Moreover, much of the misconduct being discussed isn't criminal in nature, so the notion of due process doesn't apply. People have very strong feelings on both sides of the debate. Perhaps the only #MeToo topic that gets people more upset than the due process angle is the troubling issue of redemption.

CHAPTER 10

THE REDEMPTION QUESTION

JIAN GHOMESHI MADE his first attempt at a career reboot one year and seventeen days after a judge acquitted him of sexual assault. On April 10, 2017, the fallen CBC star casually tweeted, "Hi. For those interested, here is something I've been working on." The post linked to a website called The Ideation Project, a "creative adventure" that wanted to take "a bigger picture view on newsworthy issues and culture" because "in a 140-character environment, nuance is often a casualty." The first episode, "Exiles," ran six and a half minutes and was ostensibly about the refugee crisis, but it was hard not to get the sense that Ghomeshi was telegraphing a not-so-subtle message about his own state of mind. "What does it mean to truly feel like you belong somewhere?" he began. "Or what if you don't belong anywhere? No place to receive a hand? What does it mean to feel like you have no homeland?" It was not good.

The Ideation Project was mocked into oblivion.

"We haven't missed you," someone tweeted back to Ghomeshi. "How do you even pronounce that? I. D. Ation? Idea-shun?" asked another. A third wrote, "Here's something I've been working on" (accompanied by a picture of the words "Fuck You"). That last reaction was a common one. A promised second season of Ideation never aired and Ghomeshi resumed his own exile—until he made a second attempt at re-entry seventeen months later.

On September 14, 2018, via a 3500-word essay in the prestigious *New York Review of Books*, Ghomeshi gave us "Reflections from a Hashtag," one of a trio of cover stories under the headline "The Fall of Men." The piece was an attempt to "inject nuance" into his story, Ghomeshi explained. "There has indeed been enough humiliation for a lifetime." He wrote about being fired from the CBC, his trial, the media attention, curling up in a dark room, weeping, and having suicidal thoughts. He described what it was like losing his status, his platform, his savings on legal fees, and ultimately his identity—because who was Jian Ghomeshi without all that other stuff?

Glaringly absent from this mea culpa was any real attempt to take responsibility for harming women. Rather, Ghomeshi actively distorted the facts to frame himself in a better light. For example, he wrote that "several" people had accused him of misconduct. In fact, more than twenty people had made allegations against the former radio host. He also seemed to try to downplay the accusations. He wrote that he'd been charged with "hair-pulling, hitting during intimacy" and "nonconsensual choking while making out with a woman." Although it's true that one of the complainants had testified that Ghomeshi yanked her hair, "hair-pulling" is not a criminal charge. He'd been charged with sexual assault.

Ghomeshi also failed to address any of the other serious accusations levelled against him by the *Toronto Star* and other respected news outlets, accusations that included genital grabbing, punching, and beating a woman with a belt during intercourse. (Ghomeshi, who did not respond to a request for comment from me, has denied ever being physically violent with women and said any acts of rough sexual play were consensual.) Ghomeshi ignored all this in his *NYRB* piece. He did acknowledge that he'd been "demanding on dates and in personal affairs," and that he'd "leveraged [his] influence and status to try to entice women." But this was as close as he came to confronting the outstanding claims of violence. Where those passages of personal reflection and contrition belonged, he showcased a cringeworthy lack of perspective and self-awareness. For a window into Ghomeshi's mind, recall that the only reference to the #MeToo movement in his article was to joke about being "a #MeToo pioneer."

He opted to conclude this all-important piece—his chance at winning back the hearts and minds of his haters—with an anecdote about sitting next to a "captivating and smart" single woman in her late thirties on a Paris-bound train from London. They ended up talking about music. And when the woman mentioned that she loved Leonard Cohen, Ghomeshi said he successfully battled the instinct to say, "You know, I did one of the last interviews with Leonard Cohen." Instead he just listened to her. It was, apparently, a moment of intense personal triumph for him to sit next to a woman for a prolonged period of time and not try to pick her up.

In a criminal court, Jian Ghomeshi had been found not guilty on four counts of sexual assault and one charge of choking. But with "Reflections from a Hashtag" he'd filed an appeal with the court of public opinion—and the public did not seem to believe that he was remorseful or worthy of a second chance.

The internet reacted as you'd expect, and then the fury turned on *The New York Review of Books* for giving Ghomeshi a platform in the first place. Canadaland's Jesse Brown tweeted, "The piece @JianGhomeshi wrote for @nybooks is riddled with factual inaccuracies, obfuscations and manipulations. If his editor had bothered to Google Ghomeshi before publishing him, here's what he would have learned." Brown linked to an article on his site—"Fact-Checking Jian Ghomeshi's Comeback Attempt"—that highlighted a dozen problems with the piece. Then *NYRB* editor Ian Buruma gave *Slate* a ruinous interview in which he flippantly addressed the serious criticisms that had been raised about the story, including the fact that Ghomeshi had glossed over the details of a fifth sexual assault charge brought against him by former CBC staffer Kathryn Borel, who alleged that while at work, Ghomeshi (her boss) had grabbed her hips and rubbed his pelvis against her backside, simulating sex. Ghomeshi had referenced that charge in his piece, saying it was withdrawn and settled with a peace bond—"a pledge to be on good behavior for a year. There was no criminal trial." But he failed to mention that he'd also been required to issue an apology for "sexually inappropriate" behaviour in the workplace.

Ian Buruma was pressured out of a job. "As editor of *The*

New York Review of Books I published a theme issue about #MeToo-offenders who had not been convicted in a court of law but by social media. And now I myself am publicly pilloried," Buruma told Dutch magazine *Vrij Nederland*. "Rather ironic." (The *NYRB* issued a statement denying that Buruma's firing had anything to do with a "Twitter mob." Rather, Buruma was let go because he'd excluded all of the female staff from the substantive editing process, which was a violation of their standards.)

JIAN GHOMESHI HAD delivered a master class in how not to stage a #MeToo comeback, but as I watched the backlash unfold, it left me wondering whether redemption was even a possibility for someone like him. The night that "Reflections" landed, I tweeted out the following: "Earnest question for Twitter as we all read @JianGhomeshi's piece: Is there anything he could say that would start to make it right in your eyes? Is there a path to redemption for Jian Ghomeshi?" Shockingly, most of the hundreds of replies I received were thoughtful and considered.

Several people asked why the redemption question was even being discussed at this early stage. Why did things always circle back to making things better for the men? Others countered that if there isn't a path forward for those who've committed harm, it's bad for everyone. "This redemption narrative isn't just for the assailants, it's often for survivors to believe that change can happen," wrote a woman who identified herself as an advocate for sexual assault survivors. Others noted that any apology should be delivered directly to the individuals impacted, not through the pages of a prestigious literary magazine. Moreover, any conversation about second chances has to start with genuine contrition and an apology.

Many people have pointed to the example set by Dan Harmon, creator of the television show *Community*, for his response to writer Megan Ganz. Ganz had insinuated on Twitter that she'd been mistreated by Harmon when they worked together on the show. (He had been her boss.) On his podcast Harmon issued a seven-minute apology in which he detailed his bad behaviour, took full responsibility, and never tried to justify anything. He said he'd developed feelings for Ganz, and when she rejected him, he felt humiliated. Then he did "the cowardly" thing and "wanted to teach her a lesson. . . . Just treated her cruelly, pointedly, things that I would never, ever, have done if she had been male and if I had never had those feelings for her." In the process, he'd damaged her "internal compass." He later lost his job and ruined his show, he said. He realized he could never have acted that way if he respected women. "So, I just want to say, in addition to obviously being sorry. . . . I did it by not thinking about it and I got away with it by not thinking about it. And if she hadn't mentioned something on Twitter, I would have continued to not have to think about it." Ganz tweeted a link to the apology, praised it, and told Harmon she forgave him.

In the aftermath of #MeToo I'd been thinking about the concept of justice—specifically, what that means and looks like in both a legal and a moral sense. Is justice served merely when and if the truth comes out? Does it take the form of a day in court or will only a guilty verdict suffice? Does justice mean that someone loses a job? Is it only about punishment? Does justice allow room for atonement? And what does redemption look like anyway?

In response to my tweet, BuzzFeed Canada editor Elamin Abdelmahmoud wrote that yes, a proper apology could lead to a type of redemption for someone like Ghomeshi, but that wasn't going to translate into a return to public life.

"Is it redemption though, if you don't, in some way, return to what you once did?" asked CBC columnist Robyn Urback.

"I deeply believe that anyone can be redeemed, it's a cornerstone of my faith," replied writer Nicole Cliffe. "Do I believe there is a path to resuming a highly paid public life as a media figure? Not a chance."

But how do you define highly paid? I asked. Was $50,000 okay? What about $150,000? Could someone like Ghomeshi ever have a career again, provided he wasn't famous?

Maybe not "a career," Cliffe tweeted back, but there were plenty of "jobs."

Five months after CBS fired Charlie Rose over allegations of groping and unwanted sexual advances, media icon Tina Brown revealed that she'd been asked to co-host a new show starring Rose. Together they would interview men who'd been brought down by #MeToo, men like Louis C.K. and Matt Lauer. "These guys are already planning their comebacks!" said Brown, who declined the offer.

The debate about what to do with those who've done harm is an important one. Just as there's a spectrum of bad behaviour, there should be a range of consequences. So while no one may be keen to see Harvey Weinstein back on the Oscar red carpet, surely there was a path forward for someone like Aziz Ansari?

After the January 2018 Babe.net story appeared, Ansari issued a statement saying that he was "surprised and concerned" to learn that the young woman had had a very different experience from what he'd perceived at the time, and that he would "continue to support the movement that is happening in our culture. It is necessary and long overdue." He also apologized to the woman directly. Ansari laid low for the next several months. In May he popped up at Manhattan's hallowed Comedy Cellar for a surprise set in which he didn't address the allegations. A few other small shows followed. According to media reports, he was always greeted warmly by the audiences. And then, in September and October, Ansari accelerated his resurrection plans with a mini-tour of a few dozen cities. When I spotted a Toronto stop in November, I sprang for a third-row balcony seat ($95.75 plus tax) at Roy Thomson Hall.

I wanted to see for myself how people would react to Ansari post-Babe.

THREE STEPS THROUGH the door and a security guard took my phone, sealing it inside a soft-sleeve Yondr pouch. For the next two hours there would be no texting, tweeting, or interneting of any kind for anyone inside the theatre. These devices had become popular with big-time comedians like Dave Chappelle, Ali Wong, and Chris Rock, performers who were frustrated with fans viewing their sets through a screen and then posting the content online. With Ansari, I couldn't help wondering whether the pouch came with an additional perk: message control.

There are more than 2600 seats inside Roy Thomson Hall, home to the Toronto Symphony Orchestra. After the Monday night performance sold out, Ansari's team added a second date; I went to the Tuesday show, and although I spotted a few empty seats, the place was still jammed. People seemed excited.

Still, the shadow of the Babe story noticeably loomed over the event. In the ticket line, at the concession stand, on the stairs heading to my seat, I picked up snippets of conversation— words and phrases like "#MeToo" and "allegations" and "she wanted white wine." Just before the lights went out, I turned to the couple sitting next to me and introduced myself as a journalist.

"Do you think after the show I could ask you a few questions about what you thought of the set and how you feel about Aziz in general?"

"Oh my God, yes. I am so conflicted. That story!" the woman said. "[My husband] bought me these tickets for my birthday—I have always loved Aziz—but I wasn't sure whether to come!"

The conversation stopped there as the show got underway.

Because I'd been following Ansari's tour through the media, I had an idea about the content. "To address the elephant in the room: Ansari didn't," Vulture wrote after his appearance in Milwaukee. But I noticed the allegations everywhere in his set, even without his mentioning them. Many of Ansari's jokes circled back to a critique of modern discourse and phony political posturing. The world has gone mad with people trying to "outwoke" each other, he complained.

Ansari did a bit about a recent scandal at Pizza Hut. Someone had complained that the pepperoni on their pizza had been arranged into a swastika. The customer posted a photo online and the internet went nuts. But some people thought it looked like just a regular pizza, Ansari said. He asked the audience to clap if they'd thought the photo showed a swastika. Some did. Then he asked people to clap if they'd thought it was just a regular pizza. More clapped. Ansari asked one of the "swastika" voters where he'd seen the image. "On Twitter," the man said. That's when Ansari admitted there was no Pizza Hut scandal. He'd made the whole thing up! People are so eager to voice an opinion that they'll do it about fake controversies, he said. The world is divided, but not in two—in three. On one side there are the crazy Trump supporters, who believe in wild conspiracy theories. On the other are the crazy woke police. And then in the middle are people—like him—who are scared of both groups. "At some point, they'll eat each other."

Afterwards I turned back to the couple sitting beside me. Cheryl Sugrim and Alan Sugrim were from Mississauga, a suburb about twenty minutes outside Toronto. Three weeks earlier Alan had come home from work with a surprise: for Cheryl's thirty-ninth birthday he was taking her to see Aziz Ansari, one of their favourite comedians.

"My first reaction was 'Yay!' but then I started to feel really conflicted," she told me. "We read the Babe story when it came out. We talked about it a lot. It was something that made me feel uncomfortable, and it was so hard because I genuinely like Aziz Ansari. I was like, 'Not him!'"

"What exactly did you talk about?" I asked.

"Just about what happened. The way he pressured her," Alan said. The woman clearly hadn't wanted to engage in the sexual activity and Ansari wasn't taking the hint. They felt he'd tried to leverage the power of his celebrity in that moment, which was "creep" behaviour, said Cheryl. But neither was comfortable classifying the allegations as a sexual assault. It mattered to Cheryl, for example, that when the woman said she wanted to leave, Ansari immediately phoned for an Uber.

What was interesting to me is that neither questioned the veracity of the woman's account. They believed every word.

Said Alan, "It does come down to the individual and what her truth is. To me, he could just be an awkward guy. I'm not going to boycott Aziz Ansari. . . . He's not a dirt bag. He's not Louis C.K."

(Five women told *The New York Times* that stand-up comic Louis C.K.—who once famously joked, "How do women still go out with guys, when you consider the fact that there is no greater threat to women than men?"—had masturbated or asked to masturbate in front of them. Four were up-and-coming comedians and another worked in entertainment. In all but one of the reported incidents, C.K. had asked permission first, but given the professional imbalance, the women said they weren't sure how to respond to the request. "He abused his power," said one. Several said they feared career ramifications if they talked about what had happened. Following the *Times* investigation, C.K. released a five-hundred-word statement in which he wrote, "These stories are true. At the time, I said to myself that what I did was O.K. because I never showed a woman my dick without asking first, which is also true. But what I learned later in life, too late, is that when you have power over another person, asking them to look at your dick isn't a question. It's a predicament for them.")

Cheryl and Alan agreed that they wouldn't see Louis C.K.—once another of their favourites—if he came to town, even though he'd acknowledged that he'd done wrong and apologized. They felt that the circumstances of the Ansari incident left room for him to make amends and be forgiven.

"It's just so grey. As a woman I want to support her and her feelings. But it's grey," said Cheryl. "Although, regardless of whether he sexually assaulted her or not, that scenario should not have occurred."

"It's not something I would do. I've never been in that situation," Alan added.

Both said they thought of the comedian differently after the article and weren't sure if they'd ever change their minds.

Said Cheryl, "I don't think he should be lumped in with some of these other guys. It's different. But also, I came as a fan. Being a minority myself, seeing him succeed means so much. We're fans, so it was harder."

WHAT OFTEN COMES up in discussions of whether a person is deserving of a second chance is how it shifts attention away from the individuals who've reported harm. "We spend so little energy thinking about justice for victims and so much energy thinking about the men who perpetrate sexual harassment and violence," wrote Roxane Gay in *The New York Times*. "People have asked for the #MeToo movement to provide a path to redemption for these men, as if it is the primary responsibility of the victimized to help their victimizers find redemption." As Frida Garza observed in Jezebel following the Jian Ghomeshi essay, "The subtext is: 'Okay, we've heard from the women; let's hear from the men.'"

As I read Ghomeshi's *New York Review of Books* piece, there was one woman I wanted to hear from.

Months earlier I'd spoken with Lucy DeCoutere, the first of Ghomeshi's accusers to publicly identify herself, about her life since the trial. During that interview I asked her about forgiveness. "Is there anything he could do to make it right with you?" I asked.

"I guess show some kind of sincere understanding that some damage was done and it can't continue," DeCoutere said. "But he would have to call me. We would have to have a conversation. If he just gave some interview or wrote something—no, fuck no."

So naturally, when "Reflections from a Hashtag" dropped, she was my first phone call. DeCoutere told me she'd heard rumblings that Ghomeshi might be writing something. Part of her thought he might just try to ignore the whole scandal. Maybe he was actually reviewing a book or something. She was having lunch with colleagues—she's a captain in the Royal Canadian Air Force and former actor—when she learned the link was live.

"I didn't read it right away, but I was super curious," she said. Later that day, when she was alone, DeCoutere pulled up the article. It was as disappointing as she'd feared. "He says he's developed empathy. I believe he's developed empathy—for himself. For others, I don't think so. Because if he did, he would say 'I'm really sorry, everybody, for what happened to you.' Not 'what happened to me.'"

What galls her the most, she said, is that "for sure he was on the internet watching me and the other people getting whipped to hell." Why did he not speak up? Why now, when it was all over, could he not defend them in some way? (It's worth mentioning again: Jian Ghomeshi was criminally exonerated in connection to DeCoutere's allegation and the allegations of two other women. Another complaint was settled with a peace bond and an apology for "sexually inappropriate" behaviour. The former CBC host has denied ever physically hurting women.) DeCoutere recognizes that admitting wrongdoing can open a person up to civil litigation. But she wanted something. And she wanted that something to be real and raw, and to truly acknowledge that he'd done harm. Instead, Ghomeshi's piece was entirely about the ways his life has changed. "And I've got tons of room for that," DeCoutere told me. "I have no doubt that when things shifted for him, it was catastrophic. . . . However, that was all it was." No consideration was given to the way that her life—and her fellow complainants' lives—were changed.

"How *has* your life changed?" I asked.

"I used to be a really light person to talk to, and I'm just not anymore," she said. "I get trolled every day. That used to be a problem, [but] now I don't really care. . . . For the people who talk to me directly, no one has come up to me and said, 'You lied.' That doesn't mean people don't think that. It just means no one has said that."

The trial went horribly, she acknowledged. "My testimony fell apart right before everyone's eyes." She'd gone into the process totally unprepared for what was coming and what was expected.

DeCoutere took to the witness box on Thursday, February 4, 2016, on the third day of the trial. So far the trial had been disastrous for the Crown prosecution. The first complainant was confronted with emails that contradicted her claim that she'd had no contact with Ghomeshi after he allegedly punched her in the head—a revelation that suggested the complainant was willing to withhold facts, instantly tainting the rest of her testimony.

After watching the first witness implode, DeCoutere's attorney contacted the Crown to say that her client had also had "post-assault contact" with the accused. It would be a double whammy on DeCoutere's credibility: first, because she hadn't divulged that fact earlier. Second, it appeared she'd been paying attention to media reports on the preceding trial days, which witnesses aren't supposed to do (DeCoutere said she respected the media blackout). Then during DeCoutere's testimony, the defence revealed that the day after Ghomeshi was alleged to have choked her, the two had brunch together and then spent time cuddling in Riverdale Park—and took a photo of the cuddling. That picture was presented in court. There was more: she'd sent him flowers and a handwritten letter that ended "I love your hands." All those details were absent from DeCoutere's sworn police statement. Marie Henein accused DeCoutere of leveraging her new status as sexual assault activist to further her career.

In a final devastating blow, Ghomeshi's defence revealed that DeCoutere had exchanged more than five thousand messages ahead of the trial with the third complainant. Among these emails was evidence that the two women had discussed the specific allegations. This was something the other woman had denied under oath. In the messages, they sometimes described themselves as a "team." They wanted to "sink the prick." Henein set the table for an inference of collusion.

When the not guilty verdict came down, the judge went out of his way to denounce the three complainants, branding them as liars.

The experience was humiliating, said DeCoutere. She told me she'd never intended to hide any correspondence with Ghomeshi; she had just forgotten about it. And no one had told her she wasn't allowed to speak to the other complainants, she said. As for the cuddling and the flowers, she told me that at the time, she didn't understand why those details were important. "It was never explained [to me by the police or the

Crown] that 'you might have done stuff that was embarrassing, and maybe it looks bad. It doesn't matter, just tell us everything.'" She didn't realize that you get only one chance to make a complete statement, and that everything after that would be taken as suspicious. She thought she'd have a chance to elaborate later on if needed.

"My health took a serious blow. My psyche was pretty much destroyed for a while—have you ever met Marie Henein?" DeCoutere said. "She took the worst part of me, in my opinion, and that was in the letter that I wrote to him. It would seem I had a needy, clingy insecurity. She threw it in the air, splayed it on the courtroom floor, and then tap danced on it while it was live tweeted to the world."

For months DeCoutere didn't go out. She didn't talk to friends. Strangers bombarded her with equal numbers of appreciative messages and death threats. Hundreds of women emailed her detailed stories about being raped. Now, more than two years later, DeCoutere said she's mostly pulled herself out of the pit. She's heartened by the fact that people are talking about sexual misconduct and consent in ways they never did before, and that the media is taking a more nuanced and intelligent approach to these stories. All of that came about because she and others came forward.

"He knows I was telling the truth. He knows I was getting pummelled from it. He also knows I'm having a good life. I'm an officer in the air force. I have great family and friends. That is fun."

Jian Ghomeshi twice tried to come back from his sexual assault scandal and twice failed after neglecting to show genuine contrition. People didn't believe that he was sorry about anything except losing his status.

But what about a person who has done serious harm and who later shows genuine remorse and apologizes? Are we willing to reconsider our assessment of that person? These were the questions I was hoping to answer when I sat down with Canada's most notorious (and former) judge, Robin Camp.

CHAPTER 11

JUDGING THE JUDGE

ON A SUNNY summer day in early July 2018 I scanned the crowded restaurant for a familiar face I'd never seen in person.

I suppose I expected to see former justice Robin Camp waiting with a grim expression like the one in his official judicial portrait, the one that ran alongside all those enraging headlines. In that photo Camp is dressed in the black robe of the federal court. He's square-jawed, blue-eyed, and sitting in front of a wall of law textbooks. His trim silver hair is swept neatly to the side. I imagined him to be a stern, formal person. I wondered if I would like him. Moreover, I wondered whether I'd ever be able to see him as anyone other than the judge who asked a rape complainant why she hadn't just kept her "knees together."

I'd never thought Camp would agree to an interview.

I'd gotten in touch with him a month earlier, a few weeks after the Law Society of Alberta decided to reinstate him as a lawyer. It had been a little more than a year since Camp's resignation from the bench. He made the decision after the Canadian Judicial Council recommended his removal following a very public disciplinary hearing. Now he was being given a second chance of sorts. He would never be a judge again, but his legal career wasn't over. Camp had achieved some form of redemption, and that felt significant to me.

In the same way that the Ghomeshi trial came to take on much more meaning than one single sexual assault case, so had the story of the "knees together" judge. In the eyes of many Canadians, Camp became the walking, talking personification of rape culture. I think watching his public flogging represented something of a catharsis for many.

THE CONTROVERSY GOES back to the summer of 2014, when Camp was a provincial court judge in Alberta presiding over the sexual assault trial of a twenty-six-year-old named Alexander Wagar. Wagar was accused of raping a nineteen-year-old woman, who can only be identified as JM. Both had been drunk and homeless at the time. Each had had previous troubles with the law—a relevant detail given that a criminal record can detract from credibility and that this case turned on credibility. Wagar claimed that they'd had consensual—even tender—sex in a bathroom at a house party. JM testified that Wagar had raped her, even as she told him to "stop" and that he was "hurting" her. She told the court she went to the washroom to throw up and was rinsing out her mouth in the faucet when Wagar slipped inside and shut the door. At the time, he weighed at least 215 pounds and stood more than six feet tall. She was 100 pounds and five-foot-six. JM testified that she'd been afraid of Wagar—something Camp struggled to understand. He asked the Crown: Why was JM fearful? There was no weapon. Wagar never threatened her. And why didn't she scream for help if she was so scared? There were people outside the bathroom. Camp made numerous statements like these throughout the trial that exposed his antiquated notions. Statements like "Sex and pain sometimes go together . . . that's not necessarily a bad thing" and "She knew she was drunk. Is [there] not an onus on her to be more careful?"

But the exchange that captured the most attention occurred when JM was on the stand. Camp asked her, "When he was trying to insert his penis, your bottom was down in the basin. Or am I wrong?"

"My—my vagina was not in the bowl of the basin when he was having intercourse with me," she replied.

"All right. Which then leads me to the question: Why not—why didn't you just sink your bottom down into the basin so he couldn't penetrate you?"

"I was drunk."

"And when your ankles were held together by your jeans, your skinny jeans, why couldn't you just keep your knees together?"

JM didn't say anything.

"You're shaking your head," Camp remarked.

"I don't know."

(In her testimony during the judicial inquiry, JM said of the above exchange: "What did he [Camp] get out of asking me those kind of questions? Like, what did he expect me to say to something like that. . . . He made me hate myself and he made me feel like I should have done something that . . . that I was some kind of slut.")

On September 9, 2014, Camp found Alexander Wagar not guilty. "The accused [sic] hasn't explained why she allowed the sex to happen if she didn't want it," Camp told the court. He had, of course, meant to say, "the complainant," but this was one of the numerous times that Camp inadvertently addressed JM as if she were the alleged perpetrator.

A year later, the Alberta Court of Appeal ordered a new trial on the grounds that Camp had misunderstood consent laws and perhaps fallen prey to rape myths. (In 2017, Wagar was again found not guilty, in part because of inconsistencies in JM's story.)

The entire episode may have gone unnoticed had it not been for some Canadian legal scholars who read the appeal decision and raised the alarm. Dalhousie University's Elaine Craig and the University of Calgary's Alice Woolley wrote an op-ed in *The Globe and Mail* entitled "Myths and Stereotypes: Some Judges Still Don't Get It." Outrage ensued, prompting the Canadian Judicial Council to take action. After a much-publicized inquiry, the council took the extremely rare step of recommending Camp's removal. (He was only the third judge to meet this fate since the CJC's formation in 1971.) Camp's conduct, the council concluded, had been so "manifestly and profoundly destructive of the concept of impartiality, integrity and independence" that he would be incapable of holding public confidence as a judge. Camp resigned before the body forced him out.

The public greeted the news with relief. How could Camp have remained, given the intense scrutiny and political climate?

Only a couple years earlier, Associate Chief Justice of Manitoba Lori Douglas was forced to retire after her husband had posted sexually explicit images of her online without her consent, which raised questions with the CJC about whether that undermined the integrity of the judiciary. (It's hard to imagine that case playing out the same way post #MeToo.) If Douglas, an apparent victim of horrible cyber-bullying, couldn't remain on the bench, how could Camp?

And yet I wondered how much better off the system actually was without him. Camp was hardly the only judge to have harboured outdated beliefs. And Camp seemed as though he genuinely wanted to do better. At the hearing, Camp was asked to reflect on his conduct during the Wagar trial: "I was not the good judge that I thought I was. I struck the wrong tone . . . I held onto the myth that women were supposed to fight off aggression." He apologized to the complainant and the broader Canadian judiciary as well: "I have made the difficult role of a judge, each judge in this country, more difficult, and I am sorry for that."

Camp had also proactively sought out sensitivity and legal training. He studied the history of sexism in sexual assault law with Professor Brenda Cossman. And he worked with Toronto psychologist Lori Haskell, the trauma and sexual assault expert I'd met earlier, who taught Camp about the biological origins of seemingly illogical behaviour in times of severe stress. They talked about the ways women and men are socialized differently. Justice Deborah McCawley, a senior judge in Manitoba, spent time with Camp discussing myths, stereotypes, and unconscious bias. She told the hearing she'd initially been skeptical as to whether Camp was genuine in his desire to learn, but he'd won her over. "He's not a misogynist. He is not a racist. He's extremely fair-minded, and part of my difficulty was trying to reconcile the transcript with the person in front of me and the discussions we were having," she testified. All three women vouched for his progress during the hearing.

One of the most disturbing facts to emerge during the disciplinary hearing was the abysmal amount of training required of Canadian judges. Camp was born and educated in South Africa and moved to Calgary in 1998. His legal background was primarily in contract, bankruptcy, and oil-and-gas law. And yet, after being chosen for the provincial bench, he received no education about sexual assault law in Canada. His knowledge of the country's criminal system was "nonexistent," he testified at his disciplinary hearing. What kind of system throws an oil-and-gas lawyer into a sexual assault trial with no training in this very complicated area of law? In response to the Camp controversy, former Conservative MP Rona Ambrose, then the interim leader of the Official Opposition, put forward a bill that mandated sexual assault training for new federal judges. It passed, although it has no effect on current sitting justices. Constitutional scholars warn that requiring active judges to participate in specific training is an infringement of judicial independence. Where they are concerned, the only power the public has is pressure. (As of this writing, the bill is still being held up in the Senate.)

Camp had displayed misogynist behaviour, but did that make him a misogynist? To me, his flawed thinking seemed rooted in ignorance, not malice. Getting rid of him did nothing to address all the other ill-informed judges still hearing cases. And there are plenty of them. Around the same time as Camp's

disciplinary proceedings were underway, my *Globe* colleague
Sean Fine revealed that two other Alberta judges were also
under review for their conduct during sexual assault trials.
I heard about and encountered others in my own reporting. I
investigated one case for the Unfounded series that seemed
rock solid—there had been two witnesses, physical evidence,
and the police were involved from the outset—but still the
judge acquitted. Here was one of the reasons he gave: the complainant had testified that the accused held her down during
the attack, preventing her escape. But the judge questioned her
version of events because the suspect had been naked during
the alleged attack. "Clearly [he could not undress] if he was
forcibly holding her or if she was trying to get away." It seemed
to me that this judge was displaying the same types of prejudices Camp had shown—he was just being savvier with his
wording. That judge is still on the bench. Meanwhile, Robin
Camp, who now probably knows more about sexual assault law
and the dangers of rape myths than the vast majority of sitting
Canadian justices, is no longer permitted to hear cases.

That's what I wanted to ask Camp about: notions of justice,
redemption, and what it means to be a repentant person. Most
of all, I wanted to know how a sixty-something white man
from South Africa had come to adopt a new way of thinking. In
an era where it seems people are so dug in on their positions,
how do you change someone's mind?

IN MY EMAIL requesting the interview, I'd written, "I'm sure
your knee-jerk reaction is to run as far away from this as possible, but I think there is real value in hearing from you." I was
surprised to receive a call from an out-of-province number

a few days later, and didn't immediately place the soft-spoken owner of the South African accent on the other end of the line. Camp told me he was surprised himself that he was responding to my request. He'd never spoken to a journalist about what had happened, he said, but he was intrigued by the questions I was asking. He agreed to meet me for a causal no-pressure lunch to talk off-record about his ordeal, but he let me take notes and part way through decided he was comfortable being quoted after all.

We met for lunch in a downtown Toronto restaurant in early July 2018. At first I didn't recognize Camp sitting at a table in an aqua blue button-up shirt, jeans, and Dad loafers. He smiled warmly when he saw me and extended a hand. We ordered tacos and beer and exchanged all the pleasantries you would expect from a first meeting—our families, plans for the summer, the weather—but the conversation quickly turned to serious issues.

At his disciplinary hearing, Camp had told the panel that when the scandal first erupted, he felt defensive. He recognized that his choice of words had been inappropriate, but he didn't grasp what message his questions had sent to the complainant. It was only through his sensitivity training that he realized he'd been suggesting to JM that she was to blame for not resisting. "I thought that I was intellectually honest, that I was fair-minded, that I was free of prejudice. I flattered myself," Camp had testified. "At an intellectual level, I understood issues surrounding rape myths. It has become clear to me that at a deeper instinctive level, I had not."

I asked Camp to explain this to me. Many older men I know bristle at the words "rape culture." To them, the idea is synonymous with man-hating; it's the language of radical feminists.

They tune out before the conversation ever gets going. Regular people—never mind judges in their sixties—are entrenched in their own opinions. How had Dr. Haskell and Professor Cossman and Justice McCawley broken through?

"I can only tell you in general terms," he said. "I like to think I have an inquiring mind. I like to understand things. How does this work? Why do you do this? Lori [Haskell] did nothing other than to get me to read stuff and then ask me questions. 'Why would you think that? Why would you assume that?' She gave me no conclusions. She gave me no criticism. She didn't tell me where I was wrong. . . . She got me to examine myself." There was no one eureka moment, Camp said. Each of his mentors assigned him reading lists. There was a book edited by leading feminist legal scholar Elizabeth Sheehy about women's activism and the law. An article from Western University professor Melanie Randall about "ideal" victims. Camp told me the text that stuck with him the most was a book by University of Ottawa law professor and legal historian Constance Backhouse called *Carnal Crimes*.

Carnal Crimes is a feminist history lesson disguised as a true crime book. Backhouse explores the changing laws and evolving societal attitudes around sexual violence between 1900 and 1975 by investigating and recounting the stories of sexual assault trials from each decade. In one chapter, for example, she examines the alleged 1920s rape of a young Halifax woman by a Dalhousie medical student. Although the events took place nearly a hundred years ago, the script is familiar. During the preliminary inquiry, questions were raised about the girl's romantic history, and why she hadn't appeared sufficiently hysterical afterwards (a taxi driver who took her home testified that there were "no signs" she'd been crying). The defence painted her as a woman of bad character, and the jury—of twenty-four men—dismissed the case.

In chapter after chapter, Backhouse displays the ways in which women reporting sexual violence have historically been met with suspicion. Early in the book she writes about Sir Matthew Hale, the aforementioned seventeenth-century English jurist who declared that rape was "an accusation easily to be made and hard to be proved, and harder to be defended by the party accused, tho never so innocent." This quote, Backhouse told me, is cited in almost every historical Canadian rape case she's studied—right up through the 1950s and sometimes even into the 1960s. "He was a man who presided over witch-burning trials. So it beats me how he ended up being the guru on women's lack of credibility," she said.

In reading texts such as *Carnal Crimes*, Camp said that he slowly began to understand that deep within himself, he har-boured some of those beliefs—beliefs that a victim who doesn't immediately report is likely lying; that a woman should fight off sexual advances.

Everyone likes to see themselves in a positive light, Camp told me, so acknowledging uncomfortable truths about your-self is a difficult process. And although there wasn't any one thing that brought about his evolution, he found Dr. Haskell's lessons about the body and trauma to be revelatory. "We all accept [the idea of] flight or fight. We've all experienced that," Camp told me. "[But] there's a third reaction that we rarely talk about and one we must accept because it's so obvious. The most common reaction is to freeze . . . it can cause a person to give an appearance of acquiescence." Before his training,

Camp had never heard about the neurobiology of trauma. And since he'd never really considered the ways women are socialized to be accommodating to men, he couldn't understand why a sexual assault victim wouldn't immediately scream for help if others were in earshot.

Now he did.

The change happened slowly, Camp told me. Throughout the many months that Camp was doing this work, he and Justice McCawley spoke frequently by phone about the latest readings he'd been assigned. Sometimes the conversations seemed to go in circles. Camp would become fixated on the minutiae of the law, when McCawley was pushing him to think about sexism, stereotypes, and unconscious bias. For example, in Camp's mind, there was a legal reason that he needed to ask the complainant why she didn't keep her "knees together"—he wanted to know if consent was given because of "force or fear." But in wrestling with the legal question of whether he had been right to try to establish this point, he was neglecting to think about the terrible implications of his words. McCawley would listen to his explanations and then tell him he wasn't there yet. She'd suggest that he think some more. She never offered the answer, Camp told me. And then one evening, he was at a training course in Stratford, Ontario, with other judges, when he decided to take a long walk along the river to get some ice cream. "I can't tell you why, but suddenly the penny dropped. [That comment] had been the first thing I thought about every morning when I woke up and the last thing I thought about every night before I went to sleep, and suddenly I understood the problem," he told me. "The question carried with it a criticism—a very mean-spirited criticism. I phoned Deb right away on my cell phone as I was walking. 'Is this the conclusion you were hoping I'd reach?' And she was pretty excited."

We chatted for more than two hours. After I'd finished my second bottle of beer and third taco, Camp suddenly became concerned: "Robyn—please don't take this the wrong way. Are you okay to continue? We can talk another time." At first I didn't understand what he was talking about, but then I realized he was worried that I'd had too much to drink. I chuckled, and with some effort convinced him I was sober.

As the conversation came to a close, I asked Camp if he thought he'd been treated fairly. Did he view himself as some sacrificial lamb, offered up as restitution for every judicial sin?

"You mustn't see me in that light," he said. "Yes, it was really dreadful, but I've met a bunch of people and learned a bunch of stuff. . . . My life is still good." He told me he's keenly aware that his has been a charmed life, born to loving parents in a comfortable home. He grew up white in South Africa. His father was a judge. He had the best education. He recognizes that life has been much kinder to him than it's been to others. He sees his privilege now.

"There's one more thing I'm prepared to say. If I'd been allowed to return to the bench, I would have resigned, I think," he told me. "We do need judges. There is no other system. No other viable system. But I wouldn't be able to do it, to sit in judgment of people again. . . . The reality of being judged by other people, humiliated publicly, was so much worse than the way one imagines it. I wouldn't be able to do it again."

WELL BEFORE ROBIN CAMP agreed to meet with me, I had a long conversation with Professor Backhouse about the lessons history has to offer during this moment of profound cultural change. Backhouse is the leading authority on the history of sexual assault law in Canada. In fact, on her website she's documented year-by-year legislative changes made to the Canadian Criminal Code. She's also written a number of books on the subject. *Carnal Crimes* was one of the first things I read when I started researching this book, so when Camp told me that it had had a big impact on his thinking, I knew exactly what he meant. I remember feeling so unsettled to learn how little has changed in the Canadian criminal justice system since before the First World War—when people still rode in horse-drawn carriages, when women didn't yet have the vote. So many of the issues that came up during sexual assault trials back then continue to resurface today.

In one of the first chapters, Backhouse wrote about a rape trial from 1907 that took place in London, Ontario, the same city that my first Unfounded story focused on. In modern-day London, according to *The Globe and Mail*'s data, the city's police dismissed about 30 percent of sexual complaints as baseless. I spent months investigating one particular claim involving a young woman named Ava Williams. She told me that during her first semester at Western University she was raped by a stranger on the lawn outside a keg party while she was heavily intoxicated. She'd asked him to stop, told him it was hurting, but he ignored her, she said. Some guys at the party took notice and started taking photos with their phones. The man ran off, dropping his wallet with identification in it. The video of Williams being interviewed by police several hours later is hard to watch. The detective obviously doesn't believe her. He asked her how her clothing came to be removed, because "It's not like it's torn or anything," he told the then eighteen-year-old, suggesting Williams didn't try to fight the man off. The detective told her that her judgment would have been impaired because she was drunk. He repeatedly tried to frame the encounter as consensual, and suggested that she had biologically consented because police noticed there was "discharge" in her underwear. Nothing in her file suggested that police tried to track down the eyewitnesses. The case was closed as unfounded after little investigation. According to the police report, the detective gave the man a "warning re: sexual assault."

Which brings me back to a hot July afternoon in 1907 in the same city. On that day, a local teamster named Joseph Gray delivered some firewood to the doorstep of Mary Ann Burton, the working-class wife of a tanner who earned extra money renting out the top floor of her modest row house. When Burton tried to pay Gray, he instead invited himself inside for a drink with one of her boarders. She said she refused and, to Gray's annoyance, the men drank their ale by the shed. Gray became rude. He threatened her saying he would "have" her before the night was through. Burton told him to leave and he did temporarily. Shortly after five p.m. he returned. According to Burton's testimony, Gray shoved a dirty handkerchief into her mouth, tied a rope around her neck, and violently raped her. She fainted and, after coming to, crawled out of her home, bruised and semi-conscious. Burton was found by a passerby. During cross-examination at the preliminary inquiry, defence lawyer Edmund Meredith badgered her about whether she'd been drunk at the time of the incident—she was adamant that she did not drink with the men—and then insinuated to the jury that Burton was a promiscuous woman. Without evidence,

Meredith claimed to have heard from "a most respectable person" that Burton had been spotted sneaking a man into her home, which she vehemently denied.

Meredith never called the mysterious respectable person as a witness. When it came time to question Burton about the actual alleged rape, Meredith interrogated her about the steps she took to get away. "Did you holler out?"—"Did you holler at the top of your voice?"—"How many times . . . ?" Meredith asked Burton to explain how she struggled and what she'd been doing with her hands, and then asked her to denote the specific location of her body parts during the alleged attack. "He threw you across the centre of the bed? . . . Then your legs would just be about the end?"—"What part of your legs would come there?" "Where were your clothes?" In the end, the judge ordered the jury to reach a decision of not guilty. He gave no reasons.

Although more than a century had transpired between these two cases, both Ava Williams and Mary Ann Burton had rape myths and stereotypes used against them.

Backhouse wrote that the case of Mary Ann Burton was an "ordinary, run-of-the-mill rape trial" for the day. It made me wonder if it wasn't also an ordinary, run-of-the-mill rape trial for our day.

"If you're thinking hard when you read the historical pieces," Backhouse told me, "you can see all the parallels to today. It's not like we've improved or changed much, but sometimes it's clearer and easier to think about things in the past. . . . The world has shifted, but the belief in the lack of credibility of women has not." Although the laws were changed decades ago to try to stamp out those prejudices, it didn't fix the problem because societal attitudes don't necessarily keep pace with the law, Backhouse said. Feminists and others fought successfully to remove the requirement for outside corroboration in sexual assault cases, allowing judges and juries to convict a suspect if they felt the testimony of the complainant alone proved guilt beyond a reasonable doubt. "And then research that was done after that found that police wouldn't lay charges, Crown attorneys wouldn't prosecute, and judges and juries wouldn't convict unless there was corroboration. So it doesn't matter what the law says," Backhouse said.

"So why aren't attitudes changing?" I asked.

Backhouse suspects it has to do with perpetrators not recognizing the harm they're inflicting. "They think it's just sex, and if she's had sex before, how could this be injurious?" she said. They aren't recognizing it for what it is: a complete violation of autonomy, privacy, safety—never mind any physical pain. The other big issue is the ongoing confusion about consent, Backhouse told me. Going back to the nineteenth century, if a woman didn't show up at a police station with ripped clothing and physical injuries and couldn't prove she'd fought back with all her might, then consent was assumed. And if a woman had had sex outside of marriage, then consent was assumed. There's been a successful effort to resist that by clearly defining consent in the legal sense, Backhouse said, but there's still a lack of understanding among both men and women.

Months after Backhouse and I first met, I phoned her at her Ottawa home to tell her about my interview with Robin Camp and how he'd cited her book as one of the texts that had opened his eyes. I was curious to know where she landed on the question of redemption.

"It's a contentious issue," she said. "I know that many feminists whom I have a very high regard for disagree with me—and they may be right—but I still want to cling to the belief that reform is possible, that men who have actually committed sexual violence and men who just condone it—from the bench or elsewhere—can change.

"Then the question becomes what's required to get there, and I don't think we really, fully know."

CHAPTER 12

THE GENERATIONAL DIVIDE

AUSTRALIA'S GERMAINE GREER is sometimes introduced as the Original Feminist, an undeniable icon of the women's liberation movement. The late 1960s brought feminism's "second wave," one that raged through the next decade and into the early 1980s. Greer vaulted to fame at age thirty-one after the 1970 publication of her international bestseller *The Female Eunuch*. Within its pages she took the then shocking position that women were being held prisoner by marriage and motherhood. She argued that the traditional nuclear family structure rendered women sexually repressed beings. "The housewife is an unpaid worker in her husband's house in return for the security of being a permanent employee," with no savings, few job skills, and no actual job security, she wrote. "Women have very little idea of how much men hate them." She challenged women to break free of society's chains, and to those who already felt emancipated, Greer urged them to taste their own menstrual blood: "If it makes you sick, you've a long way to go, baby."

Her ideas amazed and appalled—just as she had intended. For some, *The Female Eunuch* became a feminist bible and Greer a leading voice of the second wave. So, nearly five decades later, with the advent of the next great feminist uprising via #MeToo, people were naturally curious to hear Greer's take. They didn't like what she had to say. "If you spread your legs because [Harvey Weinstein] said, 'Be nice to me and I'll give you a job in a movie,' then I'm afraid that's tantamount to consent, and it's too late now to start whingeing about that," the seventy-eight-year-old told *The Sydney Morning Herald* in January 2018, three months after *The New York Times* investigation into Weinstein. "I want, I've always wanted, to see women react immediately. . . . I want the woman on a train who feels a man's hand where it shouldn't be . . . to be able to say quite clearly, 'Stop.'"

News outlets around the world covered the story of the prominent feminist sounding the alarm on #MeToo. Greer had made a career of spouting inflammatory statements, so her take wasn't necessarily surprising; nevertheless, some women, especially younger women, felt stung. With attacks flying her way, Greer leaned into the controversy, directly criticizing some of Weinstein's accusers who had dishonourably accepted "six-figure sums" in non-disclosure-agreement payments and then "boast[ed]" about it. These women, she added, were at risk of becoming "career rapees."

Journalists love narratives, and what made Greer's comments particularly captivating was that they echoed a broader sentiment being expressed by a number of high-profile women, women who seemed to hail from a particular generation. And it was those female voices that dominated the initial mainstream backlash to #MeToo.

Consider the hundred French women I mentioned in Chapter 1—the ones who signed that open letter decrying what they called the recent attack on men. The highest profile signatory, seventy-nine-year-old Catherine Deneuve, later issued a tepid apology after an outpouring of criticism, but other female commentators continued to express similar concerns.

These women's ages tended to skew towards the baby boomer and up bracket—born before 1965. Their complaints followed a general theme: the #MeToo movement cast women as helpless victims with no agency, incapable of standing up for themselves. Rape was one thing, they argued, but everyday sexual nuisances should be shut down with a sharp rebuke or a good slap—as they were back in their day.

For example, in an op-ed for *The New York Times*, writer Daphne Merkin declared that many "longstanding feminists" were privately rolling their eyes at the "unnuanced sense of outrage that has accompanied this cause." For some, she wrote, #MeToo had become a "witch hunt," that portrayed women to be as "frail as Victorian housewives." Most women with whom she kept company would simply yell, "Get your hands off me right now" to any man making an unwanted advance. *Globe and Mail* columnist Margaret Wente wrote something similar. "All I can say is that most of the abuse my friends and I have encountered has been relatively harmless." Most occurred in their teens and twenties, she said. Usually it amounted to catcalls, men walking too close at night, a few public flashers, "dates who wouldn't desist until we got really angry," and the odd boss trying to force a kiss. "All these things happened to me. All of them were wrong. . . . But none of it wrecked my life, and I would never call myself a victim," she wrote. "I loathe predatory men as much as anybody does. I know the devastation they can do. I also think that if we want to make some progress, we need to turn down the volume on the outrage machine." (From a male perspective, *Real Time* host Bill Maher told his audience that he was seriously concerned about the direction in which "fucking fragile" millennials were driving #MeToo.)

On the other side of this generational fault line, younger women tried to make sense of their predecessors' position. Stella Bugbee, editor-in-chief of The Cut, wrote that, like Merkin, she had grown up believing that as a feminist her job was to persevere within the patriarchy. "So I understand Merkin's desire to wear her battle wounds like signs of strength rather than seeing herself as a victim of a rigged system. But it's a fool's game . . . One of the things we need to reckon with is what women should expect from men and from themselves." Stassa Edwards in Jezebel had a less sympathetic take. "Liberal second-wave feminists have been a prominent voice in bringing the reckoning to a premature conclusion," she wrote. It's possible to discuss the nuances of #MeToo, including its failures, without trotting out "accusations of 'witch hunts' and 'feminist hysteria.'"

This feminist rift inspired a barrage of articles on the differing generational reactions to #MeToo and what it meant for the movement's success: the CBC, *The Globe and Mail*, and the *Associated Press* weighed in, as did the BBC and *The Guardian*. So did *The New York Times*, *The New Republic*, *Time*, Vox, BuzzFeed— the list goes on.

A few took the position that the gap between feminists was a myth or, at least, overplayed. "The so-called generational divide in the #MeToo debate is a pernicious fallacy. It is a form of essentialism that says all women of one age think one thing, all those of another think another," *The New Republic*'s culture writer Josephine Livingstone argued. Vox published the results of a poll from the non-partisan Morning Consult, which found that younger women and those over the age of thirty-five supported the #MeToo movement in almost equal measure (71 percent for the younger segment and 68 percent for the older). The poll, which questioned 2511 women in America over the age of seventeen, found that both groups had experienced sexual misconduct at a similar rate and had comparable views on what constituted harassment. For example, 78 percent of women thirty-five and over said sexual comments or sexual jokes that made them uncomfortable constituted harassment, with 70 percent of older women saying the same. But the poll had problems. One, it would have been more valuable if it included a third age bracket, separating out Generation Xers (those born between about 1965 and 1980) from the baby boomers. Two, it didn't get at the actual issue of contention: what specific kinds of behaviour make a person uncomfortable.

To me, it seems obvious that women from different age ranges are experiencing #MeToo in distinct ways. No group of people is monolithic, of course, but clear patterns of thinking are associated with certain age groups. When this generational debate flared up, I thought back to an exchange I'd had shortly after my Unfounded investigation launched.

In March 2017, I spoke about the series at Massey College in Toronto to mark International Women's Day. I talked about

Ava, the law student who told me she'd been raped at a keg party in her first year of university, while she had been inebriated. The detective bungled the investigation and suggested to her face that he thought she wasn't telling the truth. At the reception after my speech, a friendly looking woman with short silvery hair pulled me aside to discuss the findings. She praised my reporting, saying that these issues were finally getting the coverage they deserved. "But I have to ask," she said, "why are these women getting so drunk? They're putting themselves in dangerous situations. Don't we need to be talking about that?" I smiled politely and said something like "Well, I think the focus needs to be on the actions of men who rape women." I walked away a few minutes later, full of unspoken judgment.

That wasn't the first time I'd heard those types of comments. My inbox was brimming with stuff like this. Here's one example: a woman who described herself as a grandmother of nine university-aged girls wrote, "I know from them how much alcohol is consumed by their female peers, much more than other generations. . . . Should the victims not be held responsible for putting themselves at risk through their irresponsible behaviour?"

For a long time I felt exasperated by opinions like these. It all seemed so obvious to me and I rested smugly in my "wokeness." Couldn't these people see how backward they were being by holding women liable? Why were they making excuses for men who couldn't keep their hands to themselves? I just could not understand their line of thinking.

And then one day I came across an article in The Cut about Susan Brownmiller, author of the iconic *Against Our Will: Men, Women and Rape*. Brownmiller single-handedly changed the way we discuss sexual violence. Her 1975 book framed rape as a political issue. It stands as a sacred text not just for second-wave feminism but also for those in the movement to end sexual violence. When *Time* named twelve women as its 1975 "Person of the Year"—although the magazine's headline said "Women of the Year"—it put Brownmiller on its cover alongside eleven other trailblazing icons, including tennis champion Billie Jean King, civil rights activist Addie Wyatt, and First Lady Betty Ford. So in 2015, when a reporter with The Cut noticed Brownmiller attending the premiere of a documentary about the militarization of the police, the writer took the opportunity to ask her about the rape activism taking place on college campuses across America.

Brownmiller told her she'd been following it and was troubled. "They think they are the first people to discover rape, and the problem of consent, and they are not," she said. "They have been tremendously influenced by the idea that 'You can drink as much as you want because you are the equal of a guy,' and it is not true." Women need to be responsible for their safety and take precautions, because there are predators, Brownmiller said. "They think they can drink as much as men, which is crazy, because they *can't* drink as much as men. I find the position 'Don't blame us, we're survivors' to be appalling."

Predictably, Brownmiller was ripped apart. The headline in *Slate* read "Former Feminist Hero Somehow Thinks That Victim-Blaming Can Stop Rape."

I struggled to connect this version of Brownmiller with the passionate voice I'd heard speaking through the pages of *Against Our Will*, a voice firmly on the side of women. What had happened? I had to know—and so I sent her an email and we arranged to talk.

A few days later, I dialled Brownmiller's number at ten a.m. sharp.

"Hello," she answered in a familiar tone, as if we'd spoken many times before. I could hear the flick of a lighter a few seconds into the call. Her voice was raspy, with a soft New York twang. She didn't wait for me to bring up The Cut interview. "The whole purpose of *Against Our Will* was to stop rape," she said. That was—and continues to be—her primary goal. So why, she asked me, is it controversial to remind women that they need to take steps to protect themselves from predators? If getting "drunk as a skunk" at a fraternity party dramatically increases a woman's chances of being raped, why are people so angry at her for thinking women shouldn't do it? "My book spoke about recognizing the early warning signs and getting out, not putting yourself into a situation where you can't get out. It's not afterward, it's before, when you have to recognize the early warning signals."

I was starting to understand Brownmiller's reasoning, though she hadn't changed my mind. I still believe that putting the onus on women to prevent their own victimization is a backward approach, but I began to see why she and others like her held these types of opinions. The truth is, no matter how many times I say that women should be able to get as drunk as they want—wherever they want and as often as they want—I know I'll feel differently when it comes to my own daughter. I know that when she hits her teenage years and wants to start going to parties, I'll warn her that getting really drunk is dangerous for a lot of reasons—and becoming vulnerable is top of the list. So how do I reconcile that?

More to the point, I was struck by the irony that this

eighty-three-year-old woman, whose views in the 1970s left her marked as a radical feminist, a godmother of the second wave, was now being dismissed as an out-of-touch victim blamer. Her views hadn't changed. But time had marched past them and now she—and those like her—are being vilified.

I asked Brownmiller if I could hang out with her for a day in New York.

"Any Tuesday is good for me," she said.

THE ADDRESS BROWNMILLER gave me led to a post-war apartment building on a cobblestone street in Greenwich Village. On the elevator ride up to her penthouse suite, I tried to imagine what extravagance waited beyond the door. Susan appeared, still looking very much like the woman whose face graced the cover of *Time*. Big, warm eyes on a long, oval face, with a generous smile and a pouf of short brown hair.

"Was your flight okay? Come on in," she said, padding back to the couch and her cigarettes.

To my Toronto sensibilities, the apartment was huge—comparable in size to my narrow two-storey house—and charmingly dated. One entire side of the living room was mirrored. Built-in bookcases painted salmon pink lined the walls of the dining room that also served as a library. The shelves were crammed with hundreds of titles, including multiple copies of some of Brownmiller's own books. Splayed across the table were thumbed-through copies of *The New York Times* and *The Wall Street Journal*. The little galley kitchen, with its seafoam countertop, checkered wallpaper, and beige appliances, appeared accidentally trendy. There was an Obama '08 poster and a hodgepodge of oversized geometric art, although

Brownmiller's favourite decor seemed to be the thriving potted plants and succulents that occupied the corners and ledges of every room. As I looked around, Brownmiller volunteered that she'd been in the building for more than forty years, and that it was rent-regulated. Still, she added, she'd taken on a student roommate to cover the cost (which turned out to be less than my mortgage).

"Do you mind if I smoke?" she asked, flipping open a pack of Marlboros as she took a seat on the living room couch. The little glass ashtray on the coffee table looked as if it had been well used that day.

"Of course not," I said. "It's your place." From the little nod she gave, I could tell I'd given the right answer. She took a deep pull off her Marlboro, let it sit for a moment, then exhaled: "I worked very hard to learn how to smoke."

Brownmiller told me she was born in Brooklyn to lower-middle-class parents who spent most of their lives in a loveless marriage. Her father was an immigrant from a small town in Poland who never properly adjusted to life in the United States. Her mother was second-generation American. Both were Jewish. Her father worked in sales but wasn't particularly good at earning a living, she said, nor was he keen on his daughter attending university, given the cost. Thankfully her mother came to her defence. Brownmiller went to Cornell on scholarships but never graduated. She wanted to work. Her initial ambition was to be an actress, but instead she found entry-level jobs in editorial positions at various magazines. By 1960, when she was twenty-five, Brownmiller was working as the assistant to the managing editor at *Coronet* magazine.

"Then I went to Cuba to see the revolution, and they were

nervous about that at *Coronet*, and I believe they fired me," she said.

"Why would they fire you?"

"I wasn't covering it. I just wanted to see it . . . it was bizarre to them," she told me. "I was with a guy. We hitchhiked down to Key West and took a flight over there . . . and I realized on the way that I was pregnant."

By this point I'd been in Brownmiller's apartment for about eleven minutes.

"And we landed and found this leftist group and I spoke to someone, and he said, 'Ah, my brother is an abortion doctor,' and I went to see him—"

"In Cuba? During the revolution?"

Remember, she said, abortion was still illegal in the United States at the time. It was a bit serendipitous that she was in Cuba. She told me she remembered waking up in the clinic surrounded by other women, some from the United States, lying on cots.

"So that was my first abortion."

There would be two others. Both done at clinics in Puerto Rico for around $350.

I have friends who've had abortions. I've gone to the clinic with them. I myself have never had to make that horrible decision, but watching it through them, I've seen how painful, conflicting, and guilt-inducing it can be. I'd never heard anyone speak so cavalierly about abortion. I wasn't offended—just taken aback.

Abortion came up constantly over the four hours that Brownmiller and I spent together. She repeatedly complained that complacency among younger generations of feminists has led to rollbacks of reproductive rights. "The most important issues today are rape and abortion," she told me. But whenever she speaks with young feminists, they're preoccupied with issues like supporting sex workers, transgender bathroom rights, and women's right to dress as they please. "These are not the cutting issues," Brownmiller said. "But they don't want to get into that. They just want to say, 'Freedom, Freedom, Freedom! We can wear what we want! We can get as drunk as we want!' I think it's just unrealistic."

I asked her if she realized how controversial she was being.

"Apparently it offends an enormous amount of people when I say, 'You're not equal, and you've got to remember there are predators out there.' I say this all the time, and I'm not going to stop saying it."

I asked if she'd read the Babe.net piece about Aziz Ansari. She rolled her eyes. "It reminded me of a date I had once, a dinner date," she said. When the waiter asked what they wanted for dessert, he ordered her berries with kirsch fruit brandy. "I said, 'I don't want the kirsch.' And he said, 'Oh, yes you do' and he poured the alcohol on my berries." Brownmiller said she immediately told him the date was over. They obviously didn't have much in common. "That's what I was thinking when I was reading the Aziz story. Why didn't she say something? . . . Individual women have to develop the courage themselves. Nobody's going to do it for them."

So what did she think about #MeToo?

Overall, she said, it's been a remarkable phenomenon to watch. "We don't know if #MeToo is a movement or a moment. I hope it's a movement and I hope things change. Sure. Of course." She does worry about the emerging narrative that women have become hysterical. "There's a confusion in people's minds about due process. We're not the ones who got these guys fired. Their companies decided to cut their losses," she said.

Brownmiller came to her awakening on the crisis of sexual violence around 1970, in the early years of the women's liberation movement. She was working as a full-time journalist writing columns for the *Village Voice*. (Previously, she'd worked at *Newsweek* magazine and at ABC television as a news writer.) At that time, groups of feminists were meeting each week in each other's living rooms for "consciousness-raising" sessions, she told me. I interjected to confess that I didn't know what the term meant. She seemed amused by that, but patiently explained that these were small groups of women who'd get together at a different house each week to discuss feminist issues. Women in the circle would take turns sharing a personal experience about a particular topic. (Some later Googling on my part turned up a pamphlet from the New York Radical Feminists group—Brownmiller was a member—which explained that the goal of consciousness-raising was to "make us aware of the societal pressures that oppress women" as well as to develop pride in being a woman by identifying with female peers.)

"We'd eat, have dinner, and talk," Brownmiller said.

"It sounds a lot like my book club."

"It's like a lot of people's book clubs."

At Brownmiller's first consciousness-raising, the topic was abortion. Over subsequent weeks her group discussed harassment, pregnancy, and sexuality. ("Who knew so many women were lesbians?" she said.) And then one evening in the fall of 1970, someone brought up rape. "I fairly shrieked in dismay," she wrote of this moment in *Against Our Will*. "I knew what rape was and what it wasn't. Rape was a sex crime, a product of a diseased, deranged mind. Rape wasn't a feminist issue, rape was—well, what was it?" Before the women's movement, Brownmiller told me, rape was not regarded as a women's issue. Whenever the topic came up in progressive circles, it was in the context of black men in the South being lynched by white men over false allegations of raping white women. Nevertheless, Brownmiller's consciousness-raising group proceeded and, one by one, the women told their stories. One talked about being gang-raped while hitchhiking from one college to another. When the police arrived afterwards, they didn't believe her. "Who'd want to rape a nice girl like you?" the officer apparently said. Another woman discussed an incident in a Paris hotel room.

Brownmiller could hardly believe that so many women she knew had had to deal with this. The group put together a "speakout" at a church, lining up women to share their stories about sexual violence; reports from the time say that about thirty gave testimony. Hundreds attended. Feeling as though they were on to something, the group members decided to organize a full-blown conference with speakers, panels, academic research, and a clear objective. The work Brownmiller's group was doing was revolutionary for the time.

On a Saturday night in April 1971, Brownmiller and a friend were tacking up leaflets for the Radical Feminist Conference on Rape on Eighth Street when a man walked past and "goosed" her. She wrote about the experience in the *Village Voice*:

I never saw his face at all, just felt the expert little twiddle that always seems to find its mark. . . . The gooser stands to the left of the ogler, the lip-smacker, the animal-noise maker, and the verbal abuser, and to the right of the rapist. . . . The gooser probably is the way he is because he gets the message from the culture that the women around him are available and dying for it, but that is not his personal experience whenever he tries to get it. So he takes out his hostility by making all women available to him with his lightning strike.

It wasn't the first time Brownmiller had had this happen, she told me, but it was the first time since she'd become a feminist. She chased the man down and kicked him in the rear. (She ended up spraining her ankle, because she slammed her foot too hard back down onto the pavement.)

They held their conference in a high school auditorium. "It was astonishing. I couldn't deny it any longer that this was a real issue. I told the group I was going to write a book about rape."

Brownmiller spent four years working on *Against Our Will*. She assembled an unprecedented history of rape going back to Babylon and beyond. "From prehistoric times to the present, I believe, rape has played a critical function. It is nothing more or less than a conscious process of intimidation by which *all* men keep *all* women in a state of fear," she famously observed. Brownmiller identified four myths that men believe about female sexuality: that all women secretly want to be raped; that if a person truly doesn't want to be raped she can stop it; that "she was asking for it"; and that rape really isn't so bad—it can actually be fun if a person lets herself relax. The book was an instant success and Brownmiller became enshrined as a feminist hero. *The New York Times Book Review* described it as "chilling and monumental," and that it "deserves a place next to those rare books which force us to change the way we feel about what we know."

When Susan Brownmiller was attending her first consciousness-raising groups and when Germaine Greer was writing *The Female Eunuch*, the world was a very different place for women. Even in developed countries, women's rights were consistently subordinate to men's in practically every respect. Consider that 1970 was the year when men in France lost their long-held legal authority over the household. Prior to that, as official heads of the family, they had sole parental authority. In Italy it would be five more years until the government passed legislation abolishing a man's legal right to dominance within a marriage. In 1970 women were vastly under-represented in politics around the world. In Canada, of the 264 seats in Parliament, only one was held by a woman, New Democrat Grace MacInnis. Similarly, only one woman sat in the United States Senate, Margaret Chase Smith. In Switzerland women still weren't allowed to vote in federal elections. Irish women couldn't own their own homes.

When *The Female Eunuch* hit the shelves in 1970, abortion was still against the law almost everywhere in the world. In the United States, banks could refuse to issue a woman a credit card, the Boston Marathon didn't allow women to compete, and Dartmouth refused to admit female students. In Canada, even limited maternity benefits did not yet exist and the RCMP did not employ a single female officer. Canadian women had been considered "persons" under Canadian law only since 1929—barely forty years earlier—owing to a landmark Supreme Court ruling. Indigenous women had only been allowed to vote in federal elections for a decade. In both countries a woman could legally be fired for becoming pregnant, a wife could not refuse sex with her husband, and female workers could expect to make a fraction of what their male colleagues earned. Even in Sweden, the world's bastion of progressive policy, gender discrimination in the workplace didn't become illegal until 1980. And in the world's developing regions—where most women weren't allowed to vote, weren't taught to read, worked longer hours than men, were expected to marry young, had little to no access to family planning strategies or technologies, and enjoyed few protections from sexual or physical violence—the outlook was exponentially bleaker.

There's a reason why women in each generation are experiencing #MeToo differently: they've lived in the world differently. We are all products of our collective experiences. My generation grew up with the gains won by Brownmiller's. That this cohort of women sees us as ungrateful is as natural as my generation viewing them as out of touch. "I don't buy it," a friend of mine told me many months later at our monthly book club during a discussion about the generational divide of #MeToo. "I don't understand why these women refuse to evolve. I don't think you should get a pass for that."

Back in New York, I'd asked Brownmiller about this. "I'm stubborn," she said simply. That same trait was in evidence when she faced down an outcry over a chapter in *Against Our Will* where she deals with race and rape. Brownmiller had spent a few pages recounting the tragedy of Emmett Till, a fourteen-year-old black boy whose mutilated body was found in the Tallahatchie River in August 1955.

Brownmiller describes how Till, from Chicago, was in Mississippi visiting an uncle for the summer and supposedly had been bragging to his friends about his "exploits" with white women back home. Unconvinced, Till's friends dared him to ask out a young shopkeeper, Carolyn Bryant, at the general store, which he did, Brownmiller wrote. When she chased him away with a pistol, Till "wolf-whistled" at her, Bryant alleged. The woman's husband, Roy Bryant, and his half-brother, J.W. Milam, seized Till from his uncle's home that night. The men told authorities they had only intended to beat him up, but they claimed Till continued to brag about having "had" white women, so they shot him, weighted down his body, and threw him in the river. The men were acquitted by an all-white jury.

Till's gruesome murder garnered national attention and became a symbol of racism in the South. It emerged as a galvanizing moment leading into the civil rights movement. So when Brownmiller summed up the story by arguing that Till's actions weren't simply innocent flirtation since he'd viewed the young girl as an object he was entitled to, she earned denunciations from black leaders, including from Angela Davis.

"It was three pages [in the book]. I get outraged letters from people who say, 'You need to apologize!'. . . The way it was told, I used the best material available at the time," she said. "What am I supposed to do? Apologize and say, 'Now I'm woke'?" About a month before Brownmiller and I met, it was revealed that the Justice Department had quietly reopened Till's case after the key witness—Carolyn Bryant Donham—recanted parts of her testimony. When I asked Brownmiller if this changed anything, she was steadfast. Why would she apologize for doing the best she could given what was known at the time? "I refuse. I'm pigheaded."

"You're a very layered person," I said.

"Thank you, so are you."

ABOUT A MONTH after my first conversation with Susan Brownmiller, I met up again with legal historian Constance Backhouse. I've already mentioned that she's the preeminent expert on the evolution of sexual assault law in Canada, but she's also a sixty-six-year-old baby boomer and an unabashed feminist, so I was curious about her take on the generational divisions over #MeToo. In particular, I hoped to hear her thoughts on what Brownmiller had said about binge drinking and the idea that women need to stand up for themselves in the face of bad behaviour.

"*Against Our Will* was very important. . . . And I understand why Brownmiller says what she says [about alcohol]. She's not wrong," Backhouse told me. "But you don't then say to women 'Curtail your activity.' . . . What about the men's responsibility not to get so drunk that they get aggressive and they can't read signals? . . . I don't think the advice Susan Brownmiller gives is going to change men's behaviour at all."

In the nineteenth century, Backhouse continued, it was understood that women were the gatekeepers of sexual morality. They were expected to stop unacceptable conduct. "So, looking at it as a historian, I get really worried as soon as people start saying the responsibility lies with the women. Because I know once you go down that route, it's a step back to the nineteenth century, and none of us are safe. None of us behaves in a way that consistently protects us from sexual assault, and so if you start saying the issue is to look at the women's behaviour, dress, actions, substance use, we're all done."

As for the idea that a woman should react immediately in the face of harassment with a strong no or a swift slap, Backhouse acknowledged that this is a popular position among a significant number of women—particularly older women. But she thinks they're missing the point. "Yeah, we should all be stronger. . . . That would be good, I'd be positive about that. Agency. Autonomy. Strengthening women. That doesn't mean we then have to say to women who aren't that strong, 'You brought it on yourself. Shut up about it. Take your lumps. Go home.'" A predator will just seek out easier, more vulnerable prey, she said. People need to step back and ask what kind of society we want to live in. "We can do better."

CHAPTER 13

WHAT THE KIDS ARE SAYING

IN THE WEEKS after I came back from visiting Susan Brownmiller in New York, I kept returning to the same thought: when would *I* be the one considered out of touch? At some point in my life, it's extremely likely that I'll pick up a magazine or a newspaper (if they're still around) and not see myself or my values represented within its pages. I'll shake my head at the younger generation's newfangled philosophies. I won't get it. The culture will have moved past me.

It occurred to me as I was transcribing my Brownmiller interview that, at age thirty-four, I wasn't exactly the best snapshot of the day's youth. When was the last time I'd actually spoken with a kid in high school? I realized I had no idea what kind of conversations teenagers were having in the wake of #MeToo. Maybe I was already being left behind and I didn't even realize it.

I sent a text to Farrah Khan, the woman who'd run the frosh-week consent training at Queen's University: "Do you know anyone in high school?"

ON A CHILLY Friday in January 2019 I arrived at The 519, a community and advocacy centre in Toronto, for the Mic Drop youth forum. With just a few minutes left in their noon break, a few hundred students buzzed around the room, catching up with friends or snatching cans of pop from the lunch buffet. A cluster of teenagers walked past me into the hallway, each with a green and white nametag that included the pronouns by which they preferred to be known: he/him, she/her, they/their. Another group of students huddled near the front podium, snapping selfies beside the conference's floor-to-ceiling values banner: "No Sexism. No Racism. No Ableism. No Classism. No Ageism. No Homophobia. No Fatphobia. No Transphobia. No Xenophobia." At the back of the room a small mob of students converged around the DIY button-maker machine, hurriedly hammering out a bespoke pin before the start of the next panel. Gradually they returned to their seats with their sloganed bling: "Ally," "Feminist Killjoy," "No," "You Are Valid." One of the most popular pins was "1998" with a red line drawn through its centre—a nod to the reason we were all there.

Six months earlier, in July 2018, the Progressive Conservative government of newly elected Ontario premier Doug Ford followed through on a controversial campaign promise to scrap the province's modernized sex-ed curriculum. That long overdue update, which had rolled out in September 2015 following extensive consultations with health professionals, academics, police, students, teachers, and parents, included subjects like consent, sexting, and gender identity. With its repeal Ontario would revert to the 1998 lesson plans, created before the smartphone era. Health officials warned that this was the exact opposite direction in which sexual education should be moving, but the Ford government was heavily indebted to a small but loud socially conservative wing of the party that had demanded its return.

I spoke to seventeen-year-old Tessa Hill, one of the forum's organizers. She told me that even though she knew the repeal was coming it was no less gutting. When Hill was in grade eight, she and a classmate, Lia Valente, spearheaded a province-wide "We Give Consent" campaign to convince Kathleen Wynne, then the Liberal premier, to include the topic of consent in the new sex-ed curriculum. The petition they posted on Change.org garnered forty thousand signatures. When Wynne heard Hill and Valente talking about their work on CBC's *Metro Morning*, she invited the young teens to the Queen's Park legislature.

"I was very emotionally tied to the curriculum, and it was just such a hit that now it was gone," Hill said. "I felt super, super frustrated and overwhelmed. It felt like I needed to do something really quickly. I felt like I should put out a statement or something [on Twitter]." But at the same time, Hill told me she had become frustrated with the hollowness of social media activism. She wanted do something that felt real. "That's where the youth forum came from." Hill emailed her mentor, Farrah Khan, who recommended that she get in touch with the staff at The 519. From there Hill hooked up with other student activists across the city. She and a committee of ten others met regularly from the end of July 2018 through to

January, planning panels, speakers, and workshops with the goal of teaching students how to advocate for their beliefs. About 150 students from local high schools registered to attend. On the day's agenda: discussions about consent, colonization, and supporting survivors of sexual violence, as well as an intergenerational conversation about activism and #MeToo. That last one was the panel I'd come to watch. The five speakers were Khan, activist and black awareness educator Tina Garnett, MPP Dr. Jill Andrew (the first openly queer black woman to hold that position), Korean-Canadian artist Janice Jo Lee, and CUPE Ontario president Fred Hahn.

Because of my job, I'm often invited to speak on panels. This one looked nothing like the ones I usually attend, but it did look like the city I live in and love: four women of colour, one white guy. The discussion was lively and engaging. Students laughed, clapped, and snapped their fingers in agreement at comments. Most of the teens in the room had been brought there by their teachers. One of the questions put to the group concerned the very issue I'd been exploring: how do different generations have productive conversations about controversial topics? "With respect," was Lee's answer. Elders have wisdom to share, even if some of their ideas seem out of step with the times. Hear them out. Make your case with love. Simply yelling "That's transphobic!" isn't going to work, she said. Dr. Andrew had a different take: "Sometimes it's okay to check the elders. Don't ever feel that because you're in their space . . . that you can't challenge them," she said. "You may challenge them differently than how you might your peer . . . but it's still okay to challenge and check an adult when it's necessary."

Former premier Kathleen Wynne made a cameo appearance. The Huffington Post and CBC had reporters covering the forum. It was hard not to be impressed by these kids.

A FEW WEEKS before the event, I met up with Tessa Hill for a coffee in the city's west end. I wanted to talk to her about #MeToo, but I was also interested to know how someone so young had become involved in feminist activism.

"Going through elementary school, I was really aware of the differences of behaviour between girls and guys. Especially how guys would treat our bodies," she told me. One incident in particular stood out in her mind. She remembers being in gym class when she was about eleven. The kids were being divided up into teams for something when one of the boys called out, "Oh, great, Tessa is on our team because her boobs are so big!" Everyone—including the teacher, she said—acted as if that was a totally normal comment. What Hill was describing was the first time she noticed rape culture. She didn't yet know the term, but even as a sixth grader, she knew it felt wrong. She wanted to understand why it was happening, and in grade eight she got her chance. As part of a media studies class, each student was expected to produce a body of work related to a social justice issue by the end of the term. Hill teamed up with her best friend, Lia Valente, and the pair decided to create a documentary exploring rape culture. (It's called *Allegedly* and it's still available on YouTube.)

When they first started, she and Valente had a very traditional "white girl" idea of feminism, Hill told me, but the more people they talked to—people like Farrah Khan, whom they found by Googling "feminist, rape culture, Toronto"—the more their understanding of feminism evolved. "We learned so much in doing those interviews, like about intersectionality," Hill said.

"Intersectional" is one of those buzzy words often used by younger feminists, but the term was actually coined three decades ago by celebrated scholar and law professor Kimberlé Crenshaw. In her 1989 paper, "Demarginalizing the Intersection of Race and Sex: A Black Feminist Critique of Antidiscrimination Doctrine, Feminist Theory and Antiracist Politics," Crenshaw outlines how viewing discrimination through a single lens, whether it's race, gender, or class, erases individuals who are dealing with multiple barriers. She tells the story of Emma DeGraffenreid, who along with four other black women sued General Motors in 1976 for hiring practices that discriminated against black women. A district court judge rejected first the gender argument, as the company did hire women for secretarial and front-office work (except that they were all white), and then the racial argument, because GM did hire black people for industrial jobs (except that they were all men).

"Only if the court was able to see how these policies came together would [the judge] be able to see the double discrimination that Emma DeGraffenreid was facing. But the court refused to allow Emma to put two causes of action together to tell her story," Crenshaw said of the case during a 2016 TED Talk. Intersectionality is the acknowledgment that there is often overlap between different social injustices, and that unless you take in a full picture of all the layers, marginalized people will be missed.

To many, that's an obvious truth. But some prominent conservative cultural critics scoff at the notion, dismissing it as at best activist jargon and at worst radical and divisive. "Intersectionality is a form of identity politics in which the value of your opinion depends on how many victim groups you belong to," says Daily Wire editor-in-chief and firebrand Ben Shapiro. Writers at Quillette, the crusading "free thought" online magazine, have described intersectionality as "the latest fad" (November 2017), a notion that "fosters groupthink, and necessitates radicalism" (May 2018), and as "philosophically incoherent, sociologically mistaken, historically illiterate [and] politically dangerous" (August 2018).

But for youth like Tessa Hill, an intersectional approach is neither controversial nor negotiable. It's inherent in her understanding of feminism. This was the standard position of everyone I spoke with at Mic Drop. In fact, I found that these teens were mistrustful of those who hadn't embraced those beliefs.

A few days after the event, I met with another of the forum's organizers, sixteen-year-old Savi Gellatly-Ladd. When I asked whether she considered herself a feminist, the teenager emitted a long, loud sigh.

"I admit I wasn't expecting that," I said.

She chuckled.

"I'm completely a feminist. I believe women are equal to men—that everyone should be equal. But I make it clear, though, that I'm an intersectional feminist. Because there are a lot of people who are feminists who only care about white women's issues. They don't think about the issues that Indigenous women and women of colour and queer women face," she said. "There's such a stigma around feminism, too, because of social media. You see a lot of white women on social media saying ridiculous things."

"Like what?"

"Like feminist accounts that just quote famous, self-identified white actresses talking about pay equity in Hollywood."

Gellatly-Ladd told me she'd been involved with activism since she was young. Her two mothers, who've been together for twenty years and have always been politically engaged, began bringing her to rallies when she was a baby. Like Hill, Gellatly-Ladd said she was acutely aware of sexism growing up. When she was in grade seven the boys used to play a game called "Slap Ass Friday." The girls had to stand with their backsides facing the lockers to avoid unwanted touching. "We weren't taught a lot of good sex education in primary school, so we didn't know this was sexual harassment." The following year she became involved with a school initiative to re-evaluate the dress code. The administration didn't want girls wearing tank tops or shorts that weren't at least mid-thigh in length (which I can tell you, as a former teenage girl, even in the late 1990s those types of shorts were very difficult to find if you wanted to shop at a remotely trendy store). "We were told we don't want to create any distractions for the boys." This was the explanation of why girls' clothing was being restricted. And it didn't sit well with her.

In high school she joined the gender equity and rights club. She also helped organize her school's walkout to protest the repeal of the revised sex-ed curriculum. They were among an estimated 38,000 Ontario students who left class on September 21, 2018, to protest the Progressive Conservative government's decision to reinstate the 1998 curriculum.

These kids amazed me. I couldn't recall ever thinking about feminism in any depth when I was in high school, consumed as I was by the crises and dramas of my own little teenage world. I was curious to know if I was the only one, so at my monthly book club meeting, I asked my girlfriends. We are five women in our mid-thirties to early forties, and three of us are white. We grew up in different parts of the country in middle-class homes, urban and rural. Each of us works, or has worked, in journalism at a big mainstream newspaper. All of us strongly identify as feminists today. I put my question to the group, consciousness-raising style: "What did you think about feminism in high school?"

No one could remember ever thinking about the subject.

"I was one of those girls who didn't want to call myself a feminist, until not that long ago really," said one of my friends. "Of course I was a feminist, but I didn't realize it. I think I bought into a lot of the stereotypes." Stereotypes like: feminists hate men; feminists are angry, unpleasant women; feminists are crunchy granola bra-burners. "I had a lot of internalized patriarchy."

"I think I only heard the word in a derogatory way until university," said another.

"We weren't particularly well served by the media of the day," added a third. "Think about Clinton and Lewinsky. It's shocking today to think how Monica Lewinsky was the butt of so many jokes. She was an *intern*."

Understanding what it means to live in a patriarchal society, being aware of rape culture—these were concepts that each of us realized we'd come to relatively recently, likely around the time of Bill Cosby and Jian Ghomeshi. I was embarrassed for us.

I can't imagine my generation walking out of class by the tens of thousands over the sex-ed curriculum. Today's youth seem so much more aware of these issues than we ever were. I asked Gellatly-Ladd if she thought this was the case.

"I do know that a lot of people [in my school] are knowledgeable about the issues," she said. Most aren't concerned enough to get involved in the kind of organizing that she and her friends do, but her classmates are generally aware of the discussions happening around consent and #MeToo.

"What about the generational divide?" I asked. Was that something she and her friends ever discussed? What did they think about older feminists who criticize women for being too sensitive or putting themselves in harm's way by drinking too much, or wearing revealing clothing?

"I see a lot of older activists who are very set in their beliefs and don't think there's anything to learn from young people because they've gone through more in their lives. I also see a lot of young people not wanting to listen and learn from older folks and what they've experienced in their lives," Gellatly-Ladd said. "I think it's everyone's responsibility to try to sort of bridge the divide. We don't want to be going against each other *and* the people who are attacking our rights."

AT FIRST GLANCE, everything about the scene at The 519 the afternoon of the Mic Drop Forum pointed to a generation that doesn't need any help. They're going to straighten everything out. They're smart and thoughtful and curious and reasonable. It's not that they agree about everything, but when I asked about controversial topics that "the adults" have been warring over, the answer I heard repeatedly from those teenagers was that everyone needs to be willing to have tough, respectful conversations. I left the event feeling reassured about the future.

But there was just one problem.

That night, going through my notes, I noticed that the girls had done almost all the talking. There were plenty of boys in the room, but in the circles I'd walked into, it was the girls who dominated the discussion. Even among the forum's organizers, all but two were young women. Of the remaining two, one identified as non-binary—they view themselves as genderless; neither masculine nor feminine. There was only one guy.

"Yeah, I'm often the only one in the room," seventeen-year-old Frank Hong told me when we spoke a few days later. Like many of the others, Hong had participated in student government and politics throughout his high school career, but it was the repeal of the sex-ed curriculum that got him involved with Mic Drop. He co-founded the March for Our Education on Queen's Park in July and then helped organize the provincial walkout in September.

When the *Toronto Star* covered the event and featured a photograph of one of its female organizers, someone posted the photo on the website 4chan, Hong told me. 4chan is a message board that began as an anime fan site and has since morphed into one of the most vile, racist, misogynist Petri dishes on the internet. The anonymous poster included the girl's name and details about how to find her.

"They were calling her a slut. Saying her lips are too . . . N-word. I can't even talk about it. It's disgusting," Hong said. "She was getting legitimate rape threats: 'I know where you live. I know your school. I'm going to come and get you.' I think that was really the first time I actually witnessed misogyny and sexism in real life and understood the seriousness of the situation—because it happened to a friend of mine."

"Do you think other guys get it?" I asked him.

Hong paused. "I think young men nowadays are increasingly more conservative, and I think it's a backlash towards feminism." Some guys feel excluded, he told me, and that's making them defensive and resentful and angry. It's a form of "radicalization," Hong said.

"So what do we do?"

Making sure that men feel welcome in the conversation is important, he said. It's not about letting men take over the discussion. This is a moment when guys need to listen. But they should know that they have a role and that they're valued.

Hong's reflections reminded me of a discussion I'd had with Jeff Perera, who used to work with the White Ribbon Campaign, a male-led effort to end violence against women. In recent years, he'd transitioned into a full-time "healthy manhood" coach of sorts. Now he tours North America speaking at businesses and schools about masculinity and the traps of the "Man Box."

Beginning at a very young age, Perera told me, boys are taught that being masculine means conforming to a narrow set of traits: Men are tough. Men are strong. Men don't cry. Men like fighting. Men don't take no for an answer. There has been considerable talk, especially in the aftermath of the #MeToo movement, about the ways girls are socialized to be agreeable, likable, and compliant. But not enough attention is being paid to the way boys are conditioned, he said.

In her book *Boys: What It Means to Become a Man*, Rachel Geise recounts compelling reasons for concern. A 2015 MTV poll found that 27 percent of males between the ages of fourteen and twenty-four believe that the recent advances won by women are coming at the expense of males. Nearly half—

46 percent—felt that feminism carried negative attitudes towards men. Writes Geise: "It's not hard to understand why some boys and young men see it that way. If we only imagine gender equality as being about empowering girls, then what's in it for them? . . . In order for change to be real and lasting, feminism can't stop at transforming the lives of girls and women; it has to transform the lives of boys and men too."

For Perera, the first step is to stop passing down harmful and outdated ideas about manhood. But step two has to be creating space for grown men to talk openly about past mistakes, to learn, and to move forward. "What we need today are living, breathing examples of men who come forward and say 'I fucked up. Here's what I've learned. Here's what I'm going to do moving forward, and I'm still learning,'" he told me. "Since our warped pursuit of manhood is about being better than everyone else, we take calls towards growth as a personal attack. . . . As a man, you spend a lifetime untangling what you've been taught. It's a lifelong journey to unlearn this shit." Then boys need to see their male role models having these conversations, he said. Confiding in others, being vulnerable, asking for help—these are all traits that fall outside the Man Box.

The reality, Perera continued, is that men don't feel like they can have honest conversations about previous misdeeds without serious personal or professional ramifications. "The tool people go to in their toolbox is shame and blame. To call someone out. To post it on Twitter. . . . And then watch them get torn down. There's no interest in healing," he said. "This mentality is steeped in our everyday culture. The way we communicate is broken."

CHAPTER 14

IT'S SOCIAL MEDIA'S FAULT

THE COMMERCIAL OPENS with a montage of men, young and old, black and white, surveying themselves in the mirror to a soundtrack of reporters' voices reciting headlines from the nightly news: "Bullying," "The #MeToo movement," "Toxic masculinity." This is when the narrator comes in, turning the razor company's long-held slogan into a question: "Is this the best a man can get? Is it?" As moody, instrumental music swells, the commercial flips through shots of boys tormenting each other, a male executive speaking for a female colleague, a man grabbing a woman's behind, a row of men standing beside smoky barbecue grills chanting "Boys will be boys." Men can't hide from this behaviour anymore, the narrator says. They can't laugh it off. No more excuses. The music shifts to an uplifting tempo. There's a father telling his young daughter to repeat "I am strong" into the mirror, a man casually telling his buddy it's "not cool" to catcall a female passerby, a father breaking up a fight between a group of guys. As that man's young son looks on from a safe distance, the narrator's voice comes back: "Because the boys watching today will be the men of tomorrow."

The first time I watched this nearly two-minute Gillette ad, I cried. It was designed to make someone like me cry. It made all my girlfriends cry. In a group chat we analyzed how we felt: Yes, this was a marketing ploy designed to capitalize on the moment. The company had obviously seized an opportunity to signal the "wokeness" of its brand. And that this message was coming from Gillette—a company that charges more for its women's line of razors than its men's, making it complicit in the "pink tax"—was a bit rich. Still, we gave Gillette kudos. Baby steps were to be encouraged. Plus, anyone with a Twitter account knows that taking on the radioactive subject of toxic masculinity these days is a risky move. People were going to flip, we agreed. And they did.

The online-only ad appeared on January 13, 2019. The calls for a boycott rolled in as fast as the view counts climbed. Joe Rogan, host of *The Joe Rogan Experience*, consistently the most listened-to podcast in North America, was one of the many furious commentators: "It makes, like, every man look like a misogynist piece of shit. It's such a disturbing commercial. . . . Nobody wants to be lectured to. We're tired of that. Stop." British blowhard Piers Morgan tweeted, "Let's be clear: @gillette now wants every man to take one of their razors & cut off his testicles."

Gillette had posted the ad on Twitter, Facebook, and YouTube. People swarmed in the hundreds of thousands to register their opinions.

"Simply can't imagine why a decent, moral man would be offended over such an ad if they weren't the culprits being called out in this ad," one woman tweeted. To which someone replied: "Imagine they were to put out an ad shaming women for gossiping, making false rape claims, and all the other bad things that women do. Would you be offended?"

Then a man posted a meme with an illustration of World War II soldiers that read, "Nobody complained about Toxic Masculinity when we were saving the world from Nazis."

THE EXTRAORDINARY CULTURAL transformation playing out today has meant that social norms around sex and power have shifted. Workplace impropriety that would have been merely frowned upon a decade ago can now qualify as a fireable offence. Misbehaviour that would have once been brushed off as "just a bad date" is no longer being dismissed as insignificant. And the criminal justice system is under unprecedented pressure to get it right when it comes to sexual violence. But within these new truths lie miles of uncertainty. When does an action cross the line? What should happen to those who have committed harm? What exactly should the courts be doing differently? How do you reconcile a victim's right to call out the abuser with an accused person's right to self-defence and a fair hearing? These are questions with complex answers, and the rules are still being negotiated. Over the last four years, I've spent hundreds of hours speaking with very smart people about all of these issues. Towards the end of our conversations, I always ask the same questions: So what do we do? What does the best path forward look like? The answer is almost always the same: we need to talk to each other.

But as Jeff Perera put it, the way we communicate these days is broken.

A few months after the Gillette ad appeared, it had garnered more than 53,000 comments on its original Twitter post. On YouTube, the ad had been viewed more than 29 million times, earned 1.4 million negative votes—double the number of positive reactions—and more than 400,000 comments. I've scanned through several hundred of those posts. The exchange I cited above is a good representation, which is to say that it's not productive. Twitter isn't a place for reasoned debate. It's a place to yell—and a place to yell alongside like-minded people yelling the same thing, since most tend to follow and interact with those who have similar politics and values. No one is being swayed by a comment on social media, and yet again and again we turn to those platforms for public debate.

Although political polarization has been deepening in the United States since the early nineties, it reached a milestone in 2016 when the Pew Research Centre found that, for the first time since 1992, a majority of people in both parties held not just unfavourable but *very* unfavourable opinions of the other side. A total of 58 percent of Republicans said their impression of the Democratic Party was very unfavourable, compared with 32 percent in 2008. On the Democratic side, 55 percent said they felt very negatively about the GOP, up from 37 percent in 2008. More than 40 percent of respondents on both sides said the other party's policies "are so misguided that they threaten the nation's well-being." The Canadian political landscape is typically viewed as less polarized, but a December 2018 poll of two thousand Canadians by Abacus Data that was provided to *Maclean's* magazine painted a somewhat different picture. The survey found that 26 percent of voters "hate" the other side.

This animosity is really about tribalism. Humans are naturally tribal—we're hard-wired to seek out community—and this is a trait that carries the potential for deep division. Once a person joins a group, that person's identity becomes entwined with that group and its values. It's an us-versus-them mentality. "The tribal instinct is not just an instinct to belong. It is also an instinct to exclude," writes Yale Law professor Amy Chua in her book *Political Tribes: Group Instinct and the Fate of Nations.* "The problem is when tribalism takes over a political system—that becomes very dangerous because you start to see everything through your group's lens and you don't even realize it," she explained during a TV appearance on *The View.* "We are getting nothing done because anytime anything happens, we immediately go into our tribal positions and we start attacking the other side." What's more, she continued, studies show that people derive great pleasure in taking down the other side.

The implications of that research don't bode well for reasoned debate, especially given that one of the primary ways we interact with each other is through social media. Around the world, 1.2 billion people log in to Facebook every day. Twitter says it has 126 million daily users. The site is an essential platform for public discourse, Twitter CEO Jack Dorsey told investors earlier this year. "You can't find the conversation on Twitter anywhere else," he said. In Canada, 94 percent of those who are online have at least one social media account.

It's also one of our main sources of information. In 2018, for the first time, social media overtook newspapers as a source of news for Americans. It's a similar story in Canada, where 42 percent of the population accesses social networking sites to find news at least once per day. We are literally addicted, thanks to that little hit of dopamine that gets released every time a new notification pings on our phone. "This is the secret to Facebook's era-defining success: we compulsively check the site because we never know when the delicious ting of social affirmation may sound," writer Simon Parkin summarized in *The Guardian*. The more likes or retweets or comments, the better. And that's where things get worrisome, because research has shown that the more inflammatory a posting is, the more likely it is to be viewed and shared.

Researchers from New York University studied more than 286,000 tweets sent by American politicians ahead of the 2016 election. The aim of their study was to identify patterns in those messages that earned the most engagement. They found that posts containing moral and emotional words—"hate," "murder," and "shame," to name a few—were associated with a double-digit increase in retweets, and that was per word. Their findings suggest that the more passionate and provocative you are, the more attention you'll receive. Social media is trapping users in a twisted Pavlov's dog experiment that's conditioning us to be jerks. And it's not even productive jerkdom: another one of their research projects showed that we're screaming at people who already agree with us. People aren't trying to engage honest reactions outside of their own silo.

Dr. William Brady, who was one of the study's authors and is now a post-doctoral researcher at Yale University, told me that the use of moral and emotional language in political social media posts is associated with an increase in an "echo chamber" effect. Discussions can become more frenzied and people can be pushed to further extremes. For that, the data suggests they'll be rewarded with more likes and retweets. Other moral psychological studies have found that those who showcase their emotional responses during moral situations were found to be viewed as more trustworthy by their own group, he said.

The trendy word for this is "virtue-signalling." It's a way to let everyone know exactly where you stand on an issue.

This is where the discussions around tribalism and social media come together. Dr. Brady's work underscores how social media debate is often geared much more to seeking peer approval than trying to change opponents' minds. And these days that conclusion applies to so many of our other public-discourse platforms, whether they're magazine think pieces, podcasts, or lectures on YouTube.

GIVEN THE POLARIZATION of tribal politics and the inflammatory nature of debate on social media platforms, how do we reasonably discuss the effects of the #MeToo movement? The contentious issues at the core of this reckoning—consent, due process, redemption, reparation, gender roles, power, privilege—carry the baggage of every other left-right debate. It's a dynamic that means a person who identifies with conservative policies on something like immigration will likely naturally default to their side's arguments on #MeToo. We know this from the research that's been done on group behaviour, but also from studies of our social media habits. "With the #MeToo movement, once you start to make it a hashtag and not about the nuance about each particular case, that's when the identity as a political group member becomes highly salient," Dr. Brady told me.

Perhaps the only way to move forward, the only way to separate the principles underlying the #MeToo movement from the partisan politics, is to abide by something as simple as the Golden Rule: Do unto others as you would have them do unto you. In other words, be kind and respectful to other people. Treat them the way you'd want to be treated if you were in their shoes, if your daughter were in their shoes, if your son were in their shoes.

In Chua's *Political Tribes* she recounts instances where people were able to overcome their tribal instincts. Among her examples is the racial integration of the American military. No one thought it would work, but when the two groups were put together, the soldiers found they had much in common. "What is needed is one-on-one human engagement, which is hard precisely because of how divided we are," Chua writes. "But anything worth achieving is difficult. When people from different tribes see one another as human beings who at the end of the day want the same things—kindness, dignity, security for loved ones—hearts can change."

IF HONEST, GOOD-FAITH debate is the solution, then it's important to understand the barriers that stand in the way of that goal. The research clearly highlights the perils of virtue-signalling online—employing certain coded terms to notify like-minded others of your righteousness. Those same words can be off-putting to those who don't share those views. So, using neutral language can be helpful. If we know that the use of certain words elicits a negative response from the other side, then why not just avoid those expressions? Using neutral language doesn't mean changing the message. It means taking more care in how you explain it. The next time you're at a family function and your annoying Uncle Bob starts talking about a war on men, push back, certainly—but maybe skip using shortcut phrases like "rape culture" or "toxic masculinity."

As a journalist, I avoid the use of triggering and loaded words. This is one of the tenets of good interview techniques established by famed journalist John Sawatsky. Don't derail your question with a charged expression that will distract or put your subject on the defensive, he advises. Don't call a plan a "scheme," or a misstep a "boondoggle." It's with this logic that I don't use the word "survivor" to describe a sexual assault complainant, whether I'm writing for the *Globe* or giving a speech. In the past, individuals who had been sexually assaulted were always referred to as "victims." Then, several years ago, there came a big push to restore power to those people by referring to them as "survivors." I understand and agree with the sentiment. But as a journalist, it isn't a term I can use. It's strongly linked to the advocacy movement and a particular ideological bent. Moreover, using terms like "survivor" and "victim" concedes that the incident actually occurred. By sticking to a neutral word like "complainant," the focus stays on establishing the facts.

As a reporter I have spent the last thirteen years training myself to second-guess my conclusions. When I'm working on a story, I'm constantly asking myself: Where could I be wrong? What haven't I considered? Is this fair? This process doesn't mean I don't form conclusions. It just means I try to protect myself against tunnel vision. At the very least, understanding what's behind someone else's different perspective gives you greater clarity on your own. I don't agree with my friends that

Aziz Ansari is an unsavoury sexual aggressor. I think he could have handled himself better, but I also believe it's entirely possible that he didn't realize how uncomfortable "Grace" was that night. That said, I thoroughly enjoyed debating the topic, because it forced me to interrogate my own opinions. It made me examine things I otherwise wouldn't have. It was the same with Susan Brownmiller. I may still think she's misguided in her stance that the onus is on women to protect themselves, but in approaching that conversation with an open mind, I came to understand why she—and many like her—hold that opinion.

The #MeToo movement launched a big conversation. Much of the behaviour under discussion isn't criminal. It's unethical and rude and wrong—but not illegal. As for the misdeeds that do cross that line, we've seen how difficult it is for the police and the courts to deal with those cases, despite the progress that they've recently made. The fix we're seeking won't come from the criminal justice system. Progress will only be made by changing societal attitudes. And if that's the goal, belittling the other side or dragging them on Twitter achieves nothing. Call-out culture is toxic. We must figure out a way to talk to each other about contentious, uncomfortable topics if we're going to find a way through this crucial moment towards a better and more evolved place.

Otherwise, #MeToo is just a hashtag.

EPILOGUE

KEEPING A PROFESSIONAL distance from sources can be one of the hardest parts of the job, especially when the subject matter is so personal. I still speak frequently with many of the women I interviewed for my Unfounded investigation. I've watched them move across the country, get new jobs, graduate from law school, lose a parent, find love and heartbreak and then love again. They are special to me and I enjoy hearing about their lives. I'm not sure I would have been brave enough to trust a reporter the way they trusted me, brave enough to speak publicly about an event so horrible. I respect them.

Late in 2018, one of the girls and I were chatting on Facebook Messenger. She had been one of the first young women to agree to let me investigate her case. She'd signed a freedom of information request I'd written to access the police records from her complaint and then had the documents sent directly to me; she had no idea what they might say. We spent hours talking over Skype. After the series ran, the police reopened her case, which had been dismissed as "unfounded." She liked and trusted the new detective. But in December, she told me that the Crown had evaluated the evidence and concluded that there wasn't enough to proceed to trial. She said she felt okay about it. She believed she'd been heard and was happy that her complaint had been taken seriously. "I'm very much at peace with my situation. I'm glad it's over," she wrote to me. I told her I was happy that she'd had a good experience, finally. New Year's Eve was coming up and I told her I hoped she'd be doing something fun. "One day you will wake up at thirty-four with a toddler and think: why didn't I just go out!" I wrote, joking about my own lacklustre plans. "I'll have to take that advice tonight hehe!" she replied. Several weeks later, I learned from one of her friends that she had committed suicide not long after our conversation. Her parents asked that I not write about it at the time. I still can't think or talk about her without crying.

I won't pretend to know what caused this amazing girl to take her life, but I do know that she'd been in counselling for years. She told me she often spoke with her therapist about her rape and also about how she had been treated by police. She felt that she had been violated twice—once by the assailant and then again by the system.

People frequently point out that sexual assault doesn't often produce physical injuries; it's part of why the cases are so difficult to prosecute. But—knowing dozens of women who reported sexual assault to police—I can attest that the wounds are there. Almost everyone I interviewed was undergoing counselling. Most still are. It has an impact on their relationships. One woman struggling with PTSD lost a job because of it. Others have put their lives on hold because of pending lawsuits. In early 2019, I was giving a speech about my Unfounded investigation. Because the content is always so depressing, I typically try to end on a positive note by talking about all the progress that police services have made since the series ran. One of the complainants I wrote about attended. Afterwards, the woman—a young woman of colour—pulled me aside. "Listen, I get what you're saying. It's great that police have better training now and whatever, but just so you know, my life isn't better. My case has still never been treated seriously. And I don't see myself represented in #MeToo at all. Things are not better."

October 2019 marks two years since the launch of #MeToo. There will likely be another onslaught of commentary and columns trying to sort out how far we've come. My assessment: not that far.

Yes, it feels as if something fundamental has shifted, but narrowing down exactly what is different is challenging. Is sexual harassment in the workplace on the decline? Are fewer women being raped? Are police taking more sexual assault complaints seriously? (On that latter point, I receive a few emails each month from a woman or a girl's parent claiming otherwise.) The fear is that all that's really changed is that it's no longer socially acceptable to be blatantly dismissive of sexual impropriety—that the business community, the politicians, and the justice system officials are now expected to at least pay lip service to the notion of fair treatment.

Here's what is certain: since the Harvey Weinstein scandal broke, there has been a tidal wave of public interest and awareness relating to the issues raised by #MeToo. A study of Google searches made within the United States revealed that the number of people looking for information on how to report sexual harassment and assault was up by 30 percent. In Canada, rape crisis centres say they've seen a huge increase in demand for service. And in both countries, the number of people reporting both sexual harassment and sexual assault has increased.

Additionally, scores of high-profile men have lost their jobs or major contracts following allegations of sexually inappropriate behaviour since the dawn of the #MeToo era. One year after the #MeToo hashtag went viral, *The New York Times* published a piece that put the number of casualties at 201, about half of whom had been replaced by women. These men were actors, elected officials, business executives, professors, and media personalities. In Canada, prominent officials, including federal Liberal minister Kent Hehr, Toronto theatre titan Albert Schultz, Just for Laughs founder Gilbert Rozon, and Quebec media personality Éric Salvail, were forced out of their positions amid allegations of misconduct (MP Hehr left cabinet but not caucus). And after *The Globe and Mail* documented a pattern of alleged sexual harassment by famed Canadian winemaker Norman Hardie, his label was dropped by a number of notable restaurants and the Liquor Control Board of Ontario.

That's the argument for real progress: increased public awareness, a greater likelihood that impropriety will be reported, and a higher risk of career consequences for powerful men implicated in complaints of sexual misconduct.

But the argument for skepticism is also strong. Just months after the *Globe*'s story on Hardie appeared, the LCBO began stocking his wine again. And for all the encouraging data that suggests positive change, there's plenty on the other side that paints a much grimmer picture.

On the workplace sexual harassment front, a cross-country survey conducted in November and December 2017 by the Gandalf Group found that 94 percent of company executives didn't believe sexual harassment was a problem in their workplace. Another post #MeToo poll for the Human Resources Professionals Association found that 43 percent of women (and 12 percent of men) had been sexually harassed at work.

As for sexual consent, a survey for the Canadian Women's Foundation determined that people's understanding of consent had actually decreased in recent years, from 33 percent in 2015—before Weinstein—to 28 percent in 2018.

People seem to agree that sexual harassment is bad and needs to be dealt with, but there is little consensus on what behaviour crosses the line. A poll from Canadian firm Angus Reid found that more than 80 percent of both men and women believed that the conversations generated by #MeToo were long overdue, however when it came to the specifics, millennial men posted unsettling answers. A quarter of those respondents thought it was acceptable to comment on a colleague's body, tell "off-colour" jokes at work, and display, look at, or share "sexually suggestive" material in the office. One in five approved of giving a colleague an uninvited shoulder massage, using sexualized language in work conversation, and a boss kissing an employee's cheek. Not exactly encouraging.

And there's more disheartening news.

Facebook COO Sheryl Sandberg's LeanIn.Org, partnered with SurveyMonkey, has been tracking the impact of #MeToo in the business world. Their 2019 report found that 60 percent of male managers were uncomfortable engaging in certain activities with female employees, such as mentoring, working one-on-one, and socializing. That was up 14 percentage points compared with the previous year. These figures are in keeping with Vice President Mike Pence's reported practice of refusing to dine alone with a woman who is not his wife. It seems that some men across the financial sector have been heeding his advice. In the summer of 2018, the Canadian Press interviewed a dozen women in corporate Canada about the effects of #MeToo. "A lawyer is asked whether a male executive should leave the door open when meeting with a woman. A consultant's long-time male client will take a meeting with her only if someone else is in the room. A public relations executive hears from senior business leaders who say they are shying away from mentoring young women." A Bloomberg report from December 2018 highlighted a similar dampening effect: "No more dinners with female colleagues. Don't sit next to them on flights. Book hotel rooms on different floors. Avoid one-on-one meetings. In fact, as a wealth adviser put it, just hiring a woman these days is 'an unknown risk.'"

This is life for wealthy, well-connected (and more often than not) white women. But what about women of colour? Or women working in lower-income and blue-collar jobs? To the shame of my industry, there's been very little reporting on the impact #MeToo has had on them, even though, statistically speaking, these marginalized groups are the most likely to be victimized. "Harassers prey upon the fact that typically women working a low-wage job will be seen as very replaceable," Emily Martin, vice president for workplace justice at the National Women's Law Center, told Vox. "If you have no financial cushion, if you need every bit of your paycheck to make ends meet, you are even more vulnerable to the threat of retaliation, to the fear of losing your job."

As for the criminal justice side of things, in Canada, at least, positive steps are being taken. I've cited the fact that officers in roughly half the country's police services now receive specialized sexual assault training that incorporates a trauma-informed approach. And that dozens of police services have already adopted—or are actively working on—case review by civilians. Judges and Crowns are under pressure from the public and lawmakers to get educated about the effects of trauma, and sexual assault trials are playing out under unprecedented scrutiny. And that scrutiny is coming not just from traditional media, but also from every citizen with a smartphone and a Twitter account.

In fact, social media may just be the key to #MeToo's staying power, University of British Columbia economics professor Marina Adshade told me. "I think with the #MeToo and Time's Up movement, everybody talks about Weinstein, but I think it was coming our way regardless. I think [that with] the level of information sharing we have now, this was always going to come." Dr. Adshade, who is an expert on women in the economy, cited Glassdoor, the job recruiting site that allows employees to write anonymous reviews of their company. If there is a culture of harassment, it won't stay hidden.

"From the economic perspective, incentives have changed dramatically," Adshade continued. "For example, firms that used to let people get away with things are no longer doing that. Firms have huge incentives to not only punish offenders but to make sure there aren't offenders, [since] once something happens, you lose your venture capitalists." She pointed to the fallout at Uber after a former engineer with the company, Susan Fowler, published a nearly three-thousand-word essay on her blog detailing the rampant sexism and harassment she faced there. The February 2017 post went viral. Uber hired a law firm to investigate, and as many as twenty employees were fired. That June, co-founder and CEO Travis Kalanick was himself forced out after five of Uber's largest investors demanded his head.

I BELIEVE THE reckoning is real. But it's going to take time for people, institutions, and power structures to adjust. Even though some people talk about #MeToo as if it is a phenomenon that dropped out of the sky with the Harvey Weinstein scandal, it's clear that's not the case. For years, tectonic plates of frustration have been grinding below the surface. Weinstein was just the earthquake.

#MeToo has forced people to confront the existence of rape culture, perhaps for the first time in their lives. There's a wider understanding of the lasting damage that sexual violence, harassment, and discrimination can have on individuals and society. And just as the path to this point has been arduous, the road ahead is going to be equally formidable—and probably just as slow. The results from the public opinion polls may seem disheartening, but the fact that we're now tracking what people think about these issues is an improvement. You need to see a problem before you can fix it, and that's what #MeToo has done best: it has demanded that we acknowledge what's been in front of us all along.

The bar for what society is willing to tolerate has been moved. It might not be at the desired level yet, but it's going in the right direction. Perhaps the most positive development is that people are talking more openly, and even more importantly, listening to each other.

Because the more we hear, the more we learn, the harder it will be to turn away.

NOTES

INTRODUCTION
exactly one CEO
Jon Erlichman, "One in 100: Canada's 'embarrassing' lack of female CEOs among top TSX companies," *BNN Bloomberg*, July 6, 2018.

CHAPTER 1
arrested Kobe Bryant
Details about the basketball player's sexual assault case come from a variety of sources, primarily a number of police reports that were released a little more than a year after Bryant's arrest. These documents were posted online by The Smoking Gun: http://www.thesmoking gun.com/documents/sports/kobe-police-file-released. Marlow Stern, a senior editor with *The Daily Beast* who wrote a comprehensive piece about the Bryant rape allegation—and who also had access to the police records independent of The Smoking Gun—told me the files online are genuine. I also spoke with Doug Winters, the former Eagle County detective who ran the Bryant sexual assault investigation (he is now a Chief Investigator with the 14th Judicial District Attorney's Office) and he told me that the information appears correct to the best of his recollection. Information about the alleged incident in this book come from The Smoking Gun documents, but only if another media outlet

independently reported those details. Other stories referenced are: Adam Liptak, "Bryant Is Ordered to Stand Trial in Rape Case," *The New York Times*, October 21, 2003; Jon Sarche, "Woman who accused Bryant says NBA star ignored her pleas to stop, documents say," *Associated Press*, October 1, 2004; Dan Mangan, "Horrifying Account Bares Accuser's 'Rape Ordeal,'" the *New York Post*, October 10, 2003; Steve Henson, "Bryant and His Accuser Settle Civil Assault Case," *Los Angeles Times*, March 3, 2005; Marlow Stern, "Kobe Bryant's Disturbing Rape Case: The DNA Evidence, the Accuser's Story, and the Half-Confession," *The Daily Beast*, April 11, 2016.

"On the hardwood"
Roger O'Neil, Newscast: Kobe Bryant arrested on sexual assault charges, *NBC News: Nightly News*, July 7, 2003.

Headline in the *Los Angeles Times*
Steve Henson and Lance Pugmire, "Quiet Street, Loud Case; Alleged victim in Bryant case is a 19-year-old graduate of local high school who is said to be fun-loving, outgoing and emotional," *Los Angeles Times*, July 10, 2003.

"Sitting not far from the court"
John Nadel, "Bryant Fights Tears, Says He's Innocent," *Associated Press*, July 18, 2003.

emailed reporters' transcripts
Adam Liptak, "Papers Reveal New Details In Kobe Bryant Rape Case," *The New York Times*, August 4, 2004.

another man's semen
Adam Liptak, "Papers Reveal New Details In Kobe Bryant Rape Case," *The New York Times*, August 4, 2004.

"patently false"
Adam Liptak, "Papers Reveal New Details in Kobe Bryant Rape Case," *The New York Times*, August 4, 2004.

"The victim has informed us"
Selena Roberts, "Mistakes and Miscues Prove Too Much for Bryant's Accuser," *The New York Times*, September 2, 2004.

"Although I truly believe"
Marlow Stern, "Kobe Bryant's Disturbing Rape Case: The DNA Evidence, the Accuser's Story, and the Half-Confession," *The Daily Beast*, April 11, 2016.

"Unfounded"
Robyn Doolittle, "Why police dismiss 1 in 5 sexual assault claims as baseless", *Globe and Mail*, February 3, 2017.

at most, 8 percent
Kimberly A. Lonsway, Joanne Archambault, David Lisak, "False Reports: Moving Beyond the Issue to Successfully Investigate and Prosecute Non-Stranger Sexual Assault," National Sexual Violence Resource Center, 2009.

auto insurance claims
It's a commonly cited statistic within the insurance industry that an estimated 10 percent of claims are fraudulent. A 2017 poll by Ipsos for the Financial Services Commission of Ontario backed this up, with nearly 1 in 10 respondents admitting to either exaggerating or falsifying an auto insurance claim. This is in line with a 2010 study by KPMG which estimated that between 9 to 18 percent of claims costs are fraudulent: https://www.newswire.ca/news-releases/many-ontario-drivers-struggle -to-identify-auto-insurance-fraud-615110713.html

so drunk at the time
Robyn Doolittle, "The problem with consent: Sex-assault cases and intoxication," *The Globe and Mail*, March 17, 2017.

"Rape culture" is a term
The first published use of the term seems to have been in the New York Radical Feminists group's 1974 text: "Rape: The First Sourcebook for Women," p. 105.

had become a "witch hunt"
Peter White, "Michael Haneke On #MeToo: 'The Witch Hunt Should Be Left In The Middle Ages,'" *Deadline*, February 11, 2018.

"#MeToo has been an assault"
Nelson Branco, "Post-Patrick Brown: Jordan Peterson on the dangers of the #MeToo movement," *Toronto Sun*, March 27, 2018.

"Rape is a crime, but"
"Catherine Deneuve says men should be 'free to hit on' women," *Agence France-Presse in Paris* appearing in *The Guardian*, January 9, 2018. Note: The wording of the English translation varies slightly between publications.

18 percent of Americans
"After a year of #MeToo, American opinion has shifted against victims," *The Economist*, October 15, 2018.

CHAPTER 2
large bruise . . . "cracked rib"
Kevin Donovan, "Ghomeshi video showed woman's bruises, cracked rib," *Toronto Star*, November 12, 2014.

three women
Kevin Donovan and Jesse Brown, "CBC fires Jian Ghomeshi over sex allegations," *Toronto Star*, October 26, 2014.

"and started closed-fist pounding me"
"Transcript of interview with woman who claims Ghomeshi assaulted her," *The Globe and Mail*, October 29, 2014.

four more
Kevin Donovan and Jesse Brown, "Jian Ghomeshi: 8 women accuse former CBC host of violence, sexual abuse or harassment," *Toronto Star*, October 29, 2014.

Hannibal Buress told a joke
Dan McQuade, "Hannibal Buress on Bill Cosby: 'You're a Rapist,'" *Philadelphia* magazine, October 17, 2014. Note: the magazine's transcript of Buress's set is slightly different than the video. I have used the video, which as of June 2019 can still be found on YouTube.

"He did exactly the same thing to me"
Nicole Weisensee Egan, "MY COSBY STORY; 'He did exactly the same thing to me' California lawyer, a former fashion model, says Bill Cosby drugged her, tried to force himself on her about 30 years ago," the *Philadelphia Daily News*, February 8, 2005.

a lack of "credible" evidence
Nicole Weisensee Egan, "No criminial charge against the 'Cos,'" the
Philadelphia Daily News, February 18, 2005.

"sink the prick"
Christie Blatchford, *Life Sentence*, Doubleday Canada: 2016, p. 288.

"it's now apparent"
Christie Blatchford, "Christie Blatchford: With third accuser on stand,
Ghomeshi trial enters unsettling new territory," *National Post*, February 8,
2016.

"inconsistencies and questionable behaviour"
Ontario Court of Justice. R. v. Ghomeshi (2016 ONCJ 155).

"One of my female friends"
Jian Ghomeshi, "Reflections From A Hashtag," *The New York Review of
Books*, October 11, 2018 issue. (This was posted online on September 14,
2018.)

341 Oscar nominations
Madeline Berg, "Oscar Hero to Zero: How Harvey Weinstein's Power
Enabled Him—And Led To His Decline," *Forbes*, October 13, 2017.

"How do I get out of the room"
Jodi Kantor and Megan Twohey, "Harvey Weinstein Paid Off Sexual
Harassment Accusers for Decades," *The New York Times*, October 5, 2017.

thirteen more women
Ronan Farrow, "Aggressive Overtures to Sexual Assault: Harvey
Weinstein's Accusers Tell Their Stories," *The New Yorker*, October 10, 2017.

"You don't know me"
Katie J.M. Baker, "Here's the Powerful Letter The Stanford Victim Read
To Her Attacker," *Buzzfeed News*, June 3, 2016.

Susan Fowler wrote a blog post
Susan Fowler, "Reflecting On One Very, Very Strange Year At Uber,"
February 19, 2017. https://www.susanjfowler.com/blog/2017/2/19/
reflecting-on-one-very-strange-year-at-uber

Bill O'Reilly, was fired
Emily Steel and Michael S. Schmidt, "Bill O'Reilly Is Forced Out At Fox News," *The New York Times*, April 19, 2017.

no set "rule"
Supreme Court of Canada, R. v. D.D., (2000 SCC 43).

CHAPTER 3
"unchaste" woman
Supreme Court of Canada, R. v. Seaboyer; R. v. Gayme, ([1991] 2 SCR 577).

Maddie
In reconstructing the events around Maddie's case, I have relied upon interviews with individuals involved in the investigation and who have access to the police file. I have also obtained documents connected to the allegation from a variety of sources, including from Maddie and her family.

Kelly . . . Melodie . . . Stacey
Robyn Doolittle, "What It's Like To Report A Sexual Assault," *The Globe and Mail*, March 17, 2017.

"For the files we've reviewed"
Robyn Doolittle, "The Unfounded Effect," *The Globe and Mail*, December 8, 2017.

"We do not believe"
Robyn Doolittle, "How Police Forces Co-Ordinated One Response To The Globe's Queries," *The Globe and Mail*," June 13, 2017.

CHAPTER 4
"In July, 1856"
"Seduction," *The Daily Globe*, May 5, 1858.

"but I do not intend to send you"
"Juvenile Termed Leader As 4 Jailed in Assault," *The Globe and Mail*, November 10, 1951.

rape, attempted rape, unlawful detention, and indecent assault
Even though the charge of "rape" was repealed by Parliament in 1982 (and replaced with sexual assault), Regan was charged with rape because

the alleged incidents predated that change, as is customary with historic allegations.

"The chances of a male accused"
George Jonas, "Regan A Victim Of Matriarchal Justice," *National Post,* February 18, 2002.

"The trial of Mr. Regan"
Ian Hunter, "Even Nasty Men Deserve A Fair Trial," *The Globe and Mail,* February 27, 2002.

"Ordeal Ends"
Kevin Cox, "Ordeal Ends For Former N.S. Premier Charges Against Regan To Be Withdrawn After Decade of Investigations, Legal Battles," *The Globe and Mail,* April 18, 2002.

"Prosecutors Give Up"
Rachel Boomer, "Nova Scotia Prosecutors Give Up On Regan Case," *Vancouver Sun,* April 18, 2002.

"egg on" . . . "two to three times" . . . "she is a credible witness" . . . "bonnet and crinolines"
Court of Appeal of Alberta, R. v. Ewanchuk, (1998) ABCA 52.

"This case is not about consent"
Supreme Court of Canada, 1999, R. v. Ewanchuk, 1999 1SCR 330.

publicly slammed
Alanna Mitchell, Jill Mahoney and Sean Fine, "Legal experts outraged by personal attack on Supreme Court judge Alberta judge's suicide reference 'is about as low as it gets,'" *The Globe and Mail,* February 27, 1999.

"was just trying to give my friend"
Shawn Ohler, "Judge reiterates belief that teen wasn't assaulted," *National Post,* February 27, 1999.

It's worth noting
Chris Purdy, "Ewanchuk's first victim breaks 37-year silence: Rapist's attack on eight year old girl persuades woman to tell her story at his dangerous-offender hearing," *Edmonton Journal,* October 26, 2006.

On May 23, 2015
All information about the allegations comes from the trial transcript.
The trial was heard in Halifax provincial court, February 9 and 10, 2017.
The verdict was read March 1, 2017. It was not included in the transcript
I obtained. I received an audio recording of the decision from the Nova
Scotia Judiciary, which I transcribed.

"disgusting rapist"
Yvette d'Entremont, "Police Urge Calm After Exchange Between
Acquitted Taxi Driver, Passengers On Halifax Bus," Truro News, March
6, 2017.

"You don't know me"
Katie J.M. Baker, "Here's The Powerful Letter The Stanford Victim Read
To Her Attacker," *Buzzfeed News*, June 3, 2016.

"moderate"
Nick Anderson and Susan Svrluga, "Prosecutors urged 'substantial
prison term' in Stanford sexual assault case, records show," *The
Washington Post*, June 11, 2016.

"thrusting"
Sam Levin, "Brock Turner laughed after bystanders stopped Standford
sex assault, files show," *The Guardian*, August 26, 2016.

California lawmakers proposed new legislation
You can read more about these changes here: Jazmine Ulloa, "California
toughens laws against rape after Brown signs bills inspired by Brock
Turner case," *Los Angeles Times*, September 30, 2016.

"Under the new law"
Michael Spratt, "The Ghomeshi Rules: Bill C-51 creates Unprecedented
Case Of Reverse Disclosure," *Canadian Lawyer*, June 19, 2017.

CHAPTER 5
"I went on a date"
Katie Way, "I Went On A Date With Aziz Ansari. It Turned Into The
Worst Night Of My Life," *Babe.net*, January 14, 2018.

"There are a lot of subtle"
"Ladies and Gentlemen," *Master of None*, Season 1 Episode 7.

"Apparently, there is a whole country"
Caitlin Flanagan, "The Humiliation of Aziz Ansari," *The Atlantic*, January 14, 2018.

"I'm apparently the victim"
Bari Weiss, "Aziz Ansari Is Guilty. Of Not Being A Mind Reader," *The New York Times*, January 15, 2018.

"Perhaps what is especially threatening"
Anna North, "The Aziz Ansari Story Is Ordinary. That's Why We Have To Talk About It," *Vox*, January 16, 2018.

378 psychology students
Susan E. Hickman and Charlene L. Muehlenhard, "'By The Semi-Mystical Appearance Of A Condom': How Young Women And Men Communicate Sexual Consent In Heterosexual Situations," *The Journal of Sex Research*, August 1999.

145 heterosexual male university students
Ashton M. Lofgreen, Richard E. Mattson, Samantha A. Wagner, Edwin G. Ortiz and Matthew D. Johnson, "Situational and Dispositional Determinants of College Men's Perception of Women's Sexual Desire and Consent to Sex: A Factorial Vignette Analysis," *Journal of Interpersonal Violence*, 2017.

a man and a woman who'd never met
Antonia Abbey, "Sex differences in attributions for friendly behavior: Do males misperceive females' friendliness?" *Journal of Personality and Social Psychology*, 1982.

Dr. Barrett wrote
Lisa Feldman Barrett, "Why Men Need to Stop Relying on Non-Verbal Consent, According to a Neuroscientist," *Time*, May 11, 2018.

a 2006 study
Rachael O'Byrne, Mark Rapley and Susan Hansen, "You Couldn't Say 'No,' Could You?': Young Men's Understandings of Sexual Refusal," *Feminism & Psychology*, 2006.

Dr. Beres published a paper
Melanie Beres, "Sexual miscommunication? Untangling assumptions about sexual communication between casual sex partners," *Culture, Health & Sexuality*, July 2009.

called the document "radical"
Joe Warmington, "New Sex-Ed Curriculum Under Fire," *Toronto Sun*, February 23, 2015.

CHAPTER 6
"Credibility for police"
Robyn Doolittle, "Why police dismiss 1 in 5 sexual assault claims as baseless," *Globe and Mail*, February 3, 2017.

researchers Linda Light and Gisela Ruebsaat
Linda Light and Gisela Ruebsaat, "Police Classification of Sexual Assault Cases as Unfounded," Research and Statistics Division Department of Justice, 2006.

DNA evidence that proved the assailant's guilt
Robyn Doolittle, "Unfounded case ends with conviction 19 years after police dismissed sexual-assault complaint," *The Globe and Mail*, September 20, 2018.

"For the first time we could watch"
Bessel van der Kolk, *The Body Keeps The Score: Brain, Mind and Body in The Healing of Trauma*, Penguin Books, 2014, p. 39.

CHAPTER 7
"In the past few years"
Emily Yoffe, "The Bad Science Behind Campus Response to Sexual Assault," *The Atlantic*, September 8, 2017.

the Obama administration invoked Title IX
You can read Obama's "Dear Colleague" letter here: https://www2 .ed.gov/about/offices/list/ocr/letters/colleague-201104.pdf

a report outlining best practices
You can read "Not Alone" here: https://www.justice.gov/archives/ovw /page/file/905942/download

"The Neurobiology of Sexual Assault"
You can read a transcript of Dr. Rebecca Campbell's presentation at the National Institute of Justice in December 2012 here: https://www.nij .gov/multimedia/presenter/presenter-campbell/pages/presenter -campbell-transcript.aspx

captured many firsts
This is per a spokesperson with the Lawson Health Research Institute. Lawson is the research institute of London Health Sciences Centre and St. Joseph's Health Care London. Robarts Research Institute is the health research institute of Western University. They are two separate institutes but often work together collaboratively and both are leading institutes in the field of medical imaging. Dr. Ruth Lanius is a scientist at both Lawson and Robarts.

Dr. Lanius scanned the brains
Dr. Ruth Lanius, Dr. James W. Hopper, Dr. Ravi S. Menon, "Individual Differences in a Husband and Wife Who Developed PTSD After a Motor Vehicle Accident: A Functional MRI Case Study," the *American Journal of Psychiatry*, 2003.

put a picture to that truth
Bessel van der Kolk, *The Body Keeps The Score: Brain, Mind and Body in The Healing of Trauma*, Penguin Books, 2014, p. 41–43.

sexual assault trial of Mustafa Ururyar
All details pertaining to the testimony and facts presented during this case come from the decision, Ontario Court of Justice, R. v. Ururyar, (2016 ONCJ 448).

"Ontario Court Justice Marvin Zuker"
Catherine Porter, "'Myths of rape should be dispelled,' says judge in Mandi Gray case," *Toronto Star*, July 21, 2016.

"hope for survivors."
Rachel Giese, "Two recent sexual assault verdicts offer hope," *Chatelaine*, July 28, 2016.

"a profound and almost astonishing"
Andrea Janus, "Judgment in Mandi Gray sexual assault case 'glorious,' but change to legal system will be slow: advocates," CBC News, July 23, 2016.

"virtually incomprehensible."
Ontario Superior Court of Justice, R. v. Ururyar, (2017 ONSC 4428).

Motherisk's tests
Rachel Mendleson, "Separated by a hair," *Toronto Star/CBC,* October 19, 2017.

CHAPTER 8
twenty-eight-year-old artist
Clea Benson, Mark Fazlollah, Michael Matza and Craig R. McCoy, "Serial rape investigation widens to a sixth attack," *The Philadelphia Inquirer,* October 7, 1999.

The Philadelphia Inquirer
You can read more about the paper's investigation and coverage of Shannon Schieber's murder here: http://inquirer.philly.com/packages/crime/schieber.asp

"a nice lady" . . . "she looked like a woman"
Clea Benson, Mark Fazlollah, Michael Matza and Craig R. McCoy, "Serial rape investigation widens to a sixth attack," *The Philadelphia Inquirer,* October 7, 1999.

a twenty-five-year-old office worker . . . "end up remembering"
Clea Benson, Mark Fazlollah, Michael Matza and Craig R. McCoy, "DNA links 5th case to Rittenhouse rapist," *The Philadelphia Inquirer,* October 6, 1999.

"lying bitches unit"
Craig R. McCoy, "From old report, 4 new charges," *The Philadelphia Inquirer,* June 23, 2003.

"No way in hell"
Leonard Pitts Jr., "Kobe Has Earned Benefit of Doubt," *The Miami Herald,* July 11, 2003.

"sometimes women lie too"
Leonard Pitts Jr., "Could Kobe Bryant Do Such A Terrible Thing," *The Miami Herald,* September 3, 2004.

"and from this weakness"
P.G. Maxwell-Stuart (editing and translation), *The Malleus Maleficarum,* Manchester University Press, 2007, p. 75-76.

"an accusation easily to be made"
Sir Matthew Hale, *The History Of The Pleas Of The Crown*, Vol. I, 1736, p. 635, "ravished" p. 632.

"No judge should ever"
Elizabeth A. Sheehy, "Canadian Judges and the Law of Rape: Should the Charter Insulate Bias?," 1989, CanLIIDocs p. 776; and "the failure to complain," John Wigmore, *Wigmore on Evidence*, section 284, (3rd ed.) as cited here: Kribs et al. v. R., Ontario Court of Appeals, 1960.

"There is no shortage"
Brent Turvey and John Savino, *Rape Investigation Handbook*, Academic Press, 2011, p. 274. (Their information on false reports is detailed on page 276.)

41 percent of rape claims were bogus
Eugene J. Kanin, False rape allegations. Archives of Sexual Behavior, 1994.

I wrote about this model
Robyn Doolittle, "How do you fix a broken system?" *The Globe and Mail*, February 10, 2017.

Most rigorous study
Liz Kelly, Jo Lovett and Linda Regan, "A gap or a chasm? Attrition in reported rape cases," Home Office Research, Development and Statistics Directorate, February 2005.

In a paper Lisak co-authored
Kim Lonsway, David Lisak, and Joanne Archambault, "False Reports: Moving Beyond the Issue to Successfully Investigate and Prosecute Non-Stranger Sexual Assault," The National Center for the Prosecution of Violence Against Women, 2009.

The story was as disturbing
Sabrina Rubin Erdely, "A Rape on Campus: A Brutal Assault and Struggle for Justice at UVA," *Rolling Stone*, November 19, 2014.

in a blog post
Richard Bradley's blog was called Shots in the Dark. His website seems to have be taken down, but you can find the November 24, 2014 post here: https://web.archive.org/web/20141201000026/http://www.richard bradley.net/shotsinthedark/2014/11/24/is-the-rolling-stone-story-true

tracked down one of the people
T. Rees Shapiro, "Key elements of Rolling Stone's U-Va. gang rape allegations in doubt," *The Washington Post*, December 5, 2014.

The finished product
Sheila Coronel, Steve Coll, and Derek Kravitz, "Rolling Stone and UVA: The Columbia University Graduate School of Journalism Report," April 5, 2015.

"true at the time"
T. Rees Shapiro, "Hear U-Va.'s 'Jackie' testify about *Rolling Stone's* gang rape story," *The Washington Post*, October 26, 2016.

Ford told the *Post*
Emma Brown, "California professor, writer of confidential Brett Kavanaugh letter, speaks out about her allegation of sexual assault," *The Washington Post*, September 16, 2018.

"This is a completely false allegation"
Josh Gerstein, Andrew Restuccia, and Daniel Lippman, "'I do not know this woman': Trump allies rally to Kavanaugh's defense," *Politico*, September 16, 2018.

"Given what we know"
Laura Ingraham, "Laura Ingraham: Kavanaugh, Ford controversy—shades of Duke lacrosse rush to judgment," *Fox News*, September 19, 2018.

"Why would a woman lie"
Mona Charen, "More witnesses needed if we are to believe Kavanaugh's accuser," *Chicago Sun-Times*, September 17, 2018.

"Allegations of sexual misconduct"
Editorial, "Kavanaugh accusation lacks details, evidence," *Las Vegas Review-Journal*, September 17, 2018.

CHAPTER 9
full recounting of the alleged incident
Sarah Thomson, "Media Personality Uses His Position To Gain Sex," *Women's Post*, February 2, 2018.

CTV News reported that two women
Rachel Aiello and Glen McGregor, "Patrick Brown denies sexual

misconduct allegations from two women, resigns as Ontario PC leader,"
CTV News, January 24, 2018.

questions began to surface
Samantha Beattie, "Steve Paikin denies sexual harassment allegation
made by Sarah Thomson," *Toronto Star*, February 6, 2018.

"Beyond being brainy"
Zosia Bielski, "Steve Paikin: The Journalist Who likes Everybody," *The
Globe and Mail*, May 20, 2011.

"I don't know who's telling the truth"
Rosie DiManno, "Bravo to TVO for not caving under pressure," *Toronto
Star*, February 5, 2018.

"Shut up, girl! Really?"
Jackie Hong, "We Chatted About Horses and Viagra with Toronto
Mayoral Candidate Sarah Thomson," *Vice*, September 4, 2014.

"We posed to get our picture taken"
David Rider, "Rob Ford: Sarah Thomson wants apology after accusing
Toronto mayor of inappropriate touch," *Toronto Star*, March 8, 2013.

Ford had been high on cocaine
Don Peat, "Sarah Thomson: I thought Mayor Rob Ford was on cocaine,"
Toronto Sun, March 11, 2013.

"We need to get a picture"
"Toronto's Rob Ford calls groping claim 'completely false,'" *CBC News*,
March 8, 2013.

"There is little doubt"
You can read Rachel Turnpenney's report, which was released April 26,
2018, here: https://www.tvo.org/sites/default/files/media-library/About
-TVO/HM%20TVO%20Report%20-%20April%2026%2C%202018.PDF

Facebook messenger conversation
The Turnpenney report includes a few direct quotes from the conversation between Sarah Thomson and "Witness J," but Thomson posted the
full conversation on her website. As of this writing, the conversation was
available at: https://www.womenspost.ca/facebook-transcript/

Thomson shot back
Sarah Thomson, "Omissions from investigation into Steve Paikin," *Women's Post*, May 2, 2018. (Note: At some point after December 2018, sections of this blog post were rewritten, including the quote about being "warned" and Paikin's supposed "affair." There is no note indicating the text was changed. When writing this chapter, I saved a PDF of the text I was reviewing. I've relied on this original as my source material.)

an article in Frank
"#MeTVO?! The Trials of Saint Steve," *Frank*, February 2018.

thousands of people living in the United States
William Hirst et al., "A Ten-Year Follow-Up of a Study of Memory for the Attack of September 11, 2001: Flashbulb Memories and Memories for Flashbulb Events," *Journal of Experimental Psychology: General*, 2015.

"Read about false memories"
Daniel Bice, "Sen. Ron Johnson suggests Christine Blasey Ford may have 'false memories' of alleged assault," *Milwaukee Journal Sentinel*, September 29, 2018. (Note: the quote in the story differs slightly from the accompanying video. I have relied on the video.)

"mistaken identity" . . . "something happened to Dr. Ford"
Avi Selk, "The junk science Republicans used to discredit Christine Blasey Ford's memories," *The Washington Post*, October 7, 2018.

As Richard McNally
Rhitu Chatterjee, "How Trauma Affects Memory: Scientists Weigh In On The Kavanaugh Hearing," *NPR*, September 28, 2018.

Ford faced the Senate Judiciary Committee
I've taken quotes for this section from "Kavanaugh hearing: Transcript," *The Washington Post*, September 27, 2018. You can read it here: https://www.washingtonpost.com/news/national/wp/2018/09/27/kavanaugh-hearing-transcript/

in a letter
You can read Mark Judge's letter here: https://www.judiciary.senate.gov/imo/media/doc/2018-09-18%20Judge%20to%20Grassley,%20Feinstein%20(Kavanaugh%20Nomination).pdf

CHAPTER 10
a second attempt at re-entry
Jian Ghomeshi, "Reflections From A Hashtag," *The New York Review of Books*, October 11, 2018 issue. (This was posted online on September 14, 2018.)

more than twenty people
Jennifer MacMillan, "Jian Ghomeshi Allegation Tracker: A Timeline Of The Harassment And Assault Accusations," *Huffington Post Canada*, December 3, 2014.

Brown linked to an article
Jesse Brown, "Fact-Checking Jian Ghomeshi's Comeback Attempt," *Canadaland*, September 17, 2018.

Ian Buruma gave slate a ruinous interview
Isaac Chotiner, "Why Did the New York Review of Books Publish That Jian Ghomeshi Essay?" *Slate*, September 14, 2018.

Borel, who alleged
"Statement from Kathryn Borel on Jian Ghomeshi," *The Globe and Mail*, May 11, 2016.

"As editor of *The New York Review of Books*"
Mischa Cohen, "Ian Buruma reacts: 'I still stand behind my decision to publish,'" *Vrij Nederland*, September 20, 2018.

Tina Brown revealed
Ian Mohr, "Tina Brown says she was pitched Charlie Rose comeback show," *Page Six*, April 25, 2018.

"surprised and concerned"
Meg Swertlow, "Aziz Ansari Releases Statement After Being Accused of Sexual Misconduct," *E! News*, January 15, 2018.

"To address the elephant in the room"
Ryan Glasspiegel, "The Scene Inside One of Aziz Ansari's Recent Shows," *Vulture*, August 27, 2018.

Five women told
Melena Ryzik, Cara Buckley and Jodi Kantor, "Louis C.K. Is Accused By 5 Women Of Sexual Misconduct," *The New York Times*, November 9, 2017.

"These stories are true"
"Louis C.K. Responds to Accusations: 'These Stories Are True,'" *The New York Times*, November 10, 2017.

"We spend so little energy"
Roxane Gay, "Louis C.K. and Men Who Think Justice Takes as Long as They Want It To," *The New York Times*, August 29, 2018.

"The subtext is"
Frida Garza, "They're Here," *Jezebel*, September 14, 2018.

"post-assault contact"
Codi Wilson, "DeCoutere questioned about emails, conduct after alleged assault by Ghomeshi," CP24.com, February 4, 2016.

"I love your hands"
"Full text: The emails and handwritten letter Lucy DeCoutere sent Jian Ghomeshi after alleged assault," *National Post*, February 5, 2016.

"team" . . . "sink the prick"
Ontario Court of Justice, R. v. Ghomeshi, (2016 ONCJ 155).

CHAPTER 11

Robin Camp
Information about testimony during the Wagar trial and testimony from the judicial inquiry come from documents posted online by the Canadian Judicial Council on a page devoted to the Camp inquiry. "Inquiry Committee regarding the Honourable Robin Camp": https://www.cjc-ccm.gc.ca/english/conduct_en.asp?selMenu=conduct_inq_camp_en.asp

raised the alarm
Elaine Craig and Alice Woolley, "Myths and stereotypes: some judges still don't get it," *The Globe and Mail*, November 9, 2015.

"manifestly and profoundly"
The Canadian Judicial Council, "Canadian Judicial Council recommends that Justice Robin Camp be removed from office," March 9, 2017.

Two other Alberta judges
Sean Fine, "Third Alberta judge faces review over handling of sex-assault case," *The Globe and Mail*, September 14, 2016.

"Clearly [he could not undress]"
This was a case I investigated as part of my Unfounded series. The incident occurred in northern Manitoba. The verdict was delivered orally on June 21, 2016. That is as much detail as I can reveal about this.

women's activism and the law
Elizabeth Sheehy, *Sexual Assault in Canada; Law, Legal Practice And Women's Activism*, University of Ottawa Press, 2012.

"ideal" victims
Melanie Randall, "Sexual Assault Law, Credibility, and 'Ideal Victims': Consent, Resistance and Victim Blaming," *Canadian Journal of Women and the Law*, 2011.

Carnal Crimes
Constance Backhouse, *Carnal Crimes: Sexual Assault Law in Canada 1900-1975*, Irwin Law, 2008.

Ava Williams
Robyn Doolittle "Why Police Dismiss 1 in 5 sexual assault claims as baseless", *The Globe and Mail*, February 3, 2017.

CHAPTER 12
her international bestseller
Germaine Greer, *The Female Eunuch*, MacGibbon & Kee, 1970, "the housewife" p. 242, "women have very" p. 249, "If it makes you sick" p. 51.

"If you spread your legs"
Nick Miller, "Germaine Greer challenges #MeToo campaign," *The Sydney Morning Herald*, January 21, 2018.

"six-figure sums" . . . "career rapees"
BBC Radio 4, March 20, 2018. (Part of the interview is still online: https://www.bbc.com/news/av/uk-43472667/academic-says-women-risk-being-branded-career-rapees, but for the rest I've relied on media coverage of the interview, including: Zoe Drewett "Germaine Greer slammed for calling victims of sexual assault 'career rapees,'" *Metro*, March 20, 2018.)

"longstanding feminists"
Daphne Merkin, "Publicly, We Say #MeToo. Privately, We Have Misgivings," *The New York Times*, January 5, 2018.

"All I can say"
Margaret Wente, "Please turn down the volume on the outrage machine," *The Globe and Mail*, October 20, 2017.

"fucking fragile"
Real Time with Bill Maher, "Bari Weiss on #MeToo," February 2018. You can watch here: https://www.youtube.com/watch?v=E6lCPvwiIqo

"So I understand Merkin's"
Stella Bugbee, "Everyone Loses When We Widen The Feminist Generation Gap," *The Cut*, January 6, 2018.

"Liberal second-wave feminists"
Stassa Edwards, "The Backlash to #MeToo Is Second-Wave Feminism," *Jezebel*, January 11, 2018.

"The so-called generational divide"
Josephine Livingstone, "Time Is A Feminist Issue," *The New Republic*, February 20, 2018.

the results of a poll
Anna North, "The #MeToo Generation Gap Is A Myth," *Vox*, March 20, 2018.

"They think they are"
Katie Van Syckle, "Against Our Will Author On What Today's Rape Activists Don't Get," *The Cut*, September 17, 2015.

Headline in *Slate*
Amanda Marcotte, "Former Feminist Hero Somehow Thinks That Victim-Blaming Can Stop Rape," *Slate*, September 17, 2015.

"I fairly shrieked" . . . "From prehistoric times"
Susan Brownmiller, *Against Our Will: Men, Women And Rape*, Fawcett Books, 1975, p. 8, p. 15

"I never saw his face"
Brownmiller showed me a copy of this article, which apparently ran in *The Village Voice* under the headline "On Goosing," April 15, 1971.

CHAPTER 13
It's called *Allegedly*
You can watch Tessa Hill and Lia Valente's documentary here: https://
www.youtube.com/watch?v=d7yx-tG_UFg

"Intersectional" is one of those buzzy words
Kimberlé Crenshaw, "Demarginalizing The Intersection Of Race And
Sex: A Black Feminist Critique Of Antidiscrimination Doctrine, Feminist
Theory and Antiracist Politics," University of Chicago Legal Forum,
1989. Crenshaw added additional context in an article for *The Washington
Post*, "Why intersectionality can't wait," September 24, 2015.

"Only if the court"
Kimberlé Crenshaw, "The Urgency of Intersectionality," TED, 2016. You
can watch here: https://www.youtube.com/watch?v=akOe5-UsQ2o

"Intersectionality is a form of identity politics"
Jacob Airey, "Ben Shapiro: What Is Intersectionality?" *Daily Wire*, June 19,
2018.

"this latest fad"
Sumantra Maitra, "Intersectionality And Popper's Paradox," *Quillette*,
November 6, 2017.

"fosters groupthink"
Christian Alejandro Gonzalez, "The Illiberal Logic Of Intersectionality,"
Quillette, May 8, 2018.

"philosophically incoherent"
Christian Alejandro Gonzalez, "Intersectionality—A Review," *Quillette*,
August 14, 2018.

A 2015 MTV poll . . . "It's not hard to understand"
Rachel Giese, *Boys: What It Means To Become A Man*, Patrick Crean Editions,
2018. You can read the MTV poll—"Look Different"—that she referred
to here: http://d1fqdnmgwphrky.cloudfront.net/studies/000/000/004/
MTV-Gender-Bias-Survey-Executive-Summary.pdf?1442267441

CHAPTER 14

The commercial opens
You can watch Gillette's ad "We Believe: The Best Men Can Be," which was posted January 13, 2019, here: You can watch here: https://www.youtube.com/watch?v=koPmuEyP3ao

"It makes, like, every man"
Joe Rogan on the Gillette Toxic Masculinity Commercial, *The Joe Rogan Experience*, Posted January 15, 2019. You can watch here: https://www.youtube.com/watch?v=oJVmtaTVKPU

political polarization has been deepening
Pew Research Centre, "Partisanship and Political Animosity in 2016," June 22, 2016.

26 percent of voters "hate"
Shannon Proudfoot, "One in four Canadians hate their political opponents," *Maclean's*, January 11, 2019.

"The tribal instinct"
Amy Chua, *Political Tribes: Group Instinct And The Fate of Nations*, Penguin Press, 2018, p. 1, "what is needed" p. 201.

"The problem is when tribalism"
You can watch Amy Chua's March 2018 appearance on *The View* here: https://www.youtube.com/watch?v=fMoHZduoxCk

"You can't find"
Hamza Shaban, "Twitter reveals its daily active user numbers for the first time," *The Washington Post*, February 7, 2019.

94 percent of those who are online
Per Social Media Lab at Ryerson's Ted Rogers School of Management. Report: https://socialmedialab.ca/2018/02/25/state-of-social-media-in-canada/

social media overtook
Elisa Shearer, "Social Media Outpaces Print Newspapers In The U.S. As A News Source," Pew Research Centre, December 10, 2018.

42 percent of the population
Amy Mitchell, Katie Simmons, Katerina Eva Matsa and Laura Silver, "People In Poorer Countries Just As Likely To Use Social Media For News As Those In Wealthier Countries," Pew Research Centre, January 11, 2018.

"This is the secret to Facebook's"
Simon Parkin, "Has dopamine got us hooked on tech?" *The Guardian*, March 4, 2018.

studied more than 286,000 tweets
William J. Brady et al., "An ideological asymmetry in the diffusion of moralized content on social media among political leaders." *Journal of Experimental Psychology: General*, 2018.

another one of their research projects
William J. Brady et al., "Emotion shapes the diffusion of moralized content in social networks," *Proceedings of the National Academy of Sciences*, 2017.

EPILOGUE

A study of Google searches
Lisa Rapaport, "More Google Searches For Sexual Harassment Facts Since #MeToo," *Reuters*, December 21, 2018.

the number of casualties at 201
Audrey Carlsen et al., "#MeToo Brought Down 201 Powerful Men. Nearly Half Of Their Replacements Are Women," *The New York Times*, October 29, 2018.

a pattern of alleged sexual harassment by
Ann Hui and Ivy Knight, "Canadian winemaker Norman Hardie accused of sexual misconduct," *The Globe and Mail*, June 19, 2018.

a cross-country survey
The Gandalf Group, "The 49th Quarterly C-Suite Survey," December 12, 2017.

43 percent of women
Human Resources Professionals Association, "Doing Our Duty: Preventing Sexual Harassment In The Workplace," April 2018.

understanding of consent had actually decreased
"Survey Finds Drop In Canadians' Understanding of Consent,"
Canadian Women's Foundation, May 16, 2018.

A poll from Canadian firm
Anguis Reid, "#Metoo: Moment Or Movement," February 9, 2018.

Facebook COO Sheryl Sandberg's
Jillesa Gebhardt, "How #MeToo Has Impacted Mentorship For Women,"
LeanIn.Org and SurveyMonkey, 2019.

a dozen women in corporate Canada
Tara Deschamps, "Women Finding Themselves Locked Out Of
Corporate Canada's Boys' Club In Wake Of #MeToo," *The Globe and Mail*,
August 2, 2018.

a similar dampening effect
Gillian Tan and Katia Porzecanski, "Wall Street Rule For The #MeToo
Era: Avoid Women At All Cost," *Bloomberg*, December 3, 2018.

"Harassers prey upon the fact"
Anna North, "What I've Learned Covering Sexual Misconduct This
Year," *Vox*, December 27, 2017.

ACKNOWLEDGMENTS

OVER THE FINAL six months of writing this book, people asked me (not infrequently) how I managed to write while working full-time and caring for a toddler. The answer: my husband, Joel. Every single weekend from September through May, Joel took our daughter solo, while I toiled away at a coffee shop writing. He did this happily and without complaint and made sure to text me photos of their adventures every few hours. He's picked up my slack on the laundry, cooking, and cleaning front, too. He's a true partner in every way and I'm so lucky to have him. Joel, I love you so much and thank you for being the best husband and father and support system.

I am also very appreciative to my workplace, *The Globe and Mail*, and to all of my editors. The foundation for *Had It Coming* was the Unfounded investigation that I did for the *Globe*. And so I'm grateful that my bosses didn't just say, "yes," when I pitched that incredibly ambitious, time-consuming and expensive idea, they said, "go further." When I had my baby a few months after the series dropped, and I wanted to still be involved in following the story, they were incredibly accommodating—allowing me to drop to part-time and then switching to an actual maternity leave when I was ready. Sometimes I had my infant in the newsroom with me. No one was anything but supportive. Now that I'm back at work full-time, I am grateful for how understanding editors are to all the parents in the newsroom (dads included, my male colleagues are all super-engaged fathers) with young kids when it comes to daycare pick-up, doctor's appointments, and sick days. This is what it looks like to support women at work. So to Editor-in-Chief David Walmsley, whose passion and vision sets the tone at the *Globe*, my boss, Dennis Choquette, an incredible, brilliant editor (and guitarist), Deputy Editor Sinclair Stewart, who pushed Unfounded to be what it was, Renata D'Aliesio, the hardest worker and best coffee-walk-vent-session partner in the world, and Publisher Phillip Crawley, who steers the ship: I am in all of your debt. (Also, to the entire, large team that made Unfounded happen, thank you, especially Laura Blenkinsop, Michael Pereira, Jeremy Agius, Stephanie Chambers, Rick Cash, Terra Ciolfe, and Shengqing Wu.)

I'm so lucky to have agent Martha Webb from the CookeMcDermid agency in my corner. She is #SmartGoals, #MomGoals, #BossLadyGoals, and also just the nicest human being. To everyone at Penguin Random House, especially my wonderful (and patient) editor, Diane Turbide, the brilliant Nicole Winstanley, publisher of Penguin Canada, as well as David Ross, Justin Stoller, Celina Fazio, Kate Sinclair, Allie

McHugh, and Claire Zaya, thank you for getting behind this book, believing in it, and making it happen.

To my squad, especially Carla Wintersgill, Jenny Yang, Emily Mathieu, Diana Zlomislic, and Hannah Sung, for reading early drafts and making whip-smart suggestions—you women complete me. I'm so lucky to have so many amazing and talented friends who inspire me and make me better every day, including but not limited to: Dakshana Bascaramurty, Janean Bruhn, Daniel Dale, Renata D'Aliesio, Lauren Gosnell, Kelly Harris, Ann Hui, Emma-Kate Millar, Jayme Poisson, and of course my Trinity synchronized skating team. Thank you for your friendship and for the many amazing conversations through the years—some of which were featured in this book!

To my family: my parents; sister, Jamie; brother-in-laws, Peter and Carey; niece and nephew, Charlotte and Clark; to the most incredible mother-in-law, Judy, who has been clutch so many times when it comes to last-minute childcare; and the most caring father-in-law, Owen, I love you all so much. To Bec and Janis, strong, amazing women who I'm so glad are in my life. To my daughter, Wren, and the little one who is growing inside me as I write this: you and your dad are the joy of my existence and everything is for you.

Also to the many subject matter experts who spent time helping me understand the law or the science, I can not express enough gratitude. Many are featured in this book, but some are not. I want to particularly acknowledge Crown attorney Jill Witkin and defence attorney Danielle Robitaille, who have been so patient in explaining the law to me. I'm sure I still didn't get it perfect, but I'm learning! (Also, Jill co-authored a great book, *Prosecuting and Defending Sexual Offence Cases:*

A Practitioner's Handbook, with Dan Brown, that was very helpful.) To law professor Lisa Dufraimont and legal historian Constance Backhouse, thank you for the many quick replies to my dumb email questions. I am eternally grateful to Sunny Marriner, Elizabeth Sheehy, Holly Johnson, Blair Crew, and Melanie Randall for the constant advice and expertise during my Unfounded reporting. To psychologists Jim Hopper and Lori Haskell, and the amazing Ruth Lanius, one of the world's leading researchers on trauma and PTSD, your help was invaluable. And to all of the sources who lent their time to speak with me for *Had It Coming*, I am greatly indebted to you.

Finally, to the incredible women and the man who shared their stories with me in the Unfounded series, your bravery is awe-inspiring. I don't think people understand how terrifying it is to speak with a journalist, to open up your life to a stranger. The change that came from that investigation would not have happened without you. A story about statistics doesn't connect until you realize those numbers are people. I admire you all so much and am forever grateful that you trusted me: To Alicia, A.M., Arlene, A.S., Ava, B.B., B.D., B.W., Candice, Christina, E., Emilie, Heather, J., Jenna, Justice, K., K., Kelly, Kerra, K.S., Lisa, L.M., M., Margaret, N., R., Marley, Melodie, Paola, Shannon, S.S., Stacey, Stacie, Taylor and T.R., and the eighteen others who preferred not to be identified in any capacity, thank you.

INDEX